STUDYING LIVED RELIGION

Studying Lived Religion

Contexts and Practices

Nancy Tatom Ammerman

NEW YORK UNIVERSITY PRESS

New York

NEW YORK UNIVERSITY PRESS
New York
www.nyupress.org

References to Internet websites (URLs) were accurate at the time of writing. Neither the author nor New York University Press is responsible for URLs that may have expired or changed since the manuscript was prepared.

Library of Congress Cataloging-in-Publication Data
Names: Ammerman, Nancy Tatom, 1950–   author.
Title: Studying lived religion : contexts and practices / Nancy Tatom Ammerman.
Description: New York : New York University Press, [2021] | Includes bibliographical references and index.
Identifiers: LCCN 2021009010 | ISBN 9781479804351 (hardback) | ISBN 9781479804344 (paperback) | ISBN 9781479804337 (ebook) | ISBN 9781479804283 (ebook other)
Subjects: LCSH: Religious life. | Religion. | Religions. | Religion and sociology.
Classification: LCC BL624 .A482 2021 | DDC 204—dc23
LC record available at https://lccn.loc.gov/2021009010

New York University Press books are printed on acid-free paper, and their binding materials are chosen for strength and durability. We strive to use environmentally responsible suppliers and materials to the greatest extent possible in publishing our books.

Manufactured in the United States of America

10 9 8 7 6 5 4 3 2 1

Also available as an ebook

For Kai Erikson

whose wisdom has sustained me from the beginning

CONTENTS

Introduction

Rediscovering Religion

Look around you as you walk down almost any street or byway in the world. Somewhere, often hidden in plain sight, there will be traces of religion. Perhaps it is the person who walks past with a Christian tattoo or a Muslim hijab. Perhaps it is the poster announcing a charity auction at the local synagogue. Perhaps it is the newspaper headline about persecution of the Rohingya in Myanmar or Uyghurs in China. Perhaps it is the entrance to a worship space—whether a storefront or a cathedral. Perhaps it is people singing a spiritual song as they march in protest. Perhaps you are in one of the booming cities of Nigeria and passing new churches on nearly every corner. Or you are in a Chinese city where you hear that successful young Christians are gathering in "house churches." Perhaps you are at an environmental rally in Brazil and notice the clerical collars and the religious garb worn by the leaders. Or perhaps you just open your Instagram feed to see what inspiring images and meditations have been posted by your favorite spiritual guides to help you start your day centered and in tune with the universe.

This book is about how to pay attention to what people are doing in all those everyday places.

Much of the activity in your everyday world may be mundane, ordinary, and seemingly secular—governed by the rules of the market, the state, and science. You shop, pay your taxes, go to work, and watch the latest Netflix series. None of those things requires any special religious knowledge. None of them has anything apparent to do with religion or spirituality. Most of life can seemingly be lived without religion. The social scientists who have tracked the advance of secular social forces are right that they dominate much of how we think and act.[1]

Yet what social scientists miss when they assume that "secularization" is the big story is the continued presence and remarkable resilence of the world's diverse religious practices. Partly they miss it because social scientists often treat "religion" as synonymous with belief—accepting certain traditional tenets about God or the Bible. If more people have doubts about those things, then religion must be losing its influence. Others have tracked religion by trends in membership in churches and synagogues. When fewer people say on surveys that they are members, the conclusion is that "religion" is declining and on its way to disappearing. By many of those measures, in fact, secularization is occurring, but those big questions about "more" and "less" religion are not our primary concern here. Rather, this book invites you to look for the religion that *is* there and think about how best to understand it. Rather than treating religious movements as anomalies, or thinking of believers and lively religious communities as residuals from an earlier era, what if you paid attention to what they are doing and how they are doing it?

The other reason so many social scientists have embraced a secularization thesis and ignored religion is that they have forgotten that their own context is coloring the way they see the world. Europe and North America produce most of the academics, and what they experience in their own lives shapes how they formulate their theories. They often miss even the differences between the European model of established state churches and the US "freedom of religion" model. Even within those focused geographic domains, the social spaces occupied by women, people of color, and sexual and gender minorities are rarely part of the picture. Assumptions that are, often unconsciously, gendered and raced are at the heart of an "Enlightenment Reason and Progress" story about religion's demise. They blind us to all the places that story didn't fit.[2] As we have slowly learned, what you see depends on where you stand, and with more observers now standing in more places, we are in the midst of rediscovering religion.

Sometimes that rediscovery has come out of hard-to-ignore problems. Religious nationalism threatens to disrupt international cooperation. Terrorist attacks around the world are accompanied by declarations that "God is great!" Religious liberty itself is redefined to include social discrimination against gay marriages and abortion providers. People claiming their power and place in the world are doing so in the name of their God. This is religion that poses problems and demands attention.

Other times, we have rediscovered religion as we have seen it in every corner of the humanitarian community—settling refugees, delivering disaster aid, investing in sustainable development, and more. Closer to home, housing the homeless and providing food pantries are very likely to be happening through the leadership of people and institutions whose faith is the reason for their engagement. Even at rallies for science and protests against rights abuses, there are signs that declare the cause to be a righteous one, in keeping with sacred commands. These people, too, are engaged in practices that are inherently religious practices—often overlooked but no less real.

Religion also happens, of course, when people gather for avowedly religious purposes in religious institutions. Over the past generation, social science has rediscovered the importance of local religious gatherings—congregations of all sorts. Many venerable institutions are struggling, but other gatherings are cropping up and thriving. What we have discovered when we have looked more closely is a complex and fascinating array of formal and informal local religious organizations— from reading groups to cycling teams to immigrant festivals. In recent years, researchers have examined the gatherings that are happening in unexpected places and times, as well as in the churches, synagogues, mosques, and temples. From yoga studios to high school gyms and from dinner gatherings to contemplative communities, social energy is being generated and expended in pursuit of religious connection.[3] Whether gathering in a dusty sanctuary, a booming megachurch, a Buddhist meditation center, or even a park, religion is happening.

Even out of view, in private individual places, religion has been happening. All kinds of people in all kinds of places have engaged in spiritual practices to connect themselves and their families to the powers of the universe. As social scientists began to blur the supposed boundaries between "public" things that matter and "private" things that can be ignored, a wealth of religious practices came into view, and it became more apparent just how much they do matter. Home altars venerate ancestors and connect people to moral traditions. Healing rites can complement the doctor's orders. A morning meditation ritual can put the day's activities in perspective and generate a range of responses, from calm resignation to righteous discontent. The religious things people do in private often matter in public.

Problems and solutions, public and private, official and unofficial—when we look carefully, we are likely to find people doing religion. Religion as it happens in everyday life. Religion in action.

The implications of paying attention to religion are both intellectual and practical. Intellectually, scholars who wish to develop useful models for how the world works cannot do so while ignoring vast swaths of (religious) everyday life and equally vast slices of the world's (religious) population. When we expand our understanding of what religion is and where we should find it, we discover that just about everything else in social life becomes clearer. We see, for example, that we cannot understand the shape of a government's approach to welfare without understanding the religious traditions of those who created and support it. We cannot understand the impulse for nations to keep their citizens in line without understanding their need to regulate religion. We cannot understand humanitarianism or multiculturalism without understanding the missionary practices at their root. We cannot understand the grassroots delivery of social services in places where there isn't a strong government without understanding the grassroots presence of religious NGOs in those places. And we cannot understand how Donald Trump came to power without understanding white American evangelicalism. We have to look for religion even in unexpected places if we are going to understand the world we live in.

This is more than an intellectual problem. It is a challenge for anyone who wants to be a productive citizen and a good neighbor. The world is simply too interconnected and diverse for individuals and societies to be willfully ignorant about the lives of the people either next door or far away. Good social policy at home and good foreign policy around the world mean recognizing that religion plays a role in the lives of many people who will be affected by that policy. Likewise, managers will have better workers if religious practice is treated respectfully. Neighbors will be able to build better communities when there are physical and social spaces that make room for diverse religious practices. All of this depends on careful attention to what is all around us. Lived religion is part of our world, and understanding it is critical to living together.

Why "Lived" Religion?

How religion happens in everyday life has come to be called "lived religion." To study religion this way is to expand our lens beyond the official texts and doctrines so as to see how ideas about the sacred emerge in unofficial places. It is to include the practices of ordinary people, not just religious leaders. It is to expect to find religion both in "religious" places and in all those other everyday places. It is to focus on what people are doing, as well as what they are saying. Lived religion is dynamic and creative, and studying religion this way has opened the door to a wealth of new knowledge on which we can continue to build.

This kind of focus on lived religious experience emerged in the mid-1990s as scholars in multiple fields gravitated to the promise of an approach that could go beyond the seemingly narrow, largely Western, understanding of religion. The term "lived religion" originated with a 1994 conference hosted at Harvard University by historian David Hall. It was a gathering mostly focused on historical study of religion, but the idea of studying what ordinary people do in their everyday religious practices meant the inclusion of a few sociologists and other religious studies scholars. The group recognized that historical knowledge about religion had been limited because scholars had largely focused on ideas, and the ideas of elites, no less. They had traced patterns in traditional religious organizations, but only those substantial enough to leave historical records. But what were ordinary people actually *doing*? The conference papers, published as *Lived Religion in America* (D. Hall 1997), marked the opening salvo in a reorientation that has taken hold in history and religious studies and has resulted in an outpouring of work documenting the religious activities of people who had previously been ignored.[4]

Anthropologists, of course, have long documented religion as practiced in everyday life; but in the early days, there was an unfortunate division of labor between anthropology and other social sciences. The study of culture got divided between those on the "primitive" and "traditional" side (anthropologists and many religious studies scholars) of the divide and those on the "advanced" and "modern" side (sociologists, political scientists, psychologists). The study of religious practice was an expected part of the former and not expected in the latter. Undermining and erasing that division is part of what has helped students of society, no matter their location or discipline, to rediscover religious practice as part of social life. By the early years of this century, "lived religion" or "everyday religion" had emerged in sociology and elsewhere as one expression of an expanded scope of study.

Studying lived religion began as something of a rebellion. Where, we asked, were the religious lives of women, children, poor people, and people of color? In setting out an exploration of "Material Christianity," historian Colleen McDannell documented how theologians and privileged people often denigrated religious images and material practices as inauthentic and not truly pious and sincere. They created a hierarchy of ideas over practices. For herself, McDannell says, "I am not drawn to criticize Christians who use Lourdes water or who wear 'Praise the Lord' T-shirts. I reject, however, the opinions of those who find nothing significant in these religious gestures" (1995, 13). Other religious studies scholars agreed, turning their attention to the material objects made by ordinary people, as well as the everyday rituals that had often been dismissed as mere "folk" religion.

A similar thing was happening among theologians. Long preoccupied with the thoughts of philosophers and preachers, a few began to wonder what theologies might look like in action and what the lived theologies of ordinary people might have to tell us. A growing field of "practical theology" suggested that theologians should begin their work with an assessment of what is actually happening on the ground, bring that into conversation with existing theological ideas, and aim toward gleaning new insights that would make theology strategic in its attention to the social world. Doing all of that meant that a growing number of theologians were taking their work into the field. They were seeking to learn from the understandings of God that emerge from and engage with everyday life.[5] They, too, were rebelling, in this case against a theology that only seemed to matter to a few other theologians.

Among sociologists, the rebellion started with the failure to squeeze the world's religious reality into a universal theory of secularization. Not every society fit the model of Western-style modernization leading to European-style religious decline. If religion was still around (or maybe always was), how should we treat it? One attempt at a different explanation—quick to be discredited—was to assume that all human beings are rational actors, that religions offer rewards everyone wants, and that people will choose the best bargain for their salvation. Perhaps consumers do attempt to maximize rewards and minimize costs when buying soap, although even there, habits and traditions can explain a lot. Perhaps churchgoers, too, may opt for the service that is the most fun, if given the choice; but human religious action simply cannot be reduced to the costs and benefits of paths to salvation. Indeed, some religions aren't concerned with salvation at all. People in all religions, in fact, engage in religious action simply for its own sake. To use McDannell's example, wearing that T-shirt is more about relationships (with Jesus and one's fellow believers) than about securing salvation.

In the 1990s, across the disciplines that were studying religion, then, there seemed to be a crisis begging for response. The turn to lived religion was one response. Rather than being confined to studying words and ideas and elites and rational bargains, students of lived religion focused on what ordinary people *do*. The result has been new accounts of religious practice that have challenged old assumptions about how religion works in the social world. There is now ample evidence for arguing that discussions of secularization need to be specified, not universalized. It is a useful theory for some times and places but not one that explains the inevitable fate of religion in the modern world. Likewise, there is ample evidence that rational choices account for only a limited range of human action. Old theoretical approaches to the study of religion have been significantly undermined.

Removing those old theoretical blinders has now cleared the way for new possibilities. A rich body of research, across several disciplines, has described new people doing new (and old) things in new (and old) places. But blinders still remain. Social scientists and other scholars writing about lived religion have frequently been limited by a tendency to define their task *over against* the study of belief and doctrine, over against attention to organizations and memberships, over against the practices of elites and leaders (Ammerman 2016). That deemphasis on traditions and institutions has produced new insight, but it has also allowed research on religion to drift toward an individualist approach, as if each person is operating alone or in newly invented groups. It emphasizes choice and personal agency and expects to see a bricolage of religious ideas and practices that fit each person's individual preferences.

That emphasis on choice and individualism fits well the democratic, neoliberal context (where most lived religion scholars have been located), but it misses the many other kinds of cultural and legal contexts in which religion is practiced. The study of lived religion cannot afford to ignore its own cultural biases.

Nor can the study of lived religion afford to ignore the religious practices that take place *inside* religious institutions and those that are undertaken by religious elites. Surely religion is "lived" there, too. If we are to understand the presence of religion in the world, we need to pay attention to the official versions, as well as to the unofficial ones, to what happens inside the temples as well as what happens on the streets.

The study of lived religion began as a successful empirical and theoretical rebellion, but now it needs a more durable foundation on which to build. That foundation will allow lived religion research to live up to the global scope of our work, and it will allow social scientists and other scholars and citizens to rediscover and better understand the religious phenomena we encounter all around us. This book aims to offer that foundation and to invite you to be part of the continuing construction project.

Looking Ahead

Part 1 is about finding the right lens. If we are studying this full range of lived religion, not limiting it to seekers and bricoleurs, how should we think about that task? We begin in chapter 1 by looking at how the study of social practice can point us toward the kinds of analytical questions we should be asking of lived religion. If lived religion is about what people do, practice theories can provide a starting place for understanding the patterns of action we are observing. People who have been thinking about how social practices work can help us see lived religion more clearly. But our focus isn't just any kind of social practice, so we will suggest that it is the *spiritual* dimension of a practice that makes it distinctively religious. We will introduce the notion that the experience of engaging in any practice is, in fact, multidimensional, involving *embodiment, materiality, emotion, aesthetics, moral judgment,* and *narrative*. These are building blocks of all human social interaction and can be useful analytical angles from which to study lived religion.

What religious practices add to this list is that *spiritual* dimension. Some of these dimensions have been well studied by lived religion scholars, while others come to our attention from practice theories and other disciplines.

This foundational work in chapter 1 will be followed by the equally foundational reminder that practices happen in particular places. Chapter 2 argues that no religious practice can be understood without placing it in its particular cultural and historical context. People in different places have very different expectations about what religion looks like but also about where to find it and even how to name it. Every society has laws about which practices are allowed (or even mandated) and which are not. While the variations may seem overwhelming at first, there are some patterns that can help us get a start on understanding how to put our study of lived religion in that larger context. Studying lived religion requires that we take those constraints and opportunities into account.

The chapters in part 2 unpack each of the dimensions of practice and offer examples from actual research studies to show what we learn by focusing on each. We will travel around the world and across many traditions. We will see people doing very habitual and traditionally religious things, as well as inventing all sorts of new ways to be religious. Within each experiential dimension of practice, we will see how it is both personally experienced and socially defined. When we focus on embodiment or emotion, for example, what do we learn about how religious practice works, how it is embedded in social contexts, and how it can both constrain and liberate the people who are engaged in it? The realities of power and difference, race and class and gender, will always be in view.

These chapters are full of the evidence from research across disciplines, traditions, and places. Sometimes an example will be highlighted in some detail in a sidebar or discussed in detail within the text to help you see how practices work and how you might study them. When we encounter issues and themes that have been widely studied, notes will direct you to "Ideas for Further Study" at the end of the chapter. In other cases, specific research will simply be cited with the usual parenthetical in-text citations. There is much more good research than can be referenced in this small book, but these sources will give you good places to start your own reading list.

As we gradually add each layer to our understanding of lived religious practice, you can also think in new ways about the things you already know about, the things you see in your own everyday world. Think about how you might study them more closely. As we go along, try picking one lived religious practice and pay special attention to a single dimension of that practice. If you have a chance to do some direct observation, take advantage of it. If you love to read about religious practices, find a novel or historical account to explore. If you know someone you could interview, ask permission and then explore with them what they do. If you have access to a body of survey data and the inclination to do some statistical analysis, look for social patterns in the numbers. Look for how they might provide insight into the multiple dimensions of whatever practices the survey has asked about. Whether the practice is something done at home or in the street, in a place of worship or a place of work, think about all the dimensions.

The examples you will read about will suggest the methods you might adopt. Ethnography and interviews may be the most common, but we will encounter archival work and geographic analysis, as well. We will look at how people analyze both texts and visual evidence and even dip into the occasional survey. This is not a methods textbook, but you will learn a good deal by carefully observing what good research looks like. We will think intentionally about how each particular method allowed the researcher to learn what they did, and when you are ready to start your own work, you can dig more deeply into the sources in the methods chapter at the end. There is still a great deal of lived religion to be studied. With new lenses and examples to spark your curiosity, you can make this as a springboard to your own discoveries.

Ideas for Further Study

1. If you are interested in reading more about social science theories about secularization, you might start with a classic synthesis of the model by Peter Berger (1967). A more recent defense of that model has been put forward by Steve Bruce (2011). Stephen Warner (1993) pointed out that it is a model that works better for Europe than for the United States. Christian Smith (2003b) documented how the secularity of public life was not so much a natural evolutionary process as an intentional social movement. One of the several people to attempt a more nuanced update is Jose Casanova (1994).

2. If you are interested in the critiques that have helped to shape this turn in the study of religion, one important place to start is with Talal Asad (1993). Within the sociology of religion, the collection of articles in *Religion on the Edge* (Bender et al. 2012) has been especially helpful in pointing to the blinders in the field; and another collection of articles, edited by Grace Yukich and Penny Edgell (2020), will help you explore the many ways that "religion is raced."

3. Casper ter Kuile and Angie Thurston have initiated fascinating projects exploring and encouraging new forms of gatherings. Their 2014 report, *How We Gather*, is at https://sacred.design. My own work (Ammerman 1997a, 2005) has documented the variety and function of US congregations and the larger network of religious organizations.

4. Robert Orsi's (1985) history of Italian Catholics in New York is among the foundational lived religion sources in history. Meredith McGuire (2008) gave "lived religion" a voice in sociology with her book of the same name. There is much good work in both fields (and beyond). We will sample it throughout this book, but here are a few other pioneers for starters: among historians, Marie Griffith (1997, 2004), with her attention to women's bodies; Colleen McDannell (1995), who successfully launched historians on the study of the materiality of religious practice among ordinary people; and Laurie Maffly-Kipp and her colleagues (2006), who made sure we remembered that even American Protestants have practices. Lily Kong (2001) and other geographers have drawn attention to the spatial dimensions of religious practice, in Kong's case in Asian cities. And in anthropology, the work of Birgit Meyer (2004) exemplifies explorations of contemporary lived practice in Africa.

5. The theological field in which this attention to lived religion took hold is practical theology, with its renewed presence signaled by Don Browning's (1991) theoretical text and the collection of studies edited by Dorothy Bass (1997). Others, such as Mary McClintock Fulkerson (2007), have taken the work into congregations. And some, such as Mary Moschella (2008), along with Chris Scharen and Aana Marie Vigen (2011), have written about ethnography itself as a "pastoral practice." The link between lived religion and practical theology is even stronger among European scholars, as outlined by Ganzevoort and Roeland (2014).

PART I

The Big Picture

In the two chapters in part 1, we place the study of lived religion in two kinds of big pictures. First, we place it in the big picture that encompasses all sorts of social practices. By starting from theories about how people act in the social world, we can see how religious practices are like and unlike what people are doing when they engage in other everyday activities. How are religious practices socially defined activities that are both habitual and improvised?

Second, we increase the angle of vision. In order to think about practices in different places, we need ways to think about how the cultures and laws of those places create opportunities and constraints for religious practices. Societies around the world simply organize the practice of religion differently. People expect to find spiritual practices in different places and have different ideas about what is possible and desirable. With a framework for understanding that diversity, the study of lived religion can take context into account. We can break out of our often-limited geographic box.

1

Studying What People Do

If lived religion is about what people do, how might we think about that? Before we get to the difficult task of defining what makes something "religious," it will help to start with the bigger picture—how do we think about the *doing* and the *living*? To do that, we will turn to some of the people who study society by analyzing "practices." Sociologist Theodore Schatzki is one of them. He has defined practices as "embodied, materially mediated arrays of human activity centrally organized around shared practical understanding" (2001, 11). Another sociologist, Andreas Reckwitz, is somewhat more expansive, but sounds many of the same notes: "A 'practice' (*praktik*) is a routinized type of behaviour which consists of several elements, interconnected to one another: forms of bodily activities, forms of mental activities, 'things' and their use, a background knowledge in the form of understanding, know-how, states of emotion and motivational knowledge" (2002, 249). Note the multiple dimensions of experience they each signal. We will return to that point shortly. But for now, let's start with "arrays of human activity" and "shared practical understanding."

A practice isn't necessarily something formalized into a ritual[1]— although it might be—but it is an *array* of activity. It is *a cluster of actions that is socially recognizable in ways that allow others to know how to respond*. Think about how we greet each other. We "just know" what words to say and what gestures to make. Practices, that is, assume shared *practical* understanding—understanding that is as much in our bones as in our heads, as much a product of habitual dispositions as of critical assessment. We automatically extend a hand without thinking—until we suddenly realize that the other person's embodied practical knowledge is different or that a pandemic has changed all the rules. Studying religion, then, means noticing those arrays of activity, wherever they happen. It means noticing an airline passenger making the sign of the cross and mourners lighting candles. It means noticing yoga poses and a silent walk in the woods. It means noticing hymns sung "by heart" and prayers recited in unison. It means noticing an offering to the spirits of the marketplace and a volunteer in a homeless shelter saying a blessing at dinner.

That notion of "practical understanding" comes from theories of pragmatism. Philosophers and social scientists in this tradition see humans as practical problem solvers. Every situation requires that we figure out what's going on and that we sort through the files in our brains to find the right cue card. Deciding what's going on means making assessments of what kind of situation it is, how it is like and unlike things we have seen before. Is this large room really a mosque prayer hall? It also means assessing the people who are there and our own relationship to them. Will they recognize me or see me as a threat or try to proselytize me or welcome me home? And it means imagining how we might explain our action if we had to. Only then—all in an instant—do we employ both habit and creativity in solving the problem of what to do. Situations, that is, present themselves to us as already having structures and patterns that we didn't create.

Once we start to think about it, we may notice that those structures and patterns privilege some people more than others. One of the pioneers in practice theory[2] was the French sociologist Pierre Bourdieu (1990), and he was especially interested in how practices reinforce structures of difference and inequality. He observed that we learn our place in society and literally enact that place in our everyday practices. How we greet each other and how we share space embody both our own place and our status relative to others. Bourdieu's experience of religion was largely in the French Catholic context and in observations of colonialism, and he was keenly aware of how practices allowed some people to dominate others. Some people had literal places of honor, while others were literally outside the door.

But understanding religion as practice is not just about attending to power differences. Bourdieu was perhaps too preoccupied with structural and cultural conditioning and with status and power as primary motivations for action. While practices often reinforce structures of domination, sometimes they don't. We need to open up Bourdieu's work to see how practices work more broadly. He was right to say that practices always involve our habitual dispositions—how we act without thinking—and our cultural resources (ordinary things we know and skills we have). He was also right that practices are situated in a social "field" that structures the existing expectations for how people will act. We expect a different range of practices at the football stadium than the practices we see at a bridal shower or at shul on Saturday. There are different relationships, different kinds of knowledge, and different sources of power. Bourdieu would pay closest attention to the way a desire to protect one's own status or to dominate others was operating in every field. Our study of religious practice, however, will go beyond that question without leaving it behind.

One of the things Bourdieu missed was the way fields of interaction intersect and are not insulated from each other. The practical know-how from one place can be put to use in another. Just as work, family, and politics overlap with each other when a community organizes to seek a living wage, so religious practices are not confined to a single social space. What we learn to do in one place can spill over into other places. As a result, for example, action can be both religious and political at the same time. While it may be useful to think about distinct social domains and the cultural logics they sustain, the reality of everyday life is that practices travel across those boundaries. Another French sociologist, Michel de Certeau, said there are "formalities of practice" that "traverse the frontiers dividing time, place, and type of action. . . . Although they remain dependent upon the possibilities offered by circumstances, these *transverse tactics* do not obey the law of the place" (1984, 29). To study lived religion is to analyze those boundary-crossing tactics, as well as the possibilities—and constraints—offered by each set of circumstances.[3]

Some sources of power and difference are pervasive, however, and religious practices are often implicated in maintaining those hierarchies. Gender, race, sexuality, and social class are among the structures of power and difference that travel with us across boundaries; and as recent research has made clear, these ways of categorizing people are "intersectional." Each status reinforces the others. An African Muslim woman in Chicago may be an immigrant, a person of color, a woman, and a Muslim all at once. Understanding her religious practices requires paying attention to the way those things intersect. Just as it makes no sense to talk about gender or sexuality without talking about race and class, so it makes no sense to talk about any of those things without talking about religion—and vice versa.[4] Lived religious practice exists within the constraints offered by circumstances of difference and power, and Bourdieu was right that those circumstances are embodied in what we do. Analyzing lived religion requires attention to those dynamics and to the ways they take shape in habitual forms of action. That is something that has to remain visible as we examine everyday religious action.

But our analysis is incomplete without paying attention to the agency and creativity people can bring to any situation. The habits and instincts sometimes get overridden; the expectations get challenged. Sometimes people are intentional about subverting the rules. De Certeau suggests we look for the ways of acting that provide tactics with which to "manipulate the mechanisms of discipline and conform to them only in order to evade them" (1984, xiv). At other times, we improvise because we have to. Sociologist Ann Swidler (1986) provides a useful way to notice the places where creativity and new practices are most likely. She suggests that in "settled" times and places, where routines are not in doubt, habitual patterns take over. We don't need to explain ourselves because everyone "just knows" how to do things. When things get "unsettled"—a move to a new place, a natural disaster, a pandemic—we have to work harder to create new patterns and explain them.

Patterns of socially constructed action—practices—can be either habitual or surprising, constrained by circumstances or creative and subversive. When we look for religion in everyday lived patterns of action, we can see both the habitual structures those patterns assume and the agency of the actors. Religious practice is not uniquely structured by habit or domination, as if human beings simply perform religion without thinking or enact oppressive patterns because God told them to. But neither is religion uniquely creative, as if each person invents actions from scratch, transcending mere social conventions. Like all practice, lived religion is both structured and evolving. Looking at the religious things people do means living with a combination of orderly predictability and disorderly improvisation that varies across times and places.

Recent thinking about practice has added insight from cognitive science, as well.[5] Figuring out how to interpret a situation and remembering how to act are cognitive tasks that employ "schemas" in our brains enabling us to organize and quickly retrieve information based on past experience. The patterns we store in our brains are formed by complex webs of information about previous interactions, emotions tied to those memories, and more. This emerging research makes it clear that cognitive patterns help us to identify subtle cues that trigger our action. Scientists are now employing a range of methods to try to understand our perceptions and emotions and what links them to action. Part of what it means to understand practice as embodied and experiential is to ask how our brains organize information from the environment into cognitive models that allow us to act, often seemingly without thinking. We can then see the models in action as people act together in ways that presume these intersubjectively shared patterns and expectations. While most observers of lived religion will not be *doing* the cognitive neuroscience, being aware of that research can add to our understanding, especially when we want to understand how embodied collective action seems to happen without instruction or explanation.

Beginning with religion as practice, then, means that we start with the patterned regularities in what people do, and we seek to understand those patterns in the context of the cognitive models and the overlapping social fields of interaction that make them meaningful and allow us to act.

To say that religious action is meaningful is not necessarily to say that it fits neatly into a coherent life structure or doctrinal belief system or set of personal values. Rather than seeing religion *as* meaning making, we are saying that all actions require the kind of practical meaning that allows us to function in the world. In some cases, people do have a comprehensive internal religious meaning system that guides their action, but there are lots of other religious meanings out there, meanings that are inherent in the shared action itself, in the way we send signals to each other about what we are doing. We see someone lighting candles and recognize that there is a shrine, or we see distinctive attire and mentally categorize the wearer. The religious meanings of the actions do not require a comprehensive cognitive framework or a shared theological system. Studying lived religion simply means watching people do religious things, even when what they are doing seems fragmentary and doesn't fit neatly with other things they do, even when they aren't believers at all.

Studying lived religion as practice means that people and events and institutions get their religious identities in practice. Sometimes those practices include professing beliefs or claiming a religious identification. Those are the things that most often count on surveys. Studying religion as practice, on the other hand, sets those questions aside. We are interested in how people employ practices that signal their identification with a tradition and how they narrate their life in religious and spiritual terms when the answers aren't predetermined.[6] People are constituted by the accumulated patterns of their social practices, but that is an ongoing construction project. There may be reasons for a person to claim a certain religious identity, and when they do, we should pay attention to those practices of identity-claiming. Where and how do people say who they are and what role religion plays in their lives? Those ways of talking and reporting are themselves lived religious practices.

Similarly, we may ask about the relative pervasiveness of religious practices in a life or a society without claiming that one is inherently religious, while another is inherently secular. Are religious practices more present in one society or another, one field of action or another? Are there more religious practices in household spaces than in work spaces? Are religious practices more pervasive in immigrant communities than in native-born ones? Studying lived religion does allow attention to "more" and "less." But that assessment has to begin by being aware of religious practice wherever and whenever it happens, not by counting actions in one place as religious and actions in another as not. Whether studying individuals, social settings, or societies, a lived religion approach directs us to what people are doing—their practices. Those actions can be seen as the structured and creative, habitual and emergent ways of assessing situations and responding out of shared practical know-how.

Studying "Religion"

While religious practice is like other social practice, it is also distinctive. What makes it so? The shared human activity that concerns us here is a particular *kind* of social practice, not because it has a cosmological world-ordering character or is performed by a religious person or in a religious institution. It is a religious social practice because it has *a spiritual dimension*. That is, it incorporates—either directly or indirectly—the presence of a reality beyond the ordinary.[7] That reality may or may not be personified as a deity. It often is, but we know that many of the world's religious traditions are oriented to spirits and spiritual realms that may not be named and personified. Likewise, a "more than ordinary" reality may or may not be seen as powerful; although it mostly is, and people often ask for assistance. We would limit our vision if we only studied practices that are oriented to a powerful god. The key identifying element in lived religion is simply the (direct) consciousness of and/or (indirect) reference to an alternative, religious, reality.

This reality is something distinctive but not separate. We can speak of it as "sacralized" or "transcendent" or even "otherworldly," but it is important not to assume that those characteristics set religious realities utterly apart from everyday life.[8] The consciousness we will be looking for is more both/and than either/or. Religious practice involves consciousness of and acting within multiple layers of reality at once, recognizing the "more than" while not necessarily losing touch with the ordinary. Wherever we find patterns of social action that fit this model, we can bring our analytical questions to the table.

That kind of broad definition also leaves open the possibility for comparison across times and places. We can think about how practices are alike or different in different social settings even when the traditions themselves might seem very different. This is an "etic" (outside, analytical) definition that allows us to think about things the participants themselves might not even call religious. Think about lighting candles or bowing, for example. What might we learn by paying attention to the range of settings where those practices evoke a spiritual dimension of experience, how they are enacted in different religious traditions and settings, by individuals or by crowds?

We need not, however, simply impose categories from the outside. Religion is a recognized category that exists in the world, a category that helps to organize all those perceptual cues in our brains. But it is not a neutral universal category that includes the same things in all times and places. Our task includes paying attention to how the category is used in context. People learn from their own experiences that certain kinds of interaction are to be understood as religious. Scholars refer to those as "emic" understandings—definitions that are operative within a social setting and used by the participants themselves. Religion gets named as such, and when it does, students of lived religious practice can ask what people are doing and with whom. What organizations are understood to deserve the "religion" label? What sorts of experiences of the sacred are included and excluded, and how do authorities police the use of the "religion" category? Lived religion approaches allow us to take seriously both everyday understandings of social action and the official impositions of categories on that interaction.

Some religious practices may be claimed as such because they are personally, directly experienced as transcendent, but other, equally religious practices are named as such because of where and how they happen. Even when the actors are not personally and directly aware of a sacred presence, a practice can be religious because of how it is socially framed. That is, the spiritual dimension may be indirectly present because practices are connected to institutions, identities, and groups that represent religion. Those institutions, in turn, often produce situations that do evoke direct spiritual experience. It is important that our study of religion encompass both direct experience of sacredness and the social institutions that construct symbols and rituals that seek to establish and maintain the transcendent connections. Rather than seeing direct experience as individual authentic "spirituality" and the institutionalized patterns as merely organized "religion," we will gain greater insight by studying both individual subjective experience and socially enacted patterns.

We do not have to choose, then, between studying individual spirituality and studying organized religion. Both involve lived religious practice. Nor do we have to choose between indigenous (emic) definitions that come from the community and an etic (analytical) definition that allows us to see patterns and resemblances. Lived religious practice can be studied based on practices that include a spiritual dimension, whether or not they are labeled "religious" by actors or authorities and whether or not they are personally meaningful. Mostly, however, what we study are things people already recognize as religious.

A Multidimensional Approach to Analyzing Lived Religious Practice

Studying lived religious practice starts with these basic tools for identifying and thinking about what a religious practice is. The next step is to think about the multiple layers of human experience that go into any practice. When we say we are studying what people do, our work can benefit from a framework that encompasses and highlights the basic human qualities of the action in question. If understanding religion means more than asking people what they believe or counting how many show up for religious services, what is it about their practices—both inside religious spaces and elsewhere—that we should pay attention to?

The framework we will use builds on the foundation of research that has been done on lived religion over the past three decades. Identifying the recurring themes that have emerged gives us a place to start. What have people been paying attention to, and how has that helped us learn more about religion? A variety of categorizations have, in fact, begun to emerge. Sociologist Penny Edgell (2012) looked at the research and listed emotion, embodied practice, and narratives as the typical foci of study. Robert Wuthnow (2020) also singled out emotion and embodiment as important topics for his sociological discussion of religious practice. Mary Jo Neitz (2011), also a sociologist of religion, added spirituality, materiality, and locality, along with embodiment, as domains that should be the focus of lived religion research.

Those themes can be expanded, deepened, and given structure, however, by what we know from practice theory itself. What human capacities are implicated in everyday social practice?[9] Recall that Schatzki (2001) and Reckwitz (2002), whose definitions started this chapter, each incorporates *embodiment* as a foundational dimension of practice. Social theorist Bryan Turner (2008) writes that the body "is constitutive of our being-in-the-world," whether we analyze it as the site where nature and culture meet, the site where society regulates, the site of political struggles over identities and power, or a site of performance and representation. Lived religion research agrees; the study of religious practice, of necessity, is a study of embodiment.

Human bodies sit at the intersection of culture with the material and natural world. While it is bodies that sense, encounter, and manipulate that world, the *materiality* itself matters. Again, Schatzki's (2001) definition of practice reminds us that actions are "materially mediated," and Reckwitz (2002) points us toward "'things' and their use." Here, too, practice theory and lived religion research intersect.

Edgell's inclusion of *emotion* in her cultural sociology of religion is echoed in practice theory, as well. Emotions are bodily, but they are also cognitive and social (Ignatow 2007). They are defined and regulated by culture and context, and they help to constitute the practices enacted in those contexts. Social practice includes an inevitable emotional dimension, so lived religion's attention to feelings is both necessary and helpful.

The study of social practice suggests two additional dimensions—*aesthetics* and *morality*—that have ironically been given less attention by students of lived religion but can enrich our work. An aesthetics of practice calls for an examination of the sometimes elusive qualities of an object (or a body) and how those are interpreted as attractive or repulsive in the process of acting. Aesthetic taste is embedded in the shared understanding that shapes practice, including when the practice in question is a religious one.

Attention to aesthetics also highlights the reality that practices involve judgments, and some of those are *moral* assessments of what should and should not happen. Practices convey and embody moral meanings and expectations, in both words and actions. Sometimes collective practices are explicitly centered on moral formation, and other times religious practices engender the solidarity necessary for moral norms to be reinforced. Even in small, everyday religious practices, we should look for assumptions and judgments about what is right and wrong, worthy and not.

Practice theories are less consistent in how they treat communication, but studies of lived religion consistently point to *narrative* as central to religious practice. This is not to place words and symbols at the center of our analysis or to substitute verbal accounts for the practice itself, but it is to say both that talk itself is a practice and that implicit and explicit stories are embedded in all practices. As Margaret Somers (1994) argues, narrative takes an event and makes it part of a plot that guides action. We act within an imagined past and future, as well as in the present.

These six dimensions—embodiment, materiality, emotion, aesthetics, moral judgment, and narrative—allow deep systematic exploration of everyday human action in the social world. We can think about any social practice—from test-taking to voting to eating out or shopping—as having these multiple experiential dimensions. Religious practice, wherever it happens, bears the same marks. What makes it distinct is its *spiritual* dimension, that is, the capacity to perceive nonordinary realities intertwined with the ordinary world. While lived religious practice is experienced as a fused whole, it is fruitful to identify these parts and to assess their interrelationship. That is the work to which we will turn in part 2, but only after a necessary look at how historical and cultural and legal contexts shape lived religious practice everywhere.

Ideas for Further Study

1. For some theorists, such as Erving Goffman (1967), "practice" and "ritual" overlap considerably. Social theorist Randall Collins (2004), for example, has elaborated an "interaction ritual theory" that points to the way society depends (both for maintenance and for moments of transformation) on occasions when there is copresence, shared focus, shared emotion, and moral obligation—a ritual. Catherine Bell's (1997) work draws clearer distinctions between this sort of social practice and what are usually understood as rituals. She points to formalism, traditionalism, invariance, rule governance, sacred symbolism, and performance as the properties of the rituals she wishes to study.

2. "Practice theory" is a burgeoning theoretical field across the social sciences and philosophy. As noted, Schatzki (2001) and Reckwitz (2002) are good places to start for a definitional overview. David Swartz (1998) provides a helpful and accessible summary and interpretation of Bourdieu's theories. Recent contributors in sociology include John Levy Martin (2011) and Neil Gross (2009), both of whom make links to philosophical pragmatism. Although not framed as practice theory, Ann Swidler's (1986) classic article "Culture in Action" builds on similar ideas; and Robert Wuthnow's (2020) book on practicing religion includes a helpful history of the way practice theory and sociological theories of religion have overlapped and diverged. Among historians of US religion, Laurie Maffly-Kipp and her colleagues (Maffly-Kipp, Schmidt, and Valeri 2006) laid the foundation by describing the rise of practice theories and providing a rich collection of cases from which to draw.

3. There are several good theoretical sources for thinking about how actors bring agency and experience with them across multiple fields, that is, how practices are portable. One could start with William Sewell (1992) but also include Mustafa Emirbayer and Ann Mische (1998), along with the more recent work of Claire Decoteau (2016).

4. Since Kimberlé Crenshaw (1989) introduced the idea, "intersectionality" has been a critical addition to our understanding of how different systems of power work together to constitute and amplify each other. She and others (Cho, Crenshaw, and McCall 2013) have provided a helpful overview and assessment of how the

idea has been used over these thirty years, across disciplines and around the world. In the study of religion, a special issue of *Gender and Society* included attention to intersectional themes (Avishai, Jafar, and Rinaldo 2015), and Krista McQueeney's (2014) research is an excellent example of what this looks like in studies of religious practice. When we turn to questions of embodiment, there will be further suggestions for places to start in this very lively field.

5. Among the social scientists who have explored the links to cognitive science are Paul DiMaggio (1997) and Omar Lizardo and Michael Strand (2010). John Levi Martin (2010) has drawn extensively on this research, as well. He says that we literally don't have the cognitive capacity to create and use a comprehensive meaning system. Note how this casts doubt on the various theories of religion that start with notions like Peter Berger's (1967) "sacred canopy" or Clifford Geertz's (1973) "patterns of meaning embodied in symbols."

6. I have written elsewhere about religious identity as narrative practice, arguing that all identities are situationally specific and multilayered (Ammerman 2003). That article covers many of the theorists who contribute to understandings of religious identity.

7. This definition of religion admittedly sometimes includes ideas and practices like Big Foot followers or astrology practitioners that we might not usually think of as religious. When we are analyzing lived religious practice, however, those judgments are out of place. Calling something "religion" (or not) is often a way of judging between "acceptable" practices and ones that are deemed marginal or illegitimate. To counter this, for example, Stephen Ellis and Gerrie ter Haar (2007) insist on calling African beliefs "religion" and not "superstition" or "occult" or "magic."

8. The idea of a radical separation between sacred and profane comes from the early twentieth-century French sociologist Emile Durkheim ([1912] 1964), but it shows up in lots of other dichotomies, such as Charles Taylor's (2007) tendency to see the transcendent as essentially different from the immanent. All the terms we have at our disposal have the unfortunate tendency to suggest the Western temptation to create a binary that sets something "otherworldly" over against things "this-worldly."

9. The dimensions I propose here have resonance with what Christian Smith (2010) outlines in *What Is a Person?* His list is longer, but he identifies basic (bodily) consciousness of existence as the primary foundation of our humanity. One layer up are emotions, interests, interpretations, and memories. These are the mechanisms for filtering and framing how we interact with the world. Next are capacities for acting creatively—making things, constructing languages, and creating identities. Moral and aesthetic judgments, finally, are the "highest order" capacities in his scheme.

2

Lived Religion and Its Contexts

Lived religious practices are patterns of action that are oriented toward things that persons or groups recognize as religious, but how that assessment is made depends on *where* it is made. That's because "religion" is a socially defined category, and that means that context matters. We can observe someone kneeling and guess that they may be praying. We can observe new parents going to a religious shrine and imagine they wish to dedicate an infant. We can observe a piece of jewelry and guess something about the religious identification of the wearer. That is, we can recognize those things *if* we share some of the same cultural know-how. People in a given cultural context learn that certain kinds of cues and interaction are to be understood as religious and others are not, and some of those contexts are quite different from the places you may know best. How they—and you—make those usually unconscious assessments is shaped by history and culture but also by the governmental definitions and constraints that surround religious practices. This chapter will give you some tools with which to confront the challenge of understanding lived religion as it happens in those differing legal and cultural contexts.

Recognizing religious practices in context means beginning our work with humility. We will make mistakes, but we will make fewer if we are willing to learn from those with whom we work. We won't understand what we are seeing if we observe from within our own cultural bubble. We have to remind ourselves to avoid imposing assumptions from our own setting onto practices in another place. If our religious context is one where head coverings are required in sacred spaces, we need to recognize that our own instinct to consider a bareheaded worshiper blasphemous may not be the right interpretation of the practice we are observing. Or if our instinct is to keep religion private, we will need to avoid jumping to conclusions about very public practices that mix religion and political life.

Contexts matter. Think about prayer. Kneeling on a rug and facing toward Mecca may be the basic core action that we can observe in the

Muslim practice of *salat*. But think about how different that practice is when the call to prayer is heard by everyone in the community and everyone stops to pray. Or when there is no audible call, only an alarm on your Apple watch, and no one else in the office stops work. Or when you are one of only a few Christians or secular people in a place where Muslim prayer is mandated by law or custom. Or when the opposite is the case—prayer of any kind is forbidden or seen as ridiculous and has to be undertaken in secret. A prayer is not just a prayer, even within the same religious tradition. Understanding lived religious practice, then, will require us to pay attention to the religious ecology of the culture and to the legal systems that define what can and can't be done, what is expected and what is required.[1] The variations in these arrangements are many but not infinite, so this chapter will suggest a set of categories that can serve as a starting point for seeing how religious practices unfold differently in different times and places.

Doing this work sometimes means that we are seeking to learn something about practices by comparing things that seem similar but are enacted in different settings—as in the preceding example of Muslim prayer. What can we learn about the practice of praying by studying it in different cultures? That very notion of studying religion across contexts is a contentious one, however. Some scholars argue that the term "religion" itself is a colonial invention and that we can't really use it at all—especially beyond its North Atlantic home. They are right that much of the world didn't know they had a "religion" until imperial powers started using that concept as a tool for sorting people and governing them (Chidester 1996). Local leaders who were respected as spiritually wise were co-opted by colonial rulers into helping keep the population passive. People with different practices were sorted into different territories. And lots of people were told they didn't have a "religion" because it didn't look much like what Western powers thought religion should look like. Scholars such as cultural anthropologist Talal Asad (1993) have pointed out the dangers of this form of essentialism—seeing religion as defined by a universal phenomenon that powerful groups get to define.

From a very different angle, many Westerners today want to distance themselves from "religion" and claim "spirituality" instead. Being religious has taken on negative connotations because it is often linked to traditionalist politics or moral scandal (Hout and Fischer 2014), while being spiritual is seen as a virtue (Fetzer Institute 2020). If the people we are observing reject the term—or don't recognize it at all—we should still pay attention. What kind of action are they rejecting? What do they see as a religious practice, and what is something else?

The terms are out there, and lived religion approaches allow us to take seriously both everyday understandings of them and official impositions. As we noted in chapter 1, we do not have to choose between indigenous definitions and a definition that allows us to make comparisons. Lived religion is a useful way to approach both. We can learn from practices that share a family resemblance in their references to a spiritual reality that goes beyond the everyday empirical world. Even if they are described differently, we can analyze the way a nonordinary reality plays a role. While many yoga practitioners are explicitly participating in a Hindu religious tradition, for example, others are quite adamant that they are just exercising, and others call their practice spiritual. Understanding the experience of this practice, including these diverse narratives about it, requires attention to the contexts in which the practices take place.

In every culture, lived religious practices can happen in any corner of everyday life, whether or not they get labeled and institutionalized. Remember that lived religion can describe practices that are categorized by the participants themselves as religious—whether or not our own culture would see them that way. And lived religion can describe practices that are indirectly religious, that is, actions that people themselves do not personally and directly experience as transcendent, but nevertheless are defined as religious by their connection to institutions, identities, and groups that are understood to be religious in their culture. Religions, in other words, often take on a social reality that goes beyond individual experience and shapes the practices of those who interact within it.

If understanding lived religious practice requires paying attention to local institutions and expectations, we have to begin simply by understanding how the people in question use the category "religion." When religion is named, what are they doing and with whom? What organizations are understood to deserve the label? What sorts of experiences of the sacred are included and excluded, and how do authorities police the use of the religion category? Those are questions observers should be asking, wherever we are doing our work.

Expanding Horizons

Taking account of the variations in how societies have understood, organized, and regulated religious action may be easiest when we start to observe a culture that is very different from our own. Why does everyone get off work for something called "Pentecost Monday"? Why are people tossing coins at a gong at this Daoist temple? Are these actually *religious* practices? What difference do they make? Assumptions about what counts and how practices are organized are no less present in your home context, of course—they are just less obvious.

This blind spot has been exacerbated by the fact that most lived religion research has concerned micro-level, face-to-face social processes (Repstad 2019). In subsequent chapters of this book, we will dig deeply into those micro-level processes, looking for the multiple dimensions of cultural practice and human experience that are at work. Before we do that, however, we need to take off some blinders. Those practices happen in specific places in which there are political and cultural forces at work. Taking account of those "macro" forces—the big structures that are often invisible—is essential to reminding ourselves that a religious practice in one place is not necessarily the same as an apparently similar one somewhere else.

A first step in opening our collective eyes is to look at where we are standing. In a recent project, with the help of two of my students—Kira Ganga Kieffer and Tim Snyder—I surveyed the lived religion studies that had been published in English-language academic journals since the mid-1990s. We cataloged publications within the social sciences and humanities that used either "lived religion" or "everyday religion" in their title, abstract, or keywords. Through Google Scholar, library keyword searches, and targeted journal searches, we identified sixty-four articles that fit those criteria. They came from a broad range of disciplines and represented practices that ranged from mixed martial arts to fly fishing. There were people writing about nursing and social work and religious leadership, along with sociologists and religious studies scholars and practical theologians. But that seeming breadth masked just how limited our geographic perspective has been. Of those sixty-four articles, just three focused on Latin America, three on South Asia, and one on an African site. The remainder were situated in the "Global North" of Europe and North America. Admittedly our search did not include books or items in other languages, so we undoubtedly missed a lot. There is also important research that comes from places and disciplines—like anthropology—where "lived religion" is not the way people have been writing about the practices that would enlarge our vision. But it is a good bet that the patterns are similar. Lived religion researchers tend to be situated in a very particular vantage point.

The unfortunate consequence of standing in the Global North has been a limited understanding of lived religious practice—or, worse yet, the notion that lived religion only happens in a post-Christian context. When we actually pay attention to the larger cultural and legal horizon, we note that most lived religion research simply assumes a context of Western democracy where institutional religion is now relatively weak and individual choice is taken for granted. That assumed and unexamined context has colored what we think we know. Time to take off those blinders!

If we are to understand lived religious practice—whether in the places where it has been most studied or in the rest of the world—we need a framework for thinking about multiple social and legal contexts. Such a framework may be useful for comparison, but it is first of all simply a way of identifying the cultural assumptions and legal constraints that shape lived religious practice wherever it happens. I am proposing here that four "ideal types" (and one important hybrid type) can be identified. They can help us describe the range of religious social contexts around the world: religion can be *entangled, established, institutional,* or *interstitial,* with *postcolonial* contexts as a hybrid formed from the encounter between established forms and entangled ones. These are not "ideal" in a moral sense of that word but ideal as a conceptualization with which we can think.[2] They are not mutually exclusive, nor are they necessarily descriptive of an entire society. Rather, they identify *differences in typical expectations for the fields within which religious practices will be found and the modes of regulation that will constrain (or encourage) religious action.* A field, in this case, is an arena of social interaction within which a given set of expectations and rules apply. And within that field, how do mechanisms of power and authority set the bounds of what is possible?

Entangled Religious Fields

The first kind of context is one we will call *entangled*. People in many societies engage in religious practices that are so highly interwoven with everyday practical affairs that it is impossible to think of them as distinct forms of social life, and they certainly are not organized into separate "religious" institutions. Life-cycle events, business transactions, political organizing, and interaction with the natural world are simultaneously mundane and sacred. Hailing a taxi might be a religious practice as much as planting one's crops or blessing a new birth. Religious practice is diffuse, interwoven with all the other activities of daily life. There are few divisions—spatially, ontologically, functionally—between religious action and action that is also economic, political, or familial. Where religion happens, what kind of knowledge it represents, and what it does are intertwined with everything else. In these contexts, there is, in fact, something like what Peter Berger (1967) called a "sacred canopy," although it is more a canopy of practice than of ideas or institutions.

Social scientists who live and work in Europe and North America have long been accustomed to thinking of such settings as "traditional" societies and assuming that they have been or soon will be replaced by a modern way of doing things that insists religion is something private and set apart. It is useful to remind ourselves, however, that religiously entangled places are present in the world today and usually exist alongside otherwise-modern ways of living. People can be technologically skilled, advocate for democracy, connect with diverse others, and also engage those activities with a spiritual awareness and a range of ritual practice that they share with all or most of their compatriots.

This sort of entanglement is not the same as religion having an *influence* in secular affairs. When societies separate religious practice from other kinds of practices, it makes sense to ask if one has an effect on the other. In an entangled context, however, that separation does not exist, so the practices we observe have to be understood on their own terms. In a context like this, where religious practice penetrates all aspects of life, the term "secular" has little meaning.

This highly entangled cultural context can be seen in Stephen Ellis and Gerrie ter Haar's writing about African politics. They insist that understanding the social and political world in Africa requires an approach that recognizes "distinctive modes of acquiring knowledge about the world, characterised by a holistic approach in which the sacred and the secular can be said to constitute one organic reality" (Ellis and ter Haar 2007, 386). An African epistemology, they argue, includes both material and immaterial realms—distinguishable but not separable. Consider, for example, Ann Swidler's (2010b) analysis of economic development and humanitarian efforts in Malawi. Understanding those realities ("secular" in a Western accounting) required an understanding of the sacred role of chiefs, people who embody the identity and collective well-being of the group. Swidler writes,

> Chiefs also store up—and in some sense embody—sacred power. Their sacred power is connected to what are, or were, at least systems, specific ritual roles in communicating with the ancestors or ensuring the fertility of land, animals and people. It is difficult, however, to distinguish a chief's prestige, which comes in part from traditional cultural roles, from his sacred or spiritual powers, which in turn both reflect and protect the strength and health of his community. Chiefs' prestige in turn depends on their ability to access and contain sacred powers. (2010b, 162–163)

Chiefs' ability to tap sacred power is entangled with their political position, the group's agricultural practice, and everything else of significance, something Swidler was able to see, in part, with the help of her local research team. When researchers cross these kinds of cultural boundaries, partnerships with people on the ground become essential.

The role of religious leaders in the health of the community was especially clear when the Ebola virus wreaked havoc in much of West Africa. Experts from global health agencies brought their own ideas about the proper role of religion, perhaps shaped by notions of universal human rights but also shaped by secularized ways of thinking about the world. When their technical solutions fell short, they eventually learned to work alongside those who understood the religious practices in local communities. Writing in the medical journal *The Lancet*, Katherine Marshall and Sally Smith (2015) described what those experts and local leaders learned. These public health workers came to understand the entangled nature of religion in this context. Burying the dead and caring for the living were sacred and mundane at the same time. Understanding that entanglement was literally a matter of life and death.

Entangled Religious Practice Meets Global Health Workers

Health messages, crucial in public health approaches to infectious disease, are more readily accepted if developed with communities through two-way communication and respect for community expertise that is concentrated prominently in religious institutions. Ebola's close association with cultural and religious practices makes active community engagement especially important. Change of funeral practices was imperative to reversing the epidemic, and religious leaders (modern and traditional, Muslim and Christian) had to be involved. The resulting WHO "Safe and Dignified Burial Protocol" was vital in halting spread of the disease and laying foundations for community trust. In many respects, the protocol was a game changer in the overall trajectory of crisis response. Organisation of home care and guarantee of proper quarantine procedures likewise demand religious communities' involvement. (Marshall and Smith 2015, e25)

Perceiving and acting on spirit-infused understandings of the world is not confined to Africa, of course, nor is it exclusively the domain of "traditional" societies. There may be pockets of social life in any society where religious practice is expected to exist pervasively—times and places where the ordinary is swept aside. But more importantly, all over the world, there are subsocieties that organize themselves as religious communal enclaves (think about Orthodox Jews in Brooklyn or Amish farmers in Pennsylvania). From convents to religious utopian experiments like the Shakers, groups have long attempted to bring all of life into an entangled religious whole. In many places, it takes intentional action and enforced separation from other parts of society for such complete entanglement to survive. That separation and its implied rejection of the mainstream can mean trouble for a religious group. Living a separate life, governed by different rules, can engender hostility and clashes with legal authorities. Sometimes the issue is a specific practice (such as avoiding vaccination), but often the offense is the very notion of living a life fully entangled with spiritual practice in a society where that is not the norm.[3]

It is therefore useful to think about a continuum of religious entanglement. In its ideal typical form, entangled religion occurs in social locations where there is a high degree of overlap between religion and everyday social action that extends across a broad swath of the society or subgroup as a whole.

Established Religion

A second, rather different sort of entanglement exists where there is an organized *established* religious tradition, that is, where there is both an organized entity that claims jurisdiction over religious practice and an organized entity (a state) that legitimizes the authority of that group. Together, the organized entities create a culture that is deeply infused with religious practice, and those practices are enforced and supported collectively through laws and taxes. Again, there is a continuum, since every modern state regulates religion to some degree, and strong cultural majorities can create a kind of de facto establishment that often includes legal privileges.[4] Businesses may be required to close on Sunday, for example, supporting Christian practices—or (as in Israel) on Saturday, supporting Jewish practice—even if citizens can legally practice many traditions.

A legally established religion can exercise a good deal more power than that, of course. It can mandate prescribed or banned forms of clothing, require the payment of taxes or attendance at services, and set the shared calendar of holidays and days off. Its ability to levy taxes will allow it to support religious staff and operations and buildings, as well as cultural and social service activities; and it will probably bear the obligation to register births and deaths for the population as a whole. In addition, the state will probably control the certification of religious officials and may organize major religious festivals. When individuals participate in any of this, we can analyze their practices as religious, whether or not they personally experience anything spiritual or believe what the official religion teaches.

Sometimes this wedding of religious and national identity is intentionally fostered as a way of deepening the power of those who are in authority. Such practices can be described as religious nationalisms,[5] where citizenship is intentionally linked to religious identity. Religious nationalist practices can be relatively benign, but they always exclude. They can also be contentious and even violent. Being Hindu in India, for example, involves religious practices, but it has also become a political statement and sometimes involves violent responses to non-Hindus. Similarly, being Catholic in Bavaria or an Eastern Orthodox Christian in Serbia or evangelical Christian in the United States can become a highly contested political assertion about the legitimacy of one's place and power in the society. Religious nationalists operate within the structure of modern nation-states but surround the state with religious cultural practices, new and old. We should not overlook the *religious* nature of everyday civic and political practices in these contexts.

Theoretically, an established religion is also a monopoly, but that is rarely if ever true in practice. There are always at least some religious (and nonreligious) minorities, and the arrival of new religious minorities can precipitate difficult realignments. The presence of Muslim minorities throughout Europe has created just such a reexamination of the relation between religion and national identity (Parvez 2017). Where a nation seeks to assert a single legitimate religious or secular system, minorities must find ways to survive outside or on the margins of the law (and often in opposition to it). Indeed, when states and religions are entwined in this way, religious practice outside official limits is implicitly (or explicitly) a threat to state authority. This is true even when the established state religion is secularism or atheism, as practitioners of Falun Gong or Muslim Uyghurs have discovered in contemporary China. Doing meditative exercise in a park means one thing for a yoga class in Brooklyn and quite another for a morning gathering of Falun Gong in Beijing.

What is more common than a strict legal monopoly is what political scientist André Laliberté calls a "multiple religious establishment." This is "a particular variant . . . where the state, aware of the religious pluralism of society, asserts its prerogative to protect and even promote a limited number of different religions, where specific criteria must be met in order to benefit from the status of a religion deserving a privileged status" (Laliberté 2016, 147). Laliberté's description of Taiwan's religio-political history provides a good case study of the different ways establishments can work. In the half century before World War II, Taiwan was part of the Japanese empire. In the last years of that regime, controlling religious practice was critical to colonial rule, as it was to the Chinese rulers who followed. His attention to the legal and political history can help us remember the kinds of questions we should have in mind when we think about religious context.

Religious Establishments in Taiwan

[During its military ascendancy, the colonial government] enforced a "Japanization" movement that aimed at eliminating the practice of native religions. This latter policy affected both foreign religions like Christianity, as well as native religions such as Taoism, but less so Buddhism, which was also widely observed in Japan. But even that religion was the target of government intervention. Seeing the temples as a form of extra-governmental institution, the colonial authorities expropriated local temples to assert their control. Concurrently, and observing the weak development of Buddhism in the island prior to their arrival, Japanese Buddhist institutions sent their own monks to Taiwan to perform missionary and educational activities. . . . [Once the war was over, the Chinese Nationalists (KMT) established] a three-tiered structure of regulation for religion. . . . The first tier was recognition of a number of religions by the Ministry of Interior, a recognition the KMT made a point of presenting to the outside world as proof that the ROC [Republic of China] respected religious freedom. The second tier was a number of religious practices that state elites considered superstitions and that were harassed on the grounds that they were considered wasteful practices. Finally a third tier of religions were deemed illegal and persecuted by the government because they were suspected of being clandestine fellow travellers of the communist party, or of indulging in seditious activities because of their peace advocacy and of engaging in "immoral" behaviour. (Laliberté 2016, 155–158)

There are many ways states can regulate religious practice, and where there is an establishment—even a plural, unofficial, or legally disestablished one—both minorities and the majority know where they stand. Both are fundamentally shaped by a context where majority culture and majority politics contain countless points of connection to majority religious rituals and traditions. Majority religious culture imposes itself on everyone, meaning that routine activities of everyday life can be both civic and religious.

That mixture of civic life, cultural custom, religious symbols, and practices lingers even when the legal mechanisms are no longer present (or never were). Christmas trees are lit and Easter eggs are hidden, and we say "God bless" our country or our monarch. The religious buildings at the center of the community are preserved, and a cross on the flag is defended—even by people who consider themselves thoroughly secular. Long-entrenched practices may evolve, but it is still worth thinking about the religious dimensions of those practices, even when the individuals involved do not personally believe.[6] In monopoly or postmonopoly societies, family, culture, education, politics, and civic life are entwined with religious identity and religious practice, whether or not the individual participants believe the creeds or support their churches by attending. People may only discover how "Christian" they are when there are others around who are different. The presence of difference is often what reveals the shared practical knowledge that had been taken for granted.[7]

The Postcolonial Mix

That postestablishment situation takes on a particular character when the establishment in question was imposed as part of a colonial empire. In the often-violent encounter between indigenous religious practice (usually of the entangled variety) and colonial rule (usually of the established variety), both sides adapted. The result was something of a hybrid. Sometimes colonists co-opted local religious leaders as agents of "indirect rule."[8] Sometimes colonial culture was propagated by way of the religious schools, hospitals, and churches or temples that provided pathways for some local populations to advance in the colonial state. In most cases, preexisting sacred traditions persisted in some form.

With the exit of colonial rulers, colonial religious institutions have often been transformed by local populations into their own indigenous forms. Political struggles over the role of religious institutions have followed, as well. Inevitably, regulation of religion has been a part of the struggle for political power and national identity. Postcolonial societies ask what will properly count as religion in this new political context and what will its relationship be to the new state.

Throughout the postcolonial world, then, the practice of religion continues to bear the marks of both its long local history and the overlay of various modes of established colonial religion. In addition, dynamic new religious movements have taken hold over the past half century. As religious studies scholar Birgit Meyer says of Ghana, "African cosmologies of the relation between spirits and the physical world intersect, in complex ways, with the evangelizing work by Western mission societies, the introduction of the modern (colonial) and postcolonial state, and its transformation in our current age" (2012, 88). Those transformations, as she notes, have been significantly shaped by the explosion of Pentecostal forms of religious life, which tend toward the same entangled kinds of religious practice that had long been present in these places. When examining lived religious practice in postcolonial societies, the legal and cultural structures are likely to be shaped by more than one of our types. There are elements of entangled religion, of established religion, and of the plural institutionalized forms to which we next turn.

Institutional Religion

The third kind of context for religious belief and practice is the one that has been most commonly analyzed in existing social science research, since institutions produce things that are countable. Because religion happens in organized institutions, we can measure the number of people who participate or the way religion influences actions beyond its organizational boundaries. When religion is institutionalized, it occupies a distinct field in social life. That is, religion is supposed to happen in some places and not in others. Religion is recognized as having its own organizations that largely set their own rules, have their own separate activities, and are led by their own trained and credentialed professionals. States may set some limits but are not the dominating force. That also means that there are specialized forms of religious knowledge and religious expertise that are set apart from knowledge that is assumed to be secular.

This way of organizing the complex functions of society—economy, health, law, education, religion, and the rest—each under its own umbrella is what sociologists describe as "modern." Max Weber, an early twentieth-century sociologist, called it a "rational" system of authority, one in which social action is functionally divided and governed by the logic of each separate system. He is one of those Europeans who expected that the world would evolve eventually away from "traditional" ways of organizing (that is, around land and lineage and personal respect) and toward this sort of dividing up of the tasks and trusting the experts. Religious practices would eventually be found in religious places and perhaps in private life but not in other spheres, which were expected to operate by secular rules.[9]

There is some overlap between institutional systems and established ones, since both take on these modern organizational forms. While establishment systems may also have distinct agencies and specialized professionals, their larger connection to national history and law set them apart. In the disestablished institutional context, there are multiple religious traditions existing on a roughly level legal playing field. And as long as they play by the larger society's rules of engagement, fitting accepted criteria for what constitutes a legitimate "religion," there is room for diversity. As we noted earlier, there will always be rules and limits, and the observer of lived religious practice, even in the most apparently free context, should not ignore the way some practices are encouraged while others are outlawed.

In a context where religion takes this modern, plural, institutional form, "organized religion" is a key site for lived religious practice, even when a growing segment of the population is unaffiliated (Pew Research Center 2019). In the United States, for example, congregations and denominations and religious nonprofits are places where we expect religious action to take place. They publish lessons and worship guides, organize charitable activities, and provide spaces in which to gather. People may individually improvise and combine what they get from different places, but organizations channel practices into recognizable packages. Lived religious practice happens in the sanctuaries of these organizations and in habits they encourage. Organized modern religious traditions are sites of collective practices and sources of practices that are engaged in everyday life.

The importance of such organized religious sites has become especially apparent in the study of immigrant and other minority religious groups. To the extent that religious associations fall within a society's definition of permissible religion, organizing them allows immigrants the opportunity to create a safe, multifunctional social space, where practices are sustained but also adapted. For example, located in the heart of Little Haiti in Miami, Notre Dame D'Haiti, a Catholic parish, is a center of worship but also much more than that. Beyond regular Sunday Mass observances and annual festivals, there are many forms of practical aid and advocacy. Sociologist Margarita Mooney spent extended periods of observation in this parish and among its members. She was present in the community and learned the language, even going with parishioners back to Haiti. She writes that many of the Haitians she got to know there described it as "a *kafou*, or crossroads, where they come to worship, to meet other Haitians, and to find useful information about adapting to their new society" (Mooney 2009, 55). Hers is an excellent example of what can be learned through immersive participant observation. Among the many religious practices she observed were the prayer meetings that happened both at the church and in people's homes. These were lived religious practices given structure by organized religion and also supporting the everyday needs of the parishioners.

Immigrants and Organized Religious Practice in Miami

Charismatic prayer meetings can occur in small groups of eight to ten people in someone's home, or among much larger groups, sometimes reaching several hundred people at the weekly Charismatic prayer sessions at Notre Dame that end with Mass. During such meetings, people recite prayers together, such as the rosary. Some people pray in tongues, others then state their wishes out loud and ask for intercessory prayers. Some come forward to give testimonies and some recount how, through God's grace, they were able to overcome a serious problem. Seeing someone in a similar position who has overcome his or her problem gives others hope that they will be able to solve their own problems. . . . Notre Dame has numerous social-action-oriented groups, all of which are closely tied to one or more of the prayer groups. . . . But even those members of Notre Dame who do not participate in a social-action group perceive their continual prayer as a service they provide to the community. (Mooney 2009, 77–79)

This kind of lively and socially engaged religious practice, facilitated by organized modern religious institutions, might have surprised many early sociologists. Most of them expected that the religious sphere of social life would slowly diminish in size and importance. As we observe lived religious practices, it is worth asking whether and how that may be the case. Where and how have religious organizations lost touch with everyday religious practice? But it is also critical to look for the continuing role of religious institutions. Just as we should distinguish societies that organize religion in this "modern" way from those that link official religion with the state or entangle religious practice in everyday life, so we should avoid making assumptions about whether secularization has made organized religious institutions irrelevant. We will still need to pay attention to the ability of institutionalized religions to set the terms of practice and to sustain and adapt traditions that inform the religious things people do.

Interstitial Religious Contexts

The fourth type of social setting present in today's world is characterized by precisely the kind of religious decline expected by many social scientists. In these settings, religious authorities and institutions of all kinds are weak, and lived religious practice, where it is present at all, is more individualized, diffuse, and fluid. People are on their own to judge and select, and many opt out. In the Global North, it is precisely this religious decline and individual improvisation that has most often been the backdrop of lived religion research. If religious practices are happening at all, they are interstitial—in the cracks.

As a result of diminished institutional religious expectations in the Global North, many analysts (as well as ordinary observers) have identified a "spiritual" domain that seems to exist *in lieu of* the religious action of yore (Heelas and Woodhead 2004, Roof 1999). That work has helped to uncover the breadth of human life that can be sacralized, even in the absence of strong organized religion. From everyday mundane tasks to life-defining events, this research has highlighted the breadth of ritual action that can do the sacralizing (e.g., ter Kuile 2020). Lighting candles, meditating, walking labyrinths, doing yoga, even undertaking pilgrimages or getting a tattoo make up a bricolage that is seemingly untethered to institutional authority and subject only to the individual's creative imagination.

Especially with new communication technologies, a cornucopia of religious ideas and practices can be discovered with the click of a mouse, and compatriots and teachers can constitute Facebook and YouTube communities that are as easily disengaged as engaged. These aren't life-long affiliations or identity-defining traditions. They certainly are not set by a state authority. In a world of shifting networks, no single community seems sufficiently strong to shape a way of life, but religious experimentation persists nonetheless.

The idea that one can choose—and change—religious traditions to suit one's own needs and desires seems perfectly natural to people who live in political democracies and neoliberal economies. They live in what anthropologist Paula Pryce (2018) calls a "habitus of choice." Choice and autonomy, free of traditional constraint, neatly fit the neoliberal global order. It is up to each individual to choose whether and what to believe. The confining rules of religious traditions are cast aside, but so are collective ethical guidelines and organizations that have the social clout to stand up to economic and political systems (Carrette and King 2005). Because public life is supposed to be secular, religious justifications for moral positions lose their place in the public debate. Like other religious practices, religious discourse is confined to private life in the interstices.

Interstitial contexts are not the evolutionary end point of an inevitable process, but they do have distinct ways of shaping lived religious practice. The freedom to choose and the cultural resources to explore are a particular cultural framework to take into account. As with the other types of cultural and legal religious arrangements, however, this "ideal type" is rarely found in pure form. Some organized religious institutions remain as individuals make their way among the choices. Some legal constraints and privileges may still be imposed. Some remainders of religious cultural practices can be found. Individuals are not starting with blank slates as they engage religious practices.

It may be more useful, in fact, to think of these contexts as places that are unsettled and in transition more than simply places where organized religion has died. Social theorists Omar Lizardo and Michael Strand point to places where there are gaps in the institutional scaffolding, where people seem to be left on their own to improvise, noting that they still do not make things up out of thin air: "In these institutionally ill-defined crevices, the embodied dispositions of the habitus [ingrained skills] will be most prevalent and the implicit culture stored as embodied dispositions will be most likely to shape choices" (2010, 219). That is, the old habits that we know "in our bones" are still there. Similarly, Swidler argued that even when new ideologies are being promulgated in unsettled times, "Whatever the new ideology does not explicitly regulate still falls under the sway of the old order. Old orders are thus resilient, hiding their premises in the minutiae of everyday life" (1986, 279n15). The "ex-Catholic" seeker and bricoleur may carry more than a little of the Catholic along on the journey (Orsi 2016). An interstitial cultural setting challenges observers to see both the individual improvisations and the habits that have been shaped by a longer and larger religious history.

Thinking about gaps and unsettledness can make clear that individual and collective adaptations and innovations don't just happen in cultures where religious institutions are declining. They also happen when individuals themselves move from one cultural setting to another.[10] When religious practices are transported across cultures and geographies, they inevitably change. Like others at the social margins, people who migrate—from one nation to another or from one kind of community to another—often engage in religious practices that mix and match or simply invent. The impact of mobility and technology is visible in the burgeoning cities of the Global South, for example, where new religious communities tout practices tailored to the transformed everyday lives of their members. Note the social realities and the religious innovation that theologian Kwabena Asamoah-Gyadu describes. The people he observes have been displaced from the countryside to cities and from Ghana to North America, and their prayer practices take place in local gatherings and via radio, YouTube, Facebook, and more. People from New York and Toronto send prayer requests to Ghana. Their lived religious practice was made possible by contemporary communication technology, shaped by the religious habits they carried with them but also adapted to living in the cracks between cultures.

Transnational Religious Improvisation in Ghana

When the economies of African countries south of the Sahara started to collapse in the 1970s, following the massive corruption associated with various military dictatorial regimes, young African school graduates sought better fortunes abroad. The trend has continued since then, and by the end of the twentieth century, international travel had become one of the major aspirations of African workers, whether unskilled, skilled or professional. Religion has a part to play. Jericho Hour is a weekly "prophetic prayer service" held at the Prayer Cathedral of the Christian Action Faith Ministry (CAFM) in Accra that attracts between 3000 and 4000 people every Thursday morning between 9:00 a.m. and noon. . . . Participants in the Jericho Hour program are constantly promised breakthroughs in international travel. During one of my visits, the leader even saw a vision of angels distributing fifty KLM and fifty British Airways tickets. (Asamoah-Gyadu 2010, 91–92)

Studying lived religion means paying attention to the cultural work being done in these interstitial spaces of migration, as well as in the spaces carved out by seemingly unconstrained cultural seekers and bricoleurs. Religious practices in these settings have to be understood differently than those entangled in wholistic cultures, national systems, or bureaucratized organizations. But lived religious practices can happen in any of those contexts.

Taking Context into Account

Religious practices take place within particular kinds of social arrangements, so before we launch into the internal dynamics of those practices, these external dynamics need our attention. Which kind of cultural and legal setting is this—entangled, established, postcolonial, institutional, or interstitial? In what parts of social life do people expect to find religious practices? Do they expect organizations, rules, and professionals, or do they expect a do-it-yourself potpourri? Are there religious narratives contained within holidays and life-cycle events? Is there broad religious consensus or immense plurality and uncertainty? How does the legal system support some kinds of practice and suppress others?

The answers to these big-system questions will shape lived religious practice, including the ways in which gender, ethnic, and other social inequalities play their role. Structures of interpersonal power will be on our agenda as we examine the dimensions of everyday practice, but they too are shaped by these larger cultural and legal contexts. What are women allowed and expected to do? How are resources allocated in the population, and how do those resources affect religious practice? And what happens when lived religious practice runs contrary to the prevailing gender, racial, or social-class norms? As we will see in the coming chapters, religious practice is both shaped by the expectations and habits of the larger culture and very often subversive of those same cultural norms. Lived religious practice is a matter of both structured patterns and situational agency. Finding your place in those larger structural patterns is a necessary first step.

Ideas for Further Study

1. James Beckford (2003) is one of the relatively few social theorists of religion to keep the role of the state fully in view. Lawyer-sociologist James Richardson has also played a key role, and the articles he edited in *Regulating Religion* (2004) provide a wide-ranging overview. Fenggang Yang (2006) has kept a critical eye on the way the Chinese state regulates religion, creating what he calls "red, black, and gray markets" for religious practice.

2. Pioneering sociologist Max Weber originated the use of "ideal types." His *Theory of Social and Economic Organization* (1947) includes many examples of using them as a conceptual tool.

3. Groups that establish such separate enclaves are often called "cults" by their neighbors. As James Beckford (1985) shows, that negative label signals both the gap between their beliefs and those of the surrounding society and the gap between their way of being religious and what is considered "normal religion" in societies where religion is expected to occupy a distinct and limited role in life. During the 1960s–1980s, many scholars explored ways of life in groups like this, dubbed "new religious movements." You can find good accounts of Jonestown (J. Hall 1987), the Unification Church (Barker 1984), the Children of God (Van Zandt 1991), and the Branch Davidians (Wright 1995), among others.

4. A number of political and legal theorists have been examining these unofficial legal establishments of privilege, especially in the United States. Most basically, they point out that "freedom of religion" is never absolute. Not everyone gets to be free. For more about these observations, see Elizabeth Shakman Hurd (2015) or the authors writing in *Varieties of Religious Establishment* (Sullivan and Beaman 2016).

5. Analysis of religious nationalism includes work by Christopher Soper and Joel Fetzer (2018) and by Philip Gorski (2017). The role of religious identity and ritual in establishing nations as nations is especially clear when we think about the history of religious wars in Europe that were formative of European nation-states. Several excellent books have also addressed the rise of Donald Trump (Marti 2020) and Christian nationalism in the United States (Whitehead and Perry 2020).

6. The complicated religious histories and present political configurations in Europe are far from uniform. There is no single story of secularization or a single model of establishment. Sociologist Grace Davie's (2000) work provides an excellent introduction to the many permutations of belief and belonging there, and political

scientist Olivier Roy (2020) reflects on what the current struggles over the role of religion in public life may mean for the continent. Quebec is an equally interesting example that is analyzed by cultural sociologist Genevieve Zubrzycki (2016). If one is thinking about how religion is taught in schools, the picture is even more complicated, since the United States has just about the most secularized educational system in the world. Damon Mayrl's work (e.g., 2015) is comparative and historical and takes the intricacies of governments into account.

7. The case of Muslims in France is an excellent example of this reworking of religious and civic identity. What that looks like in practice is the subject of Fareen Parvez's (2017) excellent ethnography that compares France with India. Both are places where Muslims are a "troublesome" minority and where the state is ostensibly secular.

8. There is much good work on religious practices in Africa. Among those who have written about the role of religion in the colonial systems are Francisco Gallego and Robert Woodberry (2010), David Chidester (1988), Jean Comaroff (1991), and Karen Fields (1985). Contemporary transformations are treated by Paul Kollman (2012), Birgit Meyer (2004), and Paul Gifford (2004), among others.

9. Max Weber is one of the foundational theorists in the sociology of religion. Even though his ideas have not always held up well, we still often think with them. To brush up on those Weberian ideas, the essays collected by H. H. Gerth and C. Wright Mills (Weber 1958) are a handy place to start.

10. The study of immigrant religion in the United States has been a rich source of knowledge about lived religious practices in the interstices of cultures. The pioneering work was done by Stephen Warner and Judith Wittner (1998) and by Helen Rose Ebaugh and colleagues (Ebaugh and Chafetz 2000). More recent contributions include work by Kim Knott (2016), Peggy Levitt (2007), and many others.

PART II

Zooming In

Studying lived religion means paying careful attention to what people are actually doing, and that means that no single aspect of that action can stand for the whole. Studying lived religion isn't only the study of embodiment or materiality, for example; it encompasses a more fine-grained focus on the multifaceted range and depth of experience that constitutes our action in the world.

In part 2, we will zoom in to look at seven key dimensions of lived religious practice—first the dimension that makes it religious, namely, a connection to spiritual realities. But then we will add embodiment, materiality, emotion, aesthetics, morality, and finally narrative. Not every practice will call for attention to all the dimensions in equal measure. Nor will every research inquiry be equally focused on all seven. What this approach calls for, however, is an awareness of that full range of human experience that is at play when people engage in activities that they and others recognize as religious. The dimensions are at play with each other, and stopping to look for the full breadth may spark new insight. Taking a cue from the examples along the way, we will look for how our methods of study can make that insight possible, and in an extended example at the end of chapter 9, all the dimensions come together, along with attention to cultural context, to illustrate the fruitfulness of this approach to studying lived religion.

3

The Spiritual Dimensions of Lived Religion

The spiritual qualities of religious practice are both seemingly obvious and notoriously hard to pin down, even contentious. Theologians, social scientists, and everyone else seem to have a favorite definition, a reason to either embrace or reject this word. We have earlier argued that a spiritual dimension is the distinctive element that makes a practice religious, but that doesn't mean that religion and spirituality are the same. Religious practices have "something more" going on, but like all social practices, they are also embodied, material, emotional, aesthetic, moral, and narrative, as well. Religious social practices are patterns of action that are recognized by the participants as including experiences of more-than-ordinary realities. Sometimes that spiritual dimension is simply implied in the words and actions of a ritual, without the individual participants having any deep experience of something extra-ordinary. Other times, the actions of individuals and groups are intended to take everyone to an entirely different plane of reality. Whether represented in institutionalized rituals, in gods and spirits, or in ecstatic expressions, the spiritual dimension of lived religious practice is foundational.

As we turn our attention to this distinctive dimension of lived religious practice, some clarifications are in order before we begin. "Spirituality" is a term that is as ubiquitous as it is contentious. Scholars and practitioners, no less than ordinary citizens, have claims to make. Scholars sometimes use spirituality as another name for lived religion itself, indicating the way ordinary people do things, rather than what institutions prescribe. Popular notions about what spirituality is sometimes describe it as everything religion isn't. Studying lived religion means paying attention to those definitions and claims, but we do not have to settle for "it means whatever the individual wants it to mean." There are social patterns in the talk about spirituality. In the United States and Europe, several studies have attempted to tap the patterns in what ordinary people mean when they use the term "spirituality."[1] Each of these studies has surveyed large representative samples of the public to discover the contours of a term that is clearly in wide use but open to many interpretations. And in each survey, belief in God and identification with religious traditions are among common popular understandings of spirituality. As popular as it may be to claim to be "spiritual but not religious," most people who think of themselves as spiritual are also religiously active. Pitting the two against each other doesn't make much sense.

Going past those notions about what spirituality *isn't*, it is clear that the public does indeed have an expansive view of what is included. Surveys find people including ideas about mysterious happenings, about unspecified higher powers, as well as a sense of awe or mystical union with humanity or the natural world. People may also see spirituality in ethical terms, reflecting the individual's determination to live a life of compassion and service, being accountable to the larger world. In other ordinary usage, spirituality is taken to mean inner-focused individual enlightenment, coming to know one's true self. The European surveys, in fact, identify these self-oriented ideas and practices as by far the most common, and that leads European scholars to echo the common wisdom that spirituality is something individual and chosen that need not be connected to anything organized or collective.

US surveys show a more transcendent focus dominating over those individual inward definitions, but American scholars (including theologians) have still pointed to "spirituality" as the way of a deinstitutionalized future. In one widely cited analysis of US religion, sociologist Robert Wuthnow argues that "a traditional spirituality of inhabiting sacred places has given way to a new spirituality of seeking" (1998, 3). This implied evolution from old institutions toward contemporary seeking is also central to the influential work of Paul Heelas and Linda Woodhead (2004), whose study of a small English town led them to conclude that "religion is giving way to spirituality." Wuthnow concludes that seeker spirituality "has become increasingly common because it provides freedom to maneuver among the uncertainties of contemporary life and capitalizes on the availability of a wide variety of sources for piecing together idiosyncratic conceptions of spirituality" (1998, 168). Whatever spirituality includes, these scholars say it is flexible and individualized, as opposed to the more fixed routines and boundaries of traditional "religion." That individual focus means that interviews are ideal for studying this kind of religion, as Wade Clark Roof did in his studies of "seekers." Introducing the woman he calls Karen Potter, he recounts that she

> has found new life in a group with four other women, all of whom, she says, have taken a "leave of absence" from their churches to pursue their own spiritual depths. . . . Now, she says: "I feel my connectedness with other people. When I feel the feeling, it's very much feeling like I'm okay. And I am the source of the spirit. It's coming from within, not without, and that's what it feels like. And I feel that. I have that now with the women. We get together and we sit in a circle and we meditate and we share and spirit is there with me." . . . What she most wants is a direct experience of the divine. (1999, 21–22)

In chapter 2, we saw that those notions about spirituality are culturally situated in *interstitial* settings, where traditionally recognized religious organizations are relatively weak but also where law and custom make it likely that individuals can freely choose from a broad array of religious (and nonreligious) practices on offer. Even within those settings, being in a position to "shop" from the "spiritual marketplace" turns out to be more common among those who have more education and more resources.[2] And as with Karen Potter, they rarely go it alone.

In this chapter, we will look more closely at religious practices from across the world, among many different kinds of people, not just privileged Western seekers. We will look for the way all religious practices incorporate a spiritual dimension—whether they happen within an organized religion or within individual everyday life and whether they are directly experienced as personally extraordinary or recognized as religious because they are part of a collective spiritual tradition.

Looking for that spiritual dimension in many different kinds of practices does not mean that we are looking for a single universal human experience or a mystical "essence" that is ontologically the same at the core of all religious practice. Historian Leigh Eric Schmidt (2003) cautions against just this temptation. Western elites, at least since William James ([1936] 1994), have theorized such a common spiritual core, as have idealists the world over who want to claim that "we are one," bound together by this shared spiritual essence. That is ultimately a theological and metaphysical assertion, of course. As social science observers, our task is to look for the many different ways extraordinary realities are experienced and referenced. And because we are observing *social* practices, the particularities of the people and places will always be central to the story. That means that we will expect variation of all sorts—in the degree to which spiritual experience represents a break with ordinary consciousness, for example. Is it a rather quiet or routine awareness of "something more" that does not disrupt mundane activity in the ordinary world? Or does it transport a person into an alternative state of awareness?

The possibility of alternative states of awareness has been a frequent subject of exploration for psychologists seeking what the human psyche can tell us about spirituality. In the past, both psychologists and sociologists often fell into the trap of examining spiritual experience as if it is something abnormal or deviant—or perhaps something characteristic of people in other times and places but not in modern societies. Hearing voices or seeing visions was something to be diagnosed or sidelined. Philosopher Alfred Schutz (1945), on the other hand, argued that all of us perceive multiple realities.[3] We dream and daydream; we remember and imagine. We experience art differently from our experience of navigating the supermarket. Perceiving a situation as having a spiritual dimension is a normal part of the human experience.

More recent psychologists have been interested in how spirituality *works* in our bodies and brains. How is spirituality implicated in health and illness (Idler et al. 2003), for example? Or can we delineate the psychological correlates of an experience of "awe" (Keltner and Haidt 2003)? Ralph Hood and his various colleagues have developed psychometric scales to identify what they call a "common core" of mystical experience (Chen et al. 2011). That is, people in different places may use different words, but the psychological experience, these researchers claim, is the same. Even more recently, cognitive psychologists and neuropsychologists have shown how various hormones and other bodily processes are involved in the things people experience as a spiritual "high."[4]

This is important work, but this chapter is not focused on those psychological measurements or health effects. When insights like these are combined with close anthropological observation, however, they can be helpful.[5] Tanya Luhrmann (2012), for example, spent over two years as an ethnographic observer of a Vineyard evangelical church in Chicago, trying to understand how members had gained the cognitive ability to perceive God's presence and to sense themselves in close relationship, even in conversation, with God. To explain what she saw, she drew on insight from psychologists who study play, because play, too, is a space at the boundary between the mind and the world, where we imagine things into being.[6] When we play, we are inhabiting an alternative reality, much like what can happen in a religious ritual. Human beings, that is, can act within a space that is "liminal," somewhere between the ordinary and the extraordinary (V. Turner 1977).

One of the things Luhrmann learned was that the spiritual experiences she observed were a way of knowing, a spiritual sense of being in intimate relationship with divine beings and through that relationship knowing something that is not derived from immediate observable experience. Recall that political scientists Ellis and ter Haar (2007) argue that we can't understand politics in Africa without granting that participants act on forms of knowledge that are informed by spiritual realities. Anthropologist Knut Graw (2012) describes just such knowledge seeking in his study of Islamic divination practices in Senegal and the Gambia. The problems brought to the diviner were often everyday questions of vocation or marriage, and the result of the consultation was actionable knowledge. As with all such spiritual practices, the insight gained reframes a person's situation and allows them to imagine a different future. Note that an outside observer who inhabits a different kind of knowledge world will need to watch closely but will also need a cultural guide. Sometimes we need help understanding the spiritual dimensions of what we are seeing.

Meet the Senegalese Seeker

Several people were waiting in the courtyard of the house of the *khal-ifa*, the religious head and also de facto political head of the village, to be received for consultation. . . . [Amadou, a young football player] had come to see the marabout because of certain difficulties he had with his trainer in Dakar, and for acquiring ritual protection against a series of sport injuries he had been suffering from and which, if continuing, could bring his aspirations to a sudden end. . . .

> After the consulter's initial silent articulation of his or her reason for seeking out divinatory consultation, it is the task of the diviner to identify this reason through divinatory procedure, to spell out his findings and to indicate the right ritual measures apt to solve or counter the situation at hand. The diviner does this through a complex reading of the divinatory patterns appearing in the shells or geomantic signs. His capacity to do so is based both on apprenticeship and experience as well as inspiration and intuition ... For the person concerned the promise of the future has seemingly ceased to exist. As an answer to such situations, divination is able to offer new perspectives that can be further pursued. (Graw 2012, 21, 24)

Studying the spiritual dimension of religious practice requires that we pay attention to the way it is shaped by the shared patterns that are being enacted, the practical know-how at work. We will pay special attention to the larger cultural contexts, as well as the more immediate institutional ones. We will look for how communities expect spiritual experience to happen. Religious practice, even at its most ecstatic or mysterious, is a social practice. It can and should be analyzed as a socially patterned set of actions that are embodied, material, emotional, aesthetic, moral, and narrative, as well as spiritual. Like all practices, religious social practices—complete with their spiritual dimension—can happen across institutions, not just in religious or spiritually charged spaces. Also, like all other practices, they include both the habitual and the creative.

The Social in Spirituality: Context Matters

Different places in the world organize religious practice differently, but spirituality can still show up in a variety of ways in those practices. As we noted in chapter 2, in entangled contexts, everyday social life is awash in religious significance. Axel Michaels describes contemporary India this way:

In nearly every Hindu household, people, mostly women, worship daily to "their" gods; in the car, Gaṇeśa is invoked; merchants in small stalls or modern malls adorn their premises with a picture of the goddess Lakṣmī and with flowers and incense. Along with this vivacious everyday religiosity, there are innumerable ritual occasions and events that present to us an abounding and colorful religious life, with religious services and worship, fire sacrifices, life-cycle rituals, esoteric initiations in sects, festivals, pilgrimages, vows, and other events. (2016, 1)

That entanglement does not mean, however, that people exist in a perpetual state of spiritual ecstasy. Their connection to the spiritual dimension of practice may be as indirect and routinized as any agnostic Westerner taking communion to please their mother. The spiritual dimension is nevertheless present. That pervasive world of deities and rituals holds in trust the potential for what Tulasi Srinivas (2018) calls "wonder"—a "fracture of the ordinary" that we might call a spiritual dimension of experience. Her account of "The Cow in the Elevator" captures a ritual that has been stripped of much (but not all) of its capacity to generate wonder, but throughout her book, she documents other creative spaces where wonder can happen. In a rapidly changing society, people and their gods are adapting. Custom (*achara*) and traditional teaching (*dharma*) meet in the midst of rituals that allow participants to imagine new worlds. Srinivas's long involvement with these ceremonies allowed her to see the changes and improvisations, and her willingness to enter their "wonder" allowed her to see how everyday rituals can work as generative spaces.

Spiritual Blessings in a Malleshwaram Penthouse

In January 2009 I found myself trying to help lure a reluctant cow named Kamadhenu into a mirrored elevator. . . . I had been invited by Dandu Shastri to a *grihapravesham* (Sanskrit: lit. house entering, a house-blessing ceremony) at a high-rise luxury apartment complex. . . . A central part of the *grihapravesham*, derived from ancient Hindu agrarian customs, required a sacred cow to walk through the new house. The house to be blessed in this case was a penthouse on the eighth floor. . . . The marketing manager for the building joined us. Wrongly believing I might be an investor, he attempted to sell me an apartment by listing its many wonders: "This is best complex, Madame! Full amenities. . . . We have *purohits* [Hindu chaplains] to do all rituals, Madame."

> Despite the luxury, all of us felt the loneliness of the anomic sur-
> roundings. Dandu Shastri was unusually quiet as he issued orders to
> his assistants. No one joked or laughed. Once the *homa kunda* (Vedic
> fire pit) was prepared, he lit it with little enthusiasm and performed
> the invocations in a mechanical manner. . . . When it was her turn
> to participate Kamadhenu obediently followed directions. She wan-
> dered through the million-dollar home, climbing a short flight of
> stairs to the enormous bedrooms and lifting her hoofs to cross the
> thresholds of the walk-in baths, she stoically left a heap of dung on the
> marble floor of the kitchen, much to the delight of the participants
> for whom the cowpat was an added blessing. (Srinivas 2018, 34–36)

The entanglement of the gods and spirits in everyday life is often facilitated by ritual, that is, by formalized ways of acting that bring the
more-than-ordinary into focus. In other cultural contexts, rituals may
be less pervasive than in India, but they may still be examined for how
the spiritual dimension is present. In places where religion is officially
established or *institutionalized*, formal organizations facilitate and regulate the rituals, but a lived religion approach suggests that we still ask
about what the ordinary participants are actually doing on those occasions. Practices in institutionalized settings deserve our full attention
and may be helpful sites for understanding the interplay of established
routines and local improvisation. They challenge us to look for interactions that have a spiritual dimension, even if it is only indirectly experienced as such.

Rituals in organized settings have not been ignored by students of
lived religion, of course. They have especially been a focus for practical theologians who study liturgy.[7] While some such studies may be
full of official pronouncements and theological assertions about how
it's supposed to be done, most practical theologians who venture into
the field are eager to know how the practices of worship are actually
experienced by the participants. Don Saliers's work is a model of careful attention to all the dimensions of singing in church, for instance.
Like any practice, it is socially patterned and enacted. Notice how his
use of a group interview was especially fruitful in evoking memories
and insights, including the material and embodied and emotional dimensions of singing hymns. Notice, too, that as a theologian, he is

also attentive to the spiritual connections and how that illuminates theological understanding.

Singing and Transfiguring Grace in South Carolina

Some years ago I studied the singing practices in several Protestant churches. In Bethel United Methodist Church in Charleston, S.C., I interviewed a group of older women. After asking them to identify their favorite hymns . . . I asked them why these hymns and songs were so significant. They spoke of "hearing their grandmothers voice," of "leaning against their mother's breast," or hearing the "squeak of the parlor organ," of weddings, funerals, and Sunday evening gatherings. . . . When the Christian assembly gathers to sing in the context of worship, deep memory is required. The act of singing praise, lament, thanksgiving, and intercession to God goes beyond the surface of the words, and beyond the musical score. . . . If the text and musical form are adequate to mystery, to suffering, and to the deeper range of human emotions, the human soul is made available to the transfiguring grace of the divine life. (Saliers 2005, 337–338)

Wherever rituals occur, they are surrounded by social supports. There are specialists who lead and producers who create the necessary physical objects and set-aside places. And there are families and friends and congregations whose presence helps to make the spiritual reality come alive. These spiritual tools and social supports can lie dormant but come alive in a crisis. Where religion has been established or institutionalized, there are official keepers of the spiritual world who allow for what sociologist Grace Davie (2007) has called "vicarious religion." Even people who do not themselves engage in routine religious practices look to religious social institutions and functionaries as representatives of something they still believe is important for their society. As an observer of lived religious practices, Davie has seen this phenomenon in both the Nordic countries and her own native England, at no time more strikingly than at the time of Princess Diana's death in 1997.

What happened in Britain in the week following the car accident in Paris cannot by any stretch of the imagination be described as either rational or secular, but nor was it conventionally religious. So what was it? One point is clear: a great deal of the improvised and markedly heterogeneous rituals that emerged at that time took place in the vicinity of centrally placed churches. It was these churches, moreover, that housed books of condolence and facilities for lighting candles—ordinary people queued for hours to make use of these resources—and it was the established church (the Church of England) that took responsibility for her funeral. . . . The presence of the churches and their availability to ordinary people are simply assumed. (Davie 2015, 6–7)

Faced with tragic death, Britons signed condolence books, lit candles, sang hymns, and stood in lines. The point was not so much to explain death as to enter into a space where they could connect to each other and to something beyond themselves. What they did was spiritual, material, emotional, embodied, and aesthetic. It made moral claims, even as people attempted to make sense of the moment by telling stories. Davie is right to remind us that institutionalized and established religion has the power to shape practice.

In cultural contexts where religious practice is largely *interstitial*, those institutionalized traditions may still be available, as Diana's funeral makes clear. They may also provide pieces of the bricolage constructed by seekers, and they may linger in individual identities. Religious historian Robert Orsi is especially eloquent in his description of the lingering reality of Catholic practice for those who think they have left it behind. He speaks of a woman he calls Margaret who had become an activist nun in the 1960s, rejecting the devotional piety in which she had been raised and trained. Yet faced with imminent danger during what she described as a race riot, "all of a sudden, when her fear was extreme, she heard one of the old prayers she had memorized as a child sounding in her head. She was not 'saying' this prayer, Margaret explained. . . . [It] was 'echoing in my body'" (Orsi 2005, 108).

Because religious practices are multidimensional, one dimension (emotion, for example) can call out connection to another (embodiment, for example) and in turn to the spiritual dimension. Even when we are observing practices that seem to be highly individualized, then, we will do well to look for the social patterning. What are the shared understandings? What are the socially situated material surroundings, aesthetics, and embodied actions? What emotions are expected, and what moral commitments are deemed essential? And is there a narrative testimony that gives shape to the experience?

Interstitial contexts have also spurred a wealth of attention to practices in noninstitutional settings, "nature" among the most studied of them (Thurfjell et al. 2019). Observers have studied the practices of pilgrims (and just plain hikers)[8] on iconic journeys through natural settings, and some have even included attention to the lived-religion-like practices of fly fishers (S. Snyder 2007). The US National Parks have come into the sacred picture, as well. As religious studies scholar Kerry Mitchell argues, these public spaces create "conditions in which individuals connect with themselves and feel uplifted, recognizing their experiences as personal and private ones even as they involve a sense of connection to higher, universal realities" (2016, 5). This sense of inner "peace" is a kind of spirituality that is suitable for a "secular" space, she says. Individuals are free to improvise, but they do so in ways that have socially predictable aesthetic, embodied, and moral dimensions. Studying what people do in these natural settings, including how a spiritual dimension is present, can tell us a great deal about the social world in which those settings and practices exist.

Today's spiritual nature lovers are, of course, not new. Catherine Albanese (1990) has documented the history of "nature religion" in the United States, for example. In the nineteenth-century United States, even evangelicals were closely attuned to the role of natural spaces in bringing people closer to God. Evangelical camp meetings intentionally brought people into the spaces of nature, away from ordinary life (Messenger 1999), but they often saw all of nature itself as a bearer of spiritual insight. In Brett Grainger's history of that period—*Church in the Wild* (2019)—letters and diaries of ordinary believers reveal a spiritual fascination with all aspects of the natural world. Nature as a source and setting for religious practice is, in fact, as old as humanity.

Every aspect of the natural world has been the habitation of the spirits. Indigenous populations everywhere have situated themselves in a sacralized natural world of winds and trees and mountains and stars. As Australian anthropologist Lynne Hume writes, "Living Aborigines are tied to land and spirit in the most complex way which includes their kinship with the Ancestors, the land for which they act as caretakers and guardians, and their inextricable connection with all that exists on the land. Everything is interconnected in a vast web of sacredness. Ancestor tracks and sites, and the Dreaming stories associated with them, make up the sacred geography of Australia" (2000, 127). But many Aborigines no longer live on ancestral land and have not been tutored by Ancestors. Their practices and identities are now being adapted in ways that ironically find resonance with modern neopagans and ecospirituality practitioners from more interstitial settings. Together, they rewrite the mythology to imagine a pure precolonial ancestry that is now carried in the blood rather than in the places and stories. Their religious practices, in all their complexity, reveal not so much a pure spiritual past as the changing social world in which they now live.

The Dreaming Meets New Age Spirituality

[Among those who have been displaced from their ancestral land], there is a shift from the acquisition of knowledge gained through complete immersion in Aboriginal Law pertaining to locale and "looking after country" by being there, to a type of distanced affective intuitive knowledge. The connection, or spiritual continuity, is now being professed through blood links, intimating a kind of intuitive, or genetic, transmission of spiritual knowledge. [As one person was quoted saying], "They think we've lost our spiritual contact but we haven't; it's all inside us; it can come out of us." ... [Turning to new sources, they] are making connections between the New Age and Aboriginal world views. Some individual Aborigines are offering New Age–style workshops of self-discovery, using New Age rhetoric and practices. ... Tjanara talks about breath healing, channeling, chakras and energy centres of the body—all New Age concepts. She talks about drawing people closer to the essential force of energy which Aborigines call the Dreaming because it is "a place which is beyond space and time, beyond the physical body and this physical world." (Hume 2000, 129–131)

When we look for the spiritual in lived religious practice, then, we can observe wide variation within whatever cultural context we study. Whether the practice happens where religion is entangled in every aspect of life or whether it happens in interstitial improvisations, the patterns and social knowledge of the surrounding culture and traditions will be in play. Because practices are shaped by the shared understandings of the practitioners, the social realities surrounding those understandings are a fundamental element in our work. Studying lived religious practice means knowing something about the larger patterns of religious tradition in a given context, perhaps by examining survey data, having a local guide, or simply doing our historical homework. It also means knowing something about the individual histories and current relationships and networks of the people we observe. Practices are always situated in both macro and micro contexts.

How Spirituality Works

To understand how social networks and processes create shared practical understanding about the spiritual realities in the world, there is no better place to start than the teaching practices designed to instill such religious and spiritual sensibilities. Spiritual experts and faith communities of all sorts intentionally create spaces and experiences that are designed to encourage spiritual engagement. Whether it is a religious education teacher showing children how to kneel or a yogi teaching seekers how to breathe or a "church mother" raising her hand to signal the spirit's presence to her Black church congregation, the spiritual dimension of religious practice is no less a matter of learning than are the embodied gestures or moral imperatives. Even when the activities in question seem to be focused solely on the individual's inner being, the learned practices and the community that supports that spiritual world are concrete social realities we can observe.[9]

In an exploration of the seemingly individual "new metaphysicals" in seemingly secular Cambridge, Massachusetts, religious studies scholar Courtney Bender (2010) challenges our assumptions about the world of "spirituality." She describes the network of institutions in Cambridge and beyond that produce the practices and narratives that shape this metaphysical world where things are never just what they seem and where "synchronicity" describes the deeper spiritual meaning of ordinary everyday happenings. To find synchronicity, disciplined practices were required. Diary keeping, for example, allowed people to record their thoughts and dreams for later reference so they could see synchronicity when it happened. They also learned the established social conventions for telling stories about their spiritual experiences. Bender gives us an especially astute account that takes advantage of her immersion in the community. She did formal interviews and attended events, but she was also able to engage in the kind of informal interviewing that allowed her to hear those spiritual stories as they were told.

Bender's metaphysicals are but a tiny slice of the US religious scene, but majority-group organized traditions teach spiritual practices, as well. Nearly all organized religious groups provide programs for children, youth, and new members that are aimed at teaching the tradition. Christian and Jewish denominations publish curricula and train leaders to help them, and nearly all US congregations, in all traditions, have some sort of "Sunday school" or its equivalent (Ammerman 2005). In the early twentieth century, Roman Catholic parishes were strongly encouraged to have academic schools, as well (and many still do). Jewish communities have both after-school and Hebrew day schools, along with summer camp options. And conservative white Christians established a plethora of private schools to support their racialized religious culture in the aftermath of US desegregation. Each religious community recognizes that maintaining its religious and cultural way of life means systematic attention to learning.

And no group has done that more thoroughly than Latter-day Saints (LDS, Mormons). Their daily spiritual practices are so thorough that separate schools are unnecessary. From birth to death—and every day before school—there are rituals that sacralize each member's experience by placing it in a grand cosmic life plan. This spiritual plan "involves three overarching life worlds, beginning with pre-mortal existence, unfolding in complex patterns through mortal existence, and culminating in a post-mortal existence that is viewed as 'one eternal round'" (Hammarberg 2013, 51). Successfully navigating this plan means constantly striving for spiritual "worthiness," and at no time is that more difficult than the teenage years. Anthropologist Melvin Hammarberg has written an in-depth account of Mormon culture, the culmination of his many years of observation and interviewing. Note the overlapping and repeated practices that shape Mormon youth. There are so many related practices and accompanying social supports that they almost seem like a litany in Hammarberg's telling of it. That litany, nevertheless, describes powerful social mechanisms embodied in practice and aimed at a spiritual end.

LDS Youth Striving for Spiritual Worthiness

Standards day is an annual program in many stakes that brings together the young men and young women from the several wards of the stake in order to discuss and underscore the differences between LDS Church standards for behavior and the standards of contemporary popular culture. . . . Worthiness . . . [begins] with a bishop's informal baptismal interview of eight-year-old children, and the more formal interviews related to advancement for 12-year-old boys preparing to receive the Aaronic priesthood and girls preparing to enter the young women program. The bishop also interviews each young man and young woman annually thereafter, and twice annually for those reaching the ages of 16 and 17. These interviews provide teaching opportunities regarding the church's doctrines and practices, including regular prayer, scripture study, honoring parents, paying a full tithe, modesty in dress, refraining from any sexual activity or reading, listening to, or viewing pornographic material, obeying the Word of Wisdom, refraining from the use of illegal drugs, using vulgar expressions or taking the Lord's name in vain. The church's booklet *For the Strength of Youth* (2001) may be used to guide discussions about obeying commandments, building a testimony, and preparing to serve a mission. (Hammarberg 2013, 138–141)

Practices of organized learning are important, but no matter the context, much of the spiritual learning that happens is more a matter of imitation than explicit teaching. Practical theologian Joyce Mercer has spent time systematically observing children in Mainline Protestant congregations. Studying children is especially challenging, but Mercer's book is an excellent model for taking them and their world seriously. As a theologian, Mercer practices an engaged scholarship that aims at theologically informed change. She argues that education is more about being formed into an identity than about having the correct knowledge. Congregations, she says, should welcome children to participate in ways as simple as dropping coins in an offering plate, singing along on the hymns, and talking about the stories. The spiritual identity she hopes they will learn is one in which "practices of love, justice, hospitality, and compassion replace practices of oppression, excessive accumulation at the expense of others, and abuses of power" (Mercer 2005, 168). As she says, this is not a neutral goal. She hopes for spiritual lives no less countercultural than those of Latter-day Saints. Observers might ask what kinds of community practices would be necessary to bring about such spiritual sensibilities.

The setting is different in anthropologist Elizabeth Crocker's (2017) research on Haitian immigrants in Boston, but here too spiritual practices are learned through observation and imitation. Becoming a part of a religious community (as a child or a new member) happens mostly through being there—both for members and for observers. Crocker's anthropological study involved close, long-term connections to practitioners of Vodou, both in Boston and back on the island. She talked to them about their experiences and participated in their ceremonies. The result is a remarkable portrait of the spiritual world they inhabit and its relationship to the spaces where they live and the ways they stay connected.

Spiritual Families in Vodou Practice

While Vodou is occasionally transmitted through specific and overt lessons most of the Vodou worldview is conveyed through active participation and observation. The ritual setting is a vital way that these concepts are absorbed, honed, and acted out.... Removed from the homeland, diasporic faith communities are also removed from sacred places, people, and objects. A fete creates an as if world where they temporarily reunite with those aspects. The basement collapses space and time, as it becomes a simulacrum of the homeland where spirits and humans engage in their proper relationships.... The ritual relationship constructs a familial dynamic where initiates are spiritual siblings to one another and children of their initiatory priest. In the periods between ceremonies, they call or visit their spiritual mother once a week as part of their filial duty. Despite living in different areas, they also retain tight links to one another through new media. Technology access improvements in Haiti have meant they are even able to share videos and images with congregants in Jacmel. These dialogs often involve discussions about dreams, signs, and life decisions through the lens of their faith. For example, one of the women had been told by *Ghede* at a ceremony that he was going to help her find work. A week later she connected to her initiatory family through social media to announce she had found a job. Her first nightshift involved a dancing drunk man in a top hat and cane who she interpreted as *Ghede* stopping by to say hello. When she got home she left an offering to *Ghede* on her altar to give thanks. (Crocker 2017, 251–253)

The multidimensional approach we are taking to lived religious practice makes it more possible to see how spiritual experience works. By paying attention to the material, embodied, and emotional dimensions of practice, for example, their importance to spiritual experience becomes more apparent. When James Wellman and his multidisciplinary team set out to study the appeal of evangelical megachurches, they were not at first attuned to the spiritual nature of what they were observing. Being there changed that. Their own embodied encounter with the experience of worshiping alongside thousands of others led them to conclude that the presence of the crowd intensifies the experience, that such services can produce a spiritual high. The pull of that experience kept people coming back for more. Having been there to experience that "high," these social scientists were then able to look more closely to analyze the multiple dimensions of emotion, embodiment, and material surroundings that make it possible.

Getting a Spiritual High in a Megachurch

Insider studies of the music of these churches shows how intricate and intentional the music is in creating "the high" that is intended, and how the coordination of songs pushes human bodies toward the "wow" that most in the community say they experience.... [The presence of a crowd intensifies the experience.] Cameras scan the audience and project images of people worshiping, raising their hands with closed eyes, crying, singing, or smiling, ... which facilitates the recognition of a shared experience and mood, which contributes to the growing sense that *something is happening*. Respondents noted how powerful it was for the entire congregation to be engaged fully in the worship.... "You can stop the music and that place will *still* be vibrating because the whole congregation is singing." (Wellman, Corcoran, and Stockly-Meyerdirk 2014, 100–103)

All of this work reminds us that the religious social knowledge we are trying to understand has a powerful spiritual component, even if we can't see it. What we can see are the ways communities shape and encourage spiritual experience and how they do so in a real material and embodied world. Perceiving and acting in terms of a spiritual dimension require both intentional instruction and communities in which those realities can be observed and imitated.

The Work Spirituality Does

Skeptics looking at the spiritual dimension of religious practice may be tempted to write it off as inconsequential and "otherworldly." Perhaps, they say, it is interesting to see how spiritual practices are enacted and shaped by their social settings, but the "high" of a spiritual experience is best understood as an "opium" that deadens participants to the woes of their current life on earth (Marx [1844] 1963). These skeptics are right to challenge students of lived religion to keep the structures of power and difference in view. The spiritual dimension of religious practice works differently for some people than for others, and it can exacerbate the disempowerment of oppressed people. Differences of social class, race, and gender can make spiritual experiences either more or less accessible and accepted. Paying attention to those differences is as critical here as for any of the other dimensions of practice we will examine.

Many people claim, for example, that women seem to be "more spiritual" than men, but what does that mean? Students of lived religious practice will do well to pay attention to how spirituality works in the particular lives of particular women, analyzing the structures of patriarchy and power that shape what is perceived to be possible, but that does not mean making claims about what is always true or essential in all women's experiences (Wilcox 2012). A good example of taking gender into account comes from sociologists Eeva Sointu and Linda Woodhead (2008). Focusing on practices in "holistic spiritualities" that seek to connect mind, body, and spirit, they argue that economic and social changes have distinctively affected women and drawn them to these practices. As women in modern Western contexts are emerging from traditional gender roles into fuller labor-force participation, "holistic spirituality both legitimates and subverts traditional discourses of femininity" (Sointu and Woodhead 2008, 268), offering both practices of expressive self-care and practices of interconnection that make sense to these women at this moment in these cultures. Like Sointu and Woodhead, Kristen Aune's (2015) gender studies work has been in England, and she, too, points to the intersection of feminist sensibilities and new ways of being religious. For most of the British women these researchers have studied, participation in the established churches largely fell by the wayside as they adapted practices to fit their new realities. Aune describes one of her interviewees this way:

Attending a Christian group at university, she became critical of the way the Bible was used against women. These attitudes distanced her from the church, yet she still identifies as Roman Catholic, attends confession occasionally, and does the rosary. Christian art (especially pietas) and music move her, and she sings hymns while doing domestic chores. She likes a poem she has on her wall, Kaylin Haught's "God Says Yes to Me," which speaks about God as female. Like other participants, she values ritual. (2015, 136)

Both feminists and LGBTQ people have found themselves at odds with many traditional religious beliefs and practices, and that has often resulted in spiritual innovation. New Age, pagan, and Wiccan practices, for example, have flourished.[10] Because those spiritual groups exist outside more typical religious organizations, they are often simply called "spirituality," but like all lived religious practice, they are multidimensional and depend on shared, social, practical know-how. What they remind us as observers is that lived religious practice is shaped by structures of power and difference, as well as by the particular cultural context that supplies expectations and possibilities for how religion will be practiced.

Differences based on social class and privilege exist, as well. While some theories would predict that people at the bottom of society would be the most "religious," it matters what kinds of religious practices we are talking about. Sociologist Susan Crawford Sullivan (2011) studied the lives of mothers in the United States who experience poverty, and she discovered that they were rarely involved in organized religious activities (similarly, see Schwadel 2008). Among other things, their scarce resources and transient residences made church attendance difficult. What they did do, however, was read scripture and pray on their own, creating a sense of divine presence that was sustaining. The social work scholar Cynthia Poindexter and her colleagues (1999) found something similar when they interviewed women of color who were caring for loved ones diagnosed with AIDS. All were Protestant, and most attended services; but that's not where they got their sense of support and resources for coping.

INTERVIEWER: Who do you talk to?
STELLA: I just pray. I tell you, I talk to God like I'm talkin' to you. I
    learned that . . . you can keep your mouth closed so long, but there's
    sometime you got to open your mouth . . . to God. . . .

> As Anna explained about God's being her confidant, "It's simple. He listens. He's never tired. He's never out of town. And he never gossips. So, where else could you go? . . . And you get that relief and that peace." (Poindexter, Linsk, and Warner 1999, 234–235)

Faced with exclusion and inadequate resources, people rely on the practices they have learned to connect them with a sense of spiritual calm and inner strength.

It is important to note that this sense of inner strength can have this-worldly consequences. Paying attention to the spiritual dimension of religious practice can allow us to understand social actions that are not explainable in other terms. Meredith McGuire (2008) points out the way religious practices in many communities are premised on the idea that divine power is accessible and can produce miracles or prophetic insight in the midst of everyday life. Participants invoke sacred words or mantras or touch sacred objects or make promises, expecting that divine power will bless or heal or purify them. Subsequent individual and communal action is then premised on the expectation of that perceived power and insight. The spiritual dimension of practice can have real this-worldly consequences.

The early twentieth-century sociologist Max Weber described what can happen when a leader and their followers perceive that such extraordinary spiritual connections are at work. This spiritual knowledge can convey power and authority to the bearer—what he called "charisma" (Weber [1922] 1946)—and energy to the followers. As he pointed out, authority derived in this way is inherently disruptive to the institutional powers that are based on tradition or bureaucratic rationality. As many students of social movements have discovered, spiritual power can be at work in the practices of gathering, singing, and telling stories about a possible future. This is a power vividly described by historian Karen Fields in her research on colonial rebellions in southern Africa. When the Watchtower movement arrived there in the early twentieth century, proclaiming the coming of a New Jerusalem, followers were baptized and began to engage in the practice of *chongo* (akin to Pentecostal tongue-speaking or "shouting"). They also began to refuse to take orders or do their assigned work, disrupting economic and political systems. Colonial authorities dismissed all of this as merely troublesome preaching, but Fields argues that "by the very act of being baptized, converts received a new form of government, even before the coming of the New Jerusalem. . . . *Chongo* galvanized individuals into a group capable of taking action collectively" (1982, 345, 347). That collective spiritual action was, in fact, a key ingredient in the anticolonial insurrection of 1917–1919.

One need not go very far to find religious practices that empower people to act in extraordinary ways—and that sometimes lead to danger and destruction. From rituals before battle to rituals of mass suicide, the consequences are often horrendous. When people claim divine power on their side and evil on the side of their enemy, violence is likely to be intensified. When they shun medical advice in favor of prayer alone, the results are often tragic. Or when they engage in religious practices that inflict pain and suffering on vulnerable people, those practices are rightly condemned. To say that spiritual power is real and can have salutary effects is not to ignore the equal possibility of terror and suffering.[11]

Spirituality as Part of the Whole

The spirits themselves are beyond the reach of most research on lived religious practices, although some observers are full participants and able to bring their own experience into the picture. Because this dimension of religious practice can seem elusive, we can be tempted to set it to the side as we examine other things that seem more readily observable. What we have seen in this chapter, however, is that the spiritual in religious practice is as much a matter of shared practical knowledge as the rest. People share understandings and expectations about the gods that inhabit their world, even if those gods have been neatly shelved into seldom-used religious institutions. Others may engage practices that are much more intensely and regularly infused with spiritual presence. Even if those practices seem spontaneous and unpredictable, there are social patterns in place. Our work as observers can take us to organized religious rituals and to everyday events, to a circle of women seekers or the home of a diviner, to a household blessing or the funeral of a princess.

The spiritual dimension of practice is what distinguishes it from other social practices, but it is neither synonymous with religion nor the only reality that is relevant for research on lived religion. In each of the places we have visited in this chapter, the practices have employed bodies and material spaces. Australian aborigines claim their heritage in their bodies, even when they are not directly connected to sacred land, while pilgrims and evangelicals seek spiritual wisdom in nature. We have likewise seen emotions of longing and grief and gratitude as integral to practices as disparate as Vodou, Anglicanism, and Methodist hymn singers. Aesthetic sensibilities declared a cow pile a beautiful blessing but also shape the way those Methodist women responded to the music they love. The moral dimensions of spirituality were right on the surface of the LDS practices, urging teens to live a chaste life that could be spiritually worthy, but there are also moral claims about a better world in the spiritual activism of *chongo* or the welcoming of children in a liberal Protestant church. Both LDS youth and colonial subjects were also learning to tell a spiritual story, as were the metaphysicals in Cambridge and the displaced Aborigines. Each practice called on these dimensions in different measure, but understanding the practices means placing their spiritual character into this more complex whole.

While the spiritual dimension of religious practice often leads to surprising or disturbing power, we have also noted the differences and disparities at work. Spiritual engagement is almost always gendered, with different behavior expected for men and women. Spiritual power can substitute for worldly powerlessness, but it can also bless those who are already powerful. Religious practices that take people to another experience of reality are often an escape that reinforces the status quo.

Being fully present as an observer opens up understanding of the experiences people describe to us. Both participant observation and interviewing are foundational to the work of studying the spiritual dimension of religious practice. To place the practices in context may also mean tapping methods that give us a bigger picture, such as surveys or historical accounts. It may also be useful to take account of what psychologists and cognitive scientists have learned in trying to understand how people experience and create a spiritual high. None of those methods, however, can substitute for the basic work of examining the practices as enacted, discovering the shared practical knowledge at work, and analyzing the rich multidimensional human interaction in which spiritual experience is lodged.

Ideas for Further Study

1. Several broad-based studies have documented the range of connotations of the term "spirituality." Brian Steensland and his colleagues (2018) have provided an excellent baseline for the United States from a representative sample survey. My own work (Ammerman 2013b) was based on a qualitative study of a diverse group of ninety-five US adults. The Fetzer Institute, which promotes spirituality, conducted a wide-ranging study in the United States that they titled "What Does Spirituality Mean to Us?" (Fetzer Institute 2020). Surveying the Netherlands, Joantine Berghuijs and her colleagues (2013) arrived at still another accounting, as did Stefania Palmisano (2010), from her study of Italy. Each shows the effects of different religious cultures, but there is also a good deal of overlap in the characteristics they identify. A different kind of accounting can be found in the essays collected in *The Immanent Frame*'s "A Universe of Terms" (http://tif.ssrc.org). Religious studies and other scholars have written about "enchantment" and "spirit," among other related concepts.

2. It is always important to ask about the context in which spirituality is being studied. Jeremy Carrette and Richard King (2005) point out that the notion of "spirituality" replacing "religion" is situated in a political economy characterized by neoliberalism and consumer choice. Similarly, Joantine Berghuijs and colleagues, reflecting on their survey of the Dutch population, report, "Lower educated respondents distance themselves much more often from spirituality, and far more often they do not know what spirituality is than those who are higher educated. It appears that 'spirituality' is something of an 'elite' word" (2013, 389).

3. Schutz's phenomenological theory was foundational for his student Peter Berger's theories of religion, including Berger's last book (2014), in which he put the notion of multiple realities at the center of the argument. Those connections are argued succinctly by Silke Steets (2014), as well. The notion of human interaction with a nonordinary reality is also the starting point for theorist Robert Bellah's final book on religion and human evolution (2011).

4. Kate Stockly's (2020) appendix in *High on God* is an excellent overview of what biocultural experiments have uncovered about religious experience. She argues that these experiments show what "entrainment" (the sense of focused emotional ritual connection that Randall Collins [2004] writes about) looks like in the body.

5. Another thoughtful treatment of the interplay of bodily spiritual experience and religious social interpretations can be found in the anthropological theorizing of Julia Cassaniti and Tanya Luhrmann (2014). Luhrmann's research team has produced an impressive set of case studies from throughout the world, from which they are developing a "theory of mind" that encompasses experiences of the spirit. See the special issue of the *Journal of the Royal Anthropological Institute* edited by Luhrmann (2020b). She brings this work together in her 2020 book *How God Becomes Real*.

6. Sociologist Andre Droogers (2014) has also pointed to the parallels between religion and play. Similarly, anthropologists Robert Weller and Michael Puett teamed up with psychiatrist Bennett Simon and religious studies scholar Adam Seligman to de-

scribe the subjunctive "as if" world of ritual. They write, "Games and rituals encourage us to explore boundaries by accepting both their social reality and our ability to penetrate them" (Seligman et al. 2008, 96).

7. The field of practical theology has widely embraced ethnographic methods. A good place to start for an overview of the field is the anthology edited by Dorothy Bass and Craig Dykstra (2008). Both Martin Stringer (1999) and Mary McClintock Fulkerson (2007) have been careful observers of worship life and have shown how theology can build from that. James Nieman's (2008) writing on preaching is also deeply grounded in his empirical observations of congregational life. If you are interested in how technology reshapes worship, the work of Heidi Campbell and various colleagues will be useful to you (e.g., Campbell and DeLashmutt 2014).

8. You can read more about pilgrimage practices in John Eade and Michael Sallnow's book (2000). There are specific studies covering the Nordic (Bremborg 2013), English, and US contexts (Ivakhiv 2001; Bratton 2012), as well as work that looks at intersections with ecological concerns (Kuiper and Bryn 2012), with liturgy (Post 2011), and with processes of social change (Smelser 2009).

9. Cultivating the inner spiritual self, no less than participating in an organized ritual, is supported by teachers, publications, and communities. Sociologists Michal Pagis (2019) and Jaime Kucinskas (2019) each focus on contemplative practices that originate in Eastern traditions but have been thoroughly adapted for Western seekers and, as Kucinskas shows, adopted in countless secular settings. Anthropologist Paula Pryce's (2018) contemplatives are oriented toward Christianity but also borrow broadly. Her reflections on the challenges of studying silent practices are especially astute.

10. The practices of LGBTQ people have received a good deal of attention among students of lived religion. Melissa Wilcox (2009) and Mary Jo Neitz (2000)—in religious studies and sociology, respectively—have been among the most careful observers of the spiritual practices of queer women, while Dawne Moon's (2004) work focused on the interaction of religious communities with LGBTQ people. Both Anthony Petro (2015) and Heather White (2015) have written histories of the rise of gay rights in the United States, each showing how religious organizations and religious practices were implicated both for and against gay people. Among the most helpful places to start an exploration of religious practice on this particular margin of society is the anthology edited by sociologist Scott Thumma and ethicist Edward Gray (2004).

11. Historian Scott Appleby's work (2000) is a thoughtful exposition of the ambiguous realities inherent in claiming sacred power. To pursue such issues further, you can start with *The Oxford Handbook of Religion and Violence* (Juergensmeyer, Kitts, and Jerryson 2013). And don't forget that domestic violence in the home is itself often legitimated by religious power, as Nancy Nason-Clark (2004) has shown.

4

Embodied Religious Practice

What could be more ordinary and empirical than a human body—a collection of flesh and bones, nerves and muscles, molecules and DNA? For much of the modern era, both the social sciences and theologians left bodies to the biologists and doctors. Explaining how societies worked, like explaining how the soul worked, depended more on the human mind than on the human body, we were told. The study of lived religious practice, however, allows no such division of labor. Practices are enacted by actual bodies. We can't talk about the "lived" character of religion without attention to the physical beings doing the living. Not surprisingly, virtually every person who has written about social practices or about lived religion begins with the fact of embodiment.[1] What that means and what it tells us about how to study religion are the subject of this chapter.

To participate in a ritual, for example, is to do something real and concrete in time and space. How the body experiences that action is central to the action itself. Whether placing a consecrated communion wafer on one's tongue or celebrating the Passover Seder, taste often evokes connection to something beyond the ordinary. Clapping hands or processing to an altar, gazing at an icon or stained glass, hearing church bells or a call to prayer—all the senses are involved in the religious things we do. Religious practice is embodied just as all social practices are embodied. We act with and through our bodies. We see, taste, touch, smell, hear, and move. We feast and we dance. When we engage with others in patterns of action that presume and invoke the existence of nonordinary realities, at least some of those participants will literally feel the evidence of sacred presence in their bodies. Even outsiders will see people moving and talking, gesturing and listening. To be present is to feel the cold stone of the altar, see the intricate carving of the goddess statue, hear the music, smell the incense, taste the wine, feel aging bones protest when it is time to kneel. Lived religion is shared *embodied* know-how (to recall Schatzki's [2001] definition of practice).

To focus on embodiment is not to ignore the mind or the spirit, but it is to recognize that they can't be separated from the experiences of the bodies at work. Just as our minds help us order and navigate the world, our bodies have their own memories and ways of knowing. Cognitive scientists have taught us a good deal about how our brains work, but this is not just about synapses. It is about all the ways we take in sensations, sort them, couple them with feelings, and make them part of a narrative that may or may not come to include more-than-ordinary spiritual presence. We will add in those narrative and emotional dimensions of practice in later chapters. For now, it is the form and function of physical processes to which we turn.

Paying attention to bodies is likely to challenge the student of lived religion to be physically present, experiencing the sensations in their own body. We will explore a range of ways a researcher can gain insight into embodied practice, but being there as a participant observer is a very common approach. Musician Anne Heider and sociologist Stephen Warner, for example, are longtime participants in events that bring together singers for a "Sacred Harp Convention." Describing the practices that make up such events drew on their own embodied knowledge, as well as many years' worth of informal conversations with other participants. When they then describe these practices, note their careful attention to how bodies are arranged, move, hear, sing, and eat—and what these things feel like to the participant. In fact, they argue that these singers do not have to *believe* the same things or even believe the words they are singing for this experience to be a significant, community-creating ritual event. Their research provides us with an excellent place to start.

Embodied Presence at a Sacred Harp Singing

At a Sacred Harp singing, singers are bodily co-present, seated in tightly packed rows on benches or chairs around four sides of a "hollow square," facing in toward the center. . . . Singing is loud, and with hundreds of singers at a big convention, the volume of sound in the center of the square can be overpowering.

Each leader stands inside the hollow square, facing the tenors, who carry the tune in most songs. . . . Leaders are expected to beat time in clear, easily visible gestures, and many singers also beat time from their seats. . . . Singers and leader alike may step, tap, or stamp the rhythm and sway in time to the singing as well, but they do not clap hands or click fingers in rhythm. (Holding a wide book that weighs a good three pounds makes clapping and clicking impractical.) The singing is forthright, loud, and louder. Singers often turn and sing directly to one another the phrases they particularly relish: "I'm fettered and chained up in clay" . . . ; "Must death forever rage and reign?" . . . ; or look across the hollow square to make eye contact with members of other sections. . . .

The details of phrasing or unified breathing, so often a concern in the preparation of choral performances, are never addressed in the course of a singing, yet on favored and familiar songs the matched vowels and unanimity of phrasing in a gathering of experienced singers will produce a thrilling, ringing, well-tuned choral sound. . . .

Around the fringes of a hollow square, singers may stand rather than sit; visitors may sit and listen without singing. The boundaries to outsiders are fuzzy at the edges and become increasingly distinct as one moves toward the center; one's physical location at a singing indicates one's self-chosen centrality or peripherality to the ritual. A visitor who chooses to sit near the center will be expected and encouraged to sing. If he then persists in remaining silent, he will be told kindly that active singers would like to "move up" and that the place for listeners is back around the edges.

A traditional all-day singing will include a generous, free meal in the middle of the day. Local singers bring "a dish to pass," often several dishes, in sufficient quantity to share. Participants can and do eat as much as they like in the one hour traditionally allotted. The sheer physicality of the singing is underscored by the frequently heard assurance that "these calories don't count." They then return to the hollow square with renewed energy, ready to sing for another two to three hours. (Heider and Warner 2010, 81–84, hymn citations omitted)

Careful attention to what is experienced in religious practice demonstrates the twin realities that bodies are social and the social is embodied. We will look for all the ways those embodied religious experiences shape us and our communities but also how they both constrain and empower participants. We will look for how bodies signal memberships and boundaries but also how the practices themselves take shape in and through human bodies. Along the way, we will observe how researchers have studied practices from a variety of places and how attention to embodiment has become a fruitful way to enlarge our understanding of what happens when people call on shared practical understandings to do religious things.

Bodies Are Social

Bodies are the site where "nature" and culture meet. Biological systems and processes are at work, to be sure, but they are not just neutral receptors of stimuli from the environment. We actively *sense* and *make sense* simultaneously, and that happens in interaction with others, using the categories and filters our culture has provided us. One has only to think of the diverse range of food flavors that sometimes defy recognition to know that even our taste buds have been trained by our cultures. Our senses convey information about the environment, but all our previous experience and all the responses of the people around us tell us what those cues mean.[2] What we think we see and hear, in other words, is shaped by an active process of definition. How we then act involves aligning our perceptions with the people around us and taking our proper place in the physical and social space (Friedman 2015).

Defining and aligning happen in religious communities no less than in any other social setting. They happen in subtle ways, as people discern the implications of the gestures and movements they see around them. How far down should I bow? How loudly should I sing? Where should I sit? Defining and aligning also happen in intentional and overt ways. Masters teach postures to their disciples, and converts choose to take on new habits. While we usually study these processes by being there, traces of bodily experiences can also be unearthed in historical documents, oral history interviews, and personal memory. Historian Robert Orsi (2005) draws on all those sources to write vividly about children in mid-twentieth-century US Catholic churches. The Church (and the children's parents) hoped the children would learn to be faithful Catholics, and learning to participate in the Mass was foundational. The priests and nuns taught them the movements and responses—how to genuflect, how to receive the communion wafer on the tongue, what to do with their hands. There were cartoon sketches to illustrate what to do (and not do). Still the lessons came up against the hard reality that the Mass was long and mostly incomprehensible. Children were inevitably "restless, distracted, and bored." They might also be "dizzy and nauseated because they had been fasting since midnight as church law required," a sensation made more intense, some recalled, by the smell of incense (Orsi 2005, 94). Whether they delighted in the experience or dreaded it, this religious practice would be remembered in their bodies. Their bodies were disciplined and aligned in ways that were integral to what the community wished them to become.

Sometimes the physical memory lasts beyond the time when one actively participates. We might suspect that to be the case with some of those Catholic children, for example, but wherever religious practices foreground physical postures and movement, the body's memory may take over. McGuire quotes a not very observant Jewish friend who nevertheless felt deeply connected to lighting a candle and blessing bread at Shabbat. She "held her hands and directed her eyes exactly as in the classic prayer gesture, her expression genuinely devout. She, too, noticed that she felt different about that practice, and she exclaimed, 'It's *in* my body! That whole blessing—my body remembers it'" (McGuire 2008, 107). What she learned in her household remains available to her as shared practical know-how.

When people are present with each other, surrounding companions attune bodies to some sensations and teach us to screen out others. That is nowhere more evident than in the many forms of meditation that are practiced by traditions around the world. Emily Sigalow (2019) is a sociologist who has studied the adoption of Buddhist practices by contemporary Jews, and she writes in detail about the groups that gather to learn the physical and mental disciplines. Jaime Kucinskas (2019) expands on that observation by tracing out the networks and organizational strategies of a larger mindfulness movement. Each of them shows how groups and organizations are intentionally creating new ways to train bodies and senses. It is the work of Paula Pryce (2018), however, that perhaps shows most vividly the socially constructed bodily experience of a religious ritual. Pryce is an anthropologist and spent a number of years deeply engaged with a variety of contemporary contemplative communities. Her account again highlights the advantages of being physically present and participating in the practices we wish to understand. Here she recounts the embodied teaching of an Anglican monk and the collective experience of a religious ritual at the Society of St. John the Evangelist (SSJE). The experience might seem very individual and interior at first, but it was manifestly communal, as well. Note how carefully she documents the sights, sounds, and movements and how her own presence allows her to experience an embodied collective moment.

Collective Embodied Attunement

When silence and stillness were established, [Br. Geoffrey] guided people's awareness first to "inner bodily sensation" and then to sensation of the body in relation to its physical environment of clothing, air, floor, and chair. He encouraged the congregation to "think of how the atmosphere is charged with God's presence" and to consent to the divine by saying, "Come, Holy Spirit." Br. Geoffrey then invited his listeners to breathe in that "purifying presence" and breathe out the "impurities" of pride, anxiety, anger, selfishness. . . . He allowed time for the congregants to experiment with these body awareness practices, then asked them to try extending the realm of sensitivity outward to the collective body: "Send out active praise and thanksgiving, forgiveness, and blessing to everyone in this chapel." . . . Such exercises fostered communal contemplative senses and physical simultaneity. . . .

At the conclusion of SSJE's two-hour Maundy Thursday liturgy in 2008, the congregation of about 250 people processed in almost complete darkness from the choir to the Lady Chapel while singing a repetitive Taize chant. The chanting continued at length as the congregation slowly moved to gather about the side chapel altar, where it developed into a cyclical, seamless pulse that flowed, swelled, and receded like the breath of a solitary creature at rest. The chant had a visceral quality, just as Br. Robert had observed on other occasions. Then, without any signal or leadership or cue, not even a slowing of tempo, every single person ceased the chant simultaneously. The contrast of the lulling, rhythmic, inward tones to the newly born silence was breathtaking. Utterly still, the assembly listened as reverberations of sound gradually dissipated into the rafters. Learning such unified attentiveness and attunement was wrought in the communal practice of formalized rites. (Pryce 2018, 146–147)

What Embodied Practice Does

The embodied dimensions of lived religious practice are understood and interpreted through the language and categories our societies give us, which means that embodiment is an agent of those societies and a participant in constructing them. As with all practices, there are elements of both constraint and possibility. Our shared know-how is often habitual, but it can be challenged when we encounter the limits of what we know to do. Embodied experience continually participates in making and remaking us, both individually and collectively.

Religious practice is often foundational to how the social world is defined. It may mark time, define space, and enact membership. Marching in parades and reveling in the streets mark holiday moments that interrupt the everyday calendar. Gestures of honor and welcome mark relationships. Initiation rites physically signal movement from one status to another and may leave some enduring physical mark as a reminder.[3] Dancers can evoke remembered communal experiences (Ojo 2019). The way bodies move tells stories. In the earliest days of sociology, Emile Durkheim ([1912] 1964) wrote about how shared rituals were the site where community identity was forged. As people experienced the "collective effervescence" of a gathering honoring their totem animal, they saw themselves as part of something bigger.[4] A gathered sacred moment becomes a moment of community identity. The embodied practices in which we engage both form and signify the community and its boundaries.

No bodily practices are perhaps more signifying than food practices. Communal meals instantiate the community that physically gathers around tables. Eating kosher or halal or vegetarian may be a personal commitment, but it is taught in communal contexts and practiced with the support of a household and a community. Likewise, depriving oneself of food during a fast brings religious relationships and realities into sometimes-painful consciousness. Food also marks boundaries. Fasting during Ramadan while colleagues are feasting on appetizers at a reception marks a boundary, even if a subtle one, while gathering at an interfaith *iftar* allows the embodiment of intentional religious boundary crossing. Some religious communities, in fact, intentionally harness the power of shared meals for the sake of building new relationships

(Vanderslice 2019). Whether feasting or fasting, food is an embodied experience of devotion that is defined by the expectations of religious communities.

Paying attention to food can shed new light on the nature of the religious community itself. Susan Sered's research among elderly Israeli women revealed just how important cooking was to their religious practice and how central those practices were to the community. Rather than just going to shul, she engaged in informal conversations, structured interviews, and daily activities with the women. What she observed opened up "a religious world in which sacrality is concentrated in and radiates out from the kitchen (rather than the synagogue), in which literacy (and so study and formal prayer) is not seen as a universal value but as a male prerogative, and in which the most profane activities become sacred simply because of the manner in which they are carried out" (Sered 1988, 130). That is, paying attention to women allowed her to see the importance of the embodiment of religious practice. They literally had the necessary lived religious know-how to be properly observant.

Cooking with Jewish Grandmas

The women use food to care for the entire Jewish people, living and dead, known and unknown. Caring can be manifested in different ways, yet the women themselves emphasize that serving food to the hungry is the single most important mitzvah. The women explain that giving cooked food (as opposed to money to buy food) to the poor is the greatest religious act that a woman (not a man) can perform. . . . Being healthy enough to be able to eat good food is understood to be a gift from God. And for these women, who raised their children through times of famine (World War II and the 1948 War of Independence), having enough food to eat is indeed a sign of divine favor. . . . Many of the women have children who are no longer religiously observant and for whom eating traditional foods is a primary link with the culture and religion of their ancestors. When these elderly women prepare traditional foods for their married children and grandchildren, they consciously use food to strengthen their descendants' bonds to Judaism. . . . The women believe that food must also be prepared in the proper, that is, kosher, manner. By preparing food properly, the women also strengthen their relationship to God. The women do not doubt that God wants them to observe the laws of kashrut. . . . Although Talmudic scholars dedicate lifetimes to studying kashrut, the women claim that they never need to ask a rabbi questions involving kashrut; they already know everything that they need to know. (Sered 1988, 133)

The physical marks of membership in a religious tradition are also sometimes visible on the outside. Some of the most interesting research on lived religious practices has analyzed the way physical signs convey religious identity, even where identity is contentious. What does it mean, for example, for a woman to choose to veil in places where the hijab is banned or marks her for harassment?[5] Clothing, jewelry, hair, and tattoos are outward expressions that reinforce religious identities for the bearer of the sign and for the observer. Shaved heads, dreadlocks, long sidelocks (*peyot*), and head coverings of all sorts—from kippah to hijab to turban—are reminders of the wearer's relationship with divinity and tradition. But they are also an outward sign of belonging. Jewelry can be much more subtle but can nevertheless identify the wearer and sometimes provoke conversation, while the sacred undergarments of a faithful Mormon are signs of belonging that may never be visible to outsiders. All of these say something to the observer but also to the wearer. The act of dressing one's body is itself a lived religious practice.

Tattoos have become an especially fruitful object of study for researchers interested in lived religious practices. Tattoos have long marked community membership, whether in an Indigenous tribe or a biker gang, but they have recently emerged into mainstream acceptance in North America and Europe as personal forms of expression. No matter how personal and seemingly private, however, they still tell a story, and students of lived religion can ask about the religious aspects of those stories, as religious studies scholar Alyssa Maldonado-Estrada (2019) has done. She says of the tattooed Catholic men she interviewed in Brooklyn, "Despite the skill, virtue, or intent of the creator, [a tattoo's] use, display, and personal and communal meaning matter much more. . . . Tattoos are not just *signs* of devotion. Wearing them constitutes an *act* of devotion, much like using a sacramental or making a votive offering" (emphasis added). Not all images are so overtly tied to a tradition, however, so we should always ask about the images people choose and what audience they have in mind. Where are the images located on the body and for what purpose? Is the experience of tattooing itself a religious practice? What is the shared knowledge here?

Once we think about tattooing as a religious practice, we will need both visual and verbal evidence to explore it. Pictures of tattoos (or of items of clothing or jewelry) can be an excellent starting point for an interview. Sociologists Kevin Dougherty and Jerome Koch (2019) even enlisted their students in gathering photos of tattoos as part of a semester-long research project. They were able to analyze 752 photos and the accompanying student essays to discover a great deal about what students were communicating with their body art. While much has been written about individual choices in such bodily practices, it is worth remembering that all practices are shaped by the *shared* practical knowledge of the participants.

While religious practices create and convey identity and set the boundaries of communal membership, they are also a means of affecting the bodies that enact them. Health and healing are central religious practices across traditions, but religious and cultural differences shape just how health is understood and how religious practices relate to ways of seeking health. Recall the discussion in chapter 2 of the entangled practices of religion and health in the Ebola epidemic. No matter the context, people do religious things as part of staying well and overcoming adversity. Healthy bodies and healthy souls are often linked, even in the places where we expect religion and medicine to be separate domains.[6] Studying such practices is not just about assessing their efficacy. It is rather about discerning the way health is understood in practice and how spiritual realities are part of that understanding.

When illness strikes, medicine and spirit are likely to combine in complicated ways. In many parts of the world, scientific medicine is delivered by modern religiously affiliated institutions. In the developing world, that is disproportionately so, often a legacy of the missionary practices of the past. Today, many of those institutions have also found paths of cooperation with Indigenous healers and religious practitioners, partnerships that often yield promising advances in the health of the population.[7] In an increasingly pluralistic context in North America, medical professionals may wish they could treat bodies without having to worry about the worldviews of the persons involved, but many recognize the potentially adverse results of doing so.[8]

Nursing journals are increasingly reporting research on the practical implications and importance of taking lived religion seriously. In one such study, Sheryl Reimer-Kirkham (2009) observed that the larger social context of a presumably secular Canada tended to silence religious concerns in hospitals. Employing ethnographic methods of participant observation, interviews, and discussion groups in acute care settings, she tapped the experiences of health-care professionals, spiritual care providers, patients, and administrators to understand how religion is nevertheless present in hospitals. Focusing just on Sikh patients and professionals, she observed the way typical nursing practices (shaving arm hair to prep for an IV, for example) violated Sikh ways of life. "Moral guidance derived from Sikhism provided the patients with specific behaviors for everyday life: habits of diet, cleanliness, dress, and family relationships. With hospitalization, some patients faced considerable challenges in maintaining the practices of their faith" (Reimer-Kirkham 2009, 412). Because much of Sikh identity is represented in bodily practices, interaction with health systems inevitably involves practical negotiation.

Concerns with healing are also manifest, of course, inside religious settings themselves. Whether it is a prayer to guide the hands of the surgeons or a religious community rallying to bring casseroles to a sick member, religious traditions do not have to invoke supernatural intervention to be involved in health practices. Wherever groups are acting out of shared understandings about the relationship between physical bodies and spiritual health, there is much to be learned. Richard Callahan's (2009) historical study of Holiness religion in the eastern Kentucky coal fields is a case in point. His observation of religious practices is situated within a larger concern with the everyday experience of work, and he drew on a wide range of historical sources to describe the way work life and religious practice were mutually implicated. With a critical eye, he drew on missionary reports, travel writing, and local histories but also on the songs and stories documented by folklorists and the oral history projects that had been undertaken by the region's colleges and folk-life centers. His careful data gathering is a model for students of lived religion who hope to examine practices of the past. And among the things most clearly evident in those practices is the link between body, work, and spirit.

Bodies, Work, and Healing in the Coal Fields

There were probably a number of things that drew people to Holiness meetings and revivals, not the least of which was the spectacle of believers' physical expressiveness and the liveliness of Holiness music and preaching. Chief among the draws, whether considered authentic or fraudulent, were claims of extraordinary healing. Rumors spread throughout the coal fields of inspired preachers who had healed people of disease and, in some cases, even raised individuals from the dead. . . . [The Pentecostal-Holiness tradition is] a religious form that focused so intently on the body and healing in a setting in which broken bodies and heightened nerves were so much a part of everyday life. In the coal fields men, women, and children experienced the fragility of life daily, and they were constantly aware of the effects of the play of power—social, economic, and spiritual—on their bodies. Holiness worship's popularity emerged from and resonated with the life experiences of this place, drawing much of its energy and urgency from the structure of feeling of mining life. . . . In eastern Kentucky's coal fields, the broken body—and the power of the Holy Ghost to heal it—was an especially potent image and reality. (Callahan 2009, 141–145)

Bodies participate in lived religious practice in ways that can be transformative as well as formative. The transformation may take the shape of something experienced as physical healing, but it may also take the shape of a moral reorientation. The long tradition of immersion in water—like an observant Jewish woman's monthly trip to the *mikveh* or the Christian convert's baptism—is a practice that enacts the inner transformation of the person and the new community or status to which they belong by symbolically cleansing their body. In some Eastern Orthodox communities, it is fasting that does this moral work, and sociologist Daniel Winchester's (2016) interviews with initiates revealed a great deal about how that embodied practice changed the way they thought and acted. Note how Winchester probes in this interview to discover the concrete ways their behavior is changing and the shared practical understanding of fasting that is making that possible. His analysis is deepened by his extended ethnographic study of three parishes and his own participation in two fasts. He was able to experience in his own body some of what converts were experiencing in their practice.

Abby and Jacob Learn from Fasting

ABBY: We're finding out this is part of the learning process involved in fasting. The Holy Fathers write about the "hypocrisy of the stomach." Even when you've had plenty, you want more.

JACOB: It's this habit or addiction of always wanting more and more. . . . The Church Fathers, they say it all begins in the stomach and then it spreads from there. . . .

ABBY: I think we're programmed, at least here in the United States, to give in to our passions, to be ruled by our passions, I would say.

JACOB: Yeah, like it's some great virtue to shop your way into debt. . . . It's . . . the same thing as eating more than you really need, eating even when your belly is so full that it's bursting. Buying crap even when you don't have room in your house for all the other stuff you bought last year. That's how the passions work.

ME: And so you think fasting has helped you understand that in a new way?

JACOB: Uh-huh. Definitely.

ABBY: It's just such a tangible experience. . . . When you have to try to control one of your most basic impulses—to eat—you kind of recognize these things about your condition at a very concrete level. (Winchester 2016, 597)

Similarly, historian Kristy Nabhan-Warren described her embodied experience studying the site of Marian apparitions in Arizona:

> I touched the rosary beads, prayed, and genuflected along with the other pilgrims. . . . Mexican ballads played on the loudspeaker, and Estela's voice, coming through the loudspeaker, read the messages of the Virgin Mary as given to her. Religion was tasted, smelled, seen, heard, and touched in this shrine space. It was here at the shrine space, kneeling on a carpet remnant and holding a rosary that had been given to me by a pilgrim that my body took on the comportment of a pilgrim. Making the sign of the cross, kneeling, and murmuring Hail Marys were visible signs of devotion and were dependent on body knowledge. (Nabhan-Warren 2011, 380)

Alongside Nabhan-Warren's interviews and observations, the sensations experienced in her own body helped her to understand the body knowledge that was at work in practices she was observing.

Embodied Performances of Difference

If embodied religious practices are inherently social, forming and transforming us, they also shape our identities, which means that they mark
both memberships and exclusions. Bodies are, in fact, a primary site
where society regulates and where there are political struggles over identities and power (B. Turner 2008). That means that studying embodied
religious practice is central to understanding the exercise of power.
What practices are outlawed or shamed? How does accessibility shape
experience? How are religious practices marked as part of a society's
lines of difference?

Social order implies bodies that are under control, whether through
repressive policing or subtle shaming. As French theorist Michel Foucault ([1980] 1999) argued, religions often assist in that disciplining process with rituals of confession (Carrette 1999). Practices of confession,
he taught us, were "technologies of the self" that helped to define and
reinforce the structures of "governmentality" by which we internalize the
social order and our place in it. If we internalize religious expectations
about behavior, there is no longer a need for external enforcement. Pierre
Bourdieu's (1991) picture of religious ritual was similar. Symbolic power,
enacted in ritual, sets spatial and bodily boundaries and teaches us how
to honor the difference between ourselves and elites. Embodied religious
practice participates in sending the cues that organize our perceptions
into categories, and those categories are defined by race, gender, class,
and ability (Friedman 2015). Those same embodied practices then reinforce the differences and the hierarchies and exclusions they imply.

But often the exclusion is more than symbolic; it is physical. Spaces
are divided and reserved by category, restricting accessibility to participation. Sociologist and theologian Nancy Eiesland reminded us, "The
body practices of the church . . . are the physical discourse of inclusion
and exclusion. These practices reveal the hidden 'membership roll,' those
whose bodies matter in the shaping of liturgies and services" (1994, 112).
She observed the many ways disabled people like herself were excluded,
describing the liturgy of the Eucharist as often "restricted because of
architectural barriers, ritual practices, demeaning body aesthetics, un-
reflective speech, and bodily reactions. Hence the Eucharist becomes a
dreaded and humiliating remembrance that in the church we are tres-

passers in an able-bodied dominion" (113). Observers who are temporarily able-bodied (as she put it) may need an especially critical eye and helpful interlocutors to see these bodily exclusions.

Students of lived religion have given ample attention to other practices of bodily regulation in religious communities, and their work provides a foundation for continued exploration. Much of this work has focused on gender and sexuality. Research has documented how queer believers from various traditions struggle against religious definitions of their sexuality that labeled them as sinful and disordered, sometimes telling them to seek religious healing for what is perceived to be impure (Gerber 2011). Sociologist Bernadette Barton (2012) described the religious stigma experienced by the queer people she interviewed who lived in a Bible Belt culture where religious practices were present throughout everyday life. They could not escape the conversations and symbols that directly or indirectly labeled them as diseased, perverse, and inferior. Others have studied what happens when a gay or lesbian person comes out in a conservative religious community and must negotiate a new identity (Wedow et al. 2017; Thumma 1991). Whether creating strategies for staying in the closet or strategies for presenting a gay self to people who might shun it, a good deal of room remains for exploring the lived religion of LGBTQ people who find themselves excluded, as well as the practices that do the excluding.

Another rich vein of research has tapped the practices of queer religious communities themselves. When Edward Gray and Scott Thumma were doctoral students in Emory's Religion and Society program in the 1990s, they documented the scene at the "Gospel Hour" in an Atlanta gay bar. They described this drag performance as "fully gay and altogether Southern Evangelical." Structured like the church services most of the men remembered, its high point is the "High Church Sing-Along." The Gospel Girls lead the crowd in singing favorite hymns, and "the volume, quality, and passion of the singing would be the envy of any church. During these hymns, participants occasionally close their eyes, some bow their heads. A few others raise their hands" (Gray and Thumma 1997, 85). Gray and Thumma were present to experience the passion and brought their knowledge of religious traditions with them. Their interviews further allowed them to unpack how this practice came to be and what it meant for the participants.

Melissa Wilcox (2003, 2009) has contributed equally compelling accounts of the lived religious practices of queer women and others who challenge conventional definitions of gender and sexuality. Among her subjects, the Sisters of Perpetual Indulgence (mostly gay men in drag), claim

> to offer a perpetual indulgence to those who have been declared sinners by traditional religions—especially those in lesbian, gay, bisexual, and transgender communities. Their self-described mission is to "promulgate universal [some say omniversal] joy and expiate stigmatic guilt," and they work to raise awareness of sexual health, domestic violence, sexual assault, sex workers' rights, and other issues. . . . And although they are not technically a religious organization, many members, at least in the U.S., consider their work with the Sisters to be a part of their spiritual practice. (Wilcox 2012, 653)

As the Sisters adopt "habits" that resemble but playfully diverge from those of traditional nuns, both their activism and their celebratory performances are creative practices of resistance. It is increasingly clear that transgender people have created sustaining religious practices that redefine bodies, genders, and sexualities—practices worth much more study.[9]

Other sexualities have been on the agenda of lived religion researchers, as well. Kelsy Burke (2016) explored the world of evangelical internet sex advice, and Amy Moff Hudec (2015) studied marriage culture among the Latter-day Saints. Their collaboration (Burke and Hudec 2015), in turn, shows the fruitfulness of making studies comparative. They recognized that both communities are "gender traditional," with implications for the sex lives of women and men. They describe the practices of self-control and purity that enact masculinity before marriage and the ways those practices complicate the sex lives of men after they marry. With couples having so carefully disciplined their bodies to be celibate, marital passion is sometimes elusive. Jewish couples in observant marriages face similar issues in observing *niddah*, which prescribes seven "clean" days and physical separation of a couple during the menstrual cycle. The religious rules are seemingly clear, but couples struggle with the practice. Orit Avishai (2008) analyzed the growing presence of "niddah consultants" who help women interpret and navigate the system. As in other studies that explore sexual practices, data from the internet allowed her to "hear" conversations that might have been difficult to pursue in a face-to-face interview. Whether it is the self-control of traditional religious groups or the embodied improvisation of nontraditional ones, the experience of sexuality is often the focus of religious practice. It is worth the creative methodological work necessary to study it.

The experience of gender has also been examined by lived religion researchers. Religious practices shape and are shaped by the gendered realities of those who enact them. Both Orthodox Judaism and Islam divide the worship space into distinct gendered sections, for example, shaping the prayer practices of women and men (Chaudhry 2019). Religiously based patriarchy often reinforces the system of dominance that constrains the lives of women beyond the prayer hall, as well, and that shows up in a range of practices, including clothing and appearance. Research by Lynne Gerber (2009) and by Marie Griffith (2004) has given us careful accounts of how religious practices are employed in pursuit of thin bodies and sexual purity. Beth Graybill and Linda Arthur have focused on the role of clothing in reproducing a gender hierarchy among Mennonites. They quote a conservative Mennonite woman describing her experience of moving back into the community after being expelled: "Gradually I got back into the frame of mind that is expected and I grew to appreciate that God wants me in the church and then I no longer wanted worldly clothes. Eventually, putting on the Mennonite clothes and head covering felt right" (Graybill and Arthur 1999, 26). The woman's lived religious practice became an embodied expression of the community's gender norms.

All of these studies point to the importance of a combination of sensitive interviewing and critical analytical distance in the study of religious gender norms. Paying attention to the practices as they are lived may not reveal powerlessness and domination. It may, in fact, uncover accounts of embodied religion that is a means of agency, empowerment, and self-definition. Women sometimes freely choose hijab and other forms of modest dress, for example, to exert their own power over the men in their lives (Read and Bartkowski 2000; Mahmood 2005). And conservative Jewish women may observe *niddah* and embrace the *mikveh* as spaces that celebrate, rather than restrict, their bodies (Avishai 2008; Kaufmann 1991). Or, like the Sisters of Perpetual Indulgence, trans and queer people may simply invent their own practices. Embodied religious practice can be a fruitful site for exploring how agency and constraint are manifest, often in the same interaction.

Differences based on race and class are intertwined with religious practices, as well. Those differences are embodied and performed in everyday life. They send signals to others, but they also shape the experience itself. Historian Evelyn Brooks Higginbotham (1993) gives us an account of the "politics of respectability" adopted by Black Baptist women at the turn of the twentieth century. Central to their attempt to resist the degradation of racist white society was a crusade of "manners and morals" that encouraged habits of hygiene, dress, and middle-class manners that simultaneously imparted a sense of self-confidence and moral superiority, while also internalizing the restrictive norms of that same white society. As Africana studies scholar Anthea Butler documents, these norms had a strong spiritual dimension, as well, especially in the Church of God in Christ. Early leader Mother Robinson claimed that her "decision to 'alter a garment' [making it modest] . . . was the catalyst for the Holy Spirit to take control of her body, and she then spoke in tongues. . . . Though sanctification itself was inherently an internal affair, the external markers of Holiness dress and behavior served as signs to the community that a convert had submitted to the authority of the Spirit, of scripture, and of the leadership of the church" (Butler 2011, 79). Disciplined bodily practices send a complicated message to the person who gains acceptance at the cost of denying pleasure.

In thinking about class-based embodiment, we might bring to mind the visible physical markers of Hindu caste, but embodied class differences go far beyond that. A global culture of consumption has created new ways for people to perform their differences through religious practices. In Turkey, a burgeoning fashion industry has provided ways for women who adopt Islamic dress to display their status (Alimen 2018). And in South India, well-off people seek to display their prosperity on their bodies, but they also employ visible amulets to ward off the "evil eye" of those who disapprove (Dean 2013). Practices of dress and embodiment display both religious sensibilities and status distinctions.

Paying attention to the embodiment of religious practice means keeping those distinctions in view.

The links between religious practice and social class are seen at the bottom of the social scale, as well. We have already noted Richard Callahan's history of eastern Kentucky coal miners and how the physical brokenness of their working lives was enacted in the healing rituals of their churches. Similarly, recall the women in poverty that Susan Crawford Sullivan (2011) studied. They rarely engaged in organized religious practice because their mobility was limited by where they were forced to live; time was limited by working multiple jobs and odd shifts; and sometimes freedom was limited by incarceration. Each of these studies demonstrates that analyzing lived religious practice has to take full account of the economic, occupational, and consumption patterns that sometimes separate one group from another and shape the religious practices themselves.

Bodies are the bearers of systems of exclusion, systems abundantly clear in the continuing realities of racism in the United States. The existence of a distinct African American religious tradition is testimony to a history of enforced racial segregation (Lincoln and Mamiya 1990; Marti 2020). That tradition, in turn, produced an enormous array of distinctive embodied religious practices, not just the gendered practices we have already noted but ways of singing, moving, praying, and eating.[10] Black churches emerged in the nineteenth century as a space that was relatively safe from white intrusion. As a cultural space where African Americans are in charge, the shared know-how of the churches undergirds a wide range of practices that require no explanation for insiders. That thick presence of Black cultural expectations can show up when non-Black congregations attempt to become "multicultural" and succeed only in co-opting a few symbolic practices.[11]

Black church communities have always known that bodies matter and that race matters. Despite the wide range of attention to the history and present realities of African American religious life, studies of lived religion have included less attention to these practices. Sociologist Marla Frederick's (2003) work is, however, an excellent counterexample. She accompanied a group of African American Baptist women into the everyday ways they try to make a difference in the world, noting both the role of their churches as "alternative spaces" and the growing role of media spaces that undercut that role with a "prosperity gospel" of individual achievement. Race, economy, and struggles for power are never far from the embodied practices of religious people—Black or white.

The Challenges of Studying Embodied Religious Practice

Research on embodied religious practices in communities of color is abundant, but it is rarely labeled "lived religion." That label has too often been confined to the privileged choices of those who have left institutional religion behind. Where we stand as researchers matters, and sometimes it is our own bodies that remind us of that fact. Studying the embodied dimensions of practices almost always means that we are physically present, and that means that our relationship to the people we are observing matters. Dynamics of difference and implicit power shape that presence. Religious studies scholar Beth Dougherty (2018), for example, was interested in how rituals get constructed, and she observed both Taizé worship in a Catholic church and ritual activities in Reclaiming Witchcraft camps. In both spaces, she paid attention to the times when her position as a midwestern Lutheran produced discomfort in her own bodily experience.

> At my last UK Reclaiming ritual, I found myself uncomfortable. My memo after the event read: ". . . something just felt off. I just had to stand there, watching, as people were encouraged to roll on the ground, enacting something that made little sense to me. It felt debasing. Wrong. It just didn't work for me." I literally took myself out of the ritual because I could not perform, the sense of wrongness was so strong. Both bodily limitations and an ingrained sense of dignity kept me standing and feeling awkward. (Dougherty 2018, 122)

Her body told her about the cultural gap between herself and the people she was observing, allowing her to think about the implications of that gap.

A similar thing happened to Timothy Nelson (2005) when he, a white middle-class guy, was observing an African American church in an impoverished neighborhood in Charleston, South Carolina. He listened to one of the church mothers testify about finding a lump in her breast, crying out to God for help, and miraculously being guided in removing it. The embodied dimensions of lived religious practices have a history, in this case a history of racism that makes Mother Gadsden's strategy comprehensible. When we find ourselves uncomprehending, it just may be because we do not have the shared practical understanding on which the practice rests.

> ### Divine Healing or the Hospital: Confronting Assumptions in Charleston
>
> Why, I wondered, didn't she just go see a doctor, at least to determine whether or not it was cancerous? The disorientation I experienced over this incident signaled my arrival onto the terra incognita of real cultural difference.... What perplexed me most was not that Mother Gadsden had turned to God for healing, but that she hadn't seemed to even consider consulting a doctor at all. It was only later that I traced the source of our differences to the profound division of race and class that had formed each of our responses to this situation. Most members of Eastside Chapel could not afford adequate medical insurance (if any at all) and had to rely on the local county hospital and free medical clinic for treatment. They were openly critical of the care they received from these institutions and harbored a strong suspicion that the largely white medical staff performed clandestine experiments on their African American patients. (Nelson 2005, 173)

Paying attention to bodies—our own and others'—can be revelatory. Being physically present, talking to people, and gathering visual images can give researchers closer access to the embodied dimensions of what people are doing when they do religion. Seeing, feeling, and sensing are integral to the practices we observe. Because societies shape and regulate those bodies, we must always place what we see in the context of the norms and divisions present in those societies. But because bodies can also be sites of innovation and resistance, it is worth paying attention to how people enact religious lives that redefine what and who they are presumed to be. Studying embodied religious practice means paying attention to how people are formed but also to how they are transformed and how they transform the way their world works.

Ideas for Further Study

1. Sociologist Meredith McGuire's field-defining book includes a helpful chapter on "Why Bodies Matter" (2008). Anthropologists have long studied embodied religious practices, even if not labeled "lived religion" (e.g., Csordas 1990). The more recent focus on embodiment is not surprising given the parallel between the rise of lived religion research and of feminist approaches in the social sciences more generally (Davis 1997; Neitz 2003). Students of lived religious practice, then, can benefit from attention to the themes brought to the fore by feminist researchers.

2. A "sociology of the senses" has recently emerged, led by social scientists such as Phillip Vannini, Dennis Waskul, and Simon Gottschalk. In their introductory text, they say that "sensing and sense-making are necessarily conjoined, code-termined, and mutually emergent in active and reflexive practices" (Vannini, Waskul, and Gottschalk 2011, 15). See also the work of David Howes (2003) and of Asia Friedman (2015).

3. Among the anthropological studies often picked up by students of lived religion are those by Arnold van Gannep (1960) on rites of passage and Victor Turner (1977) on liminality. At *The Immanent Frame*'s "A Universe of Terms" feature, you can find essays on "body" and on "race," among others (http://tif.ssrc.org).

4. Randall Collins (2004) has built on Durkheim's theories to show the central role of shared embodied action and awareness in building societies of all sorts.

5. Veiling practices, and responses to them, have been widely studied, from Indonesia (Rinaldo 2013) to Pakistan (Zubair and Zubair 2017). Changes in American Muslim women's post-9/11 practices were documented by Yvonne Haddad (2007), among others. You can learn more about legal struggles from Paul Chambers (2007) and in the special issue of *Sociology of Religion* edited by Jen'nan Read (2007). Two important anthropologists, Lila Abu-Lughod (2002) and Saba Mahmood (2005), have eloquently called on Western feminists not to impose their values and assumptions on the veiled Muslim women they study.

6. Healing rituals have long been a focus for anthropological work but have only recently been taken up by scholars who are studying "modern" contexts. The volume edited by religious studies scholars Linda Barnes and Susan Sered (2004) provides a good place to start, while sociologist Lindsay Glassman's article (2018) includes an excellent review of the current sociological literature on religion and health practices. Religious studies scholar Kira Ganga Kieffer's (2020) ongoing examination of the "anti-vaxx" movement is a fascinating example of what happens when we pay attention to the religious dimensions of health practices.

7. Public health researcher Jill Olivier (2015) was at the forefront of the movement to take account of religious practice in African health care. Sociologists Jenny Trinitapoli and Alexander Weinreb's (2012) study of religion and AIDS in Africa is also helpful. Iddo Tavory and Ann Swidler's (2009) sociological analysis of the practice of condom use (or rejection thereof) is a good example of how attention

to practices is critical to understanding health (as also attested by *The Lancet*'s account of religious practice in the Ebola epidemic [Marshall and Smith 2015]). A poignant account of cultural differences in the United States can be found in journalist Anne Fadiman's *The Spirit Catches You and You Fall Down* (1997).

8. Wendy Cadge's (2013) sociological study of spiritual care provision in hospitals is a model of attention to religious practice and its intersection with medical systems of care. She and colleagues are taking that knowledge into practice with their Chaplaincy Innovation Lab (https://chaplaincyinnovation.org).

9. Social ethicist Benae Beamon's (2020) dissertation makes a strong argument for learning from both the constraints of transgender lives and the way the practices of Black trans women have ethical lessons to teach.

10. There are many excellent studies of Black Church cultural practices—too many to cover fully here. To get started, look at James Abbingdon (2001) on music; Jualynne Dodson and Cheryl Gilkes (1995) on food; and Mary Pattillo-McCoy (1998) on the infusion of Black Church practices into local political organizing. Books by Cheryl Townsend Gilkes (2001) and Anthea Butler (2011) are the place to start for attention to the roles of women. Sandra Barnes (2005) documents the presence and effects of some of these practices using data from a survey of congregations.

11. Michael Emerson, along with various coauthors, has been at the forefront of documenting the racial divide in US religion (Christerson, Edwards, and Emerson 2005; Emerson and Smith 2000; Shelton and Emerson 2012). Gerardo Marti (2012) and Korie Edwards (2009) have each written about the way that shows up in worship styles. Edwards has joined with Rebecca Kim (2019) to explore how race works in "multicultural" contexts. Their study is noteworthy for including Asian Americans in the picture.

5

The Materiality of Lived Religion

The shared practical knowledge that is embodied in lived religion is situated knowledge, situated in real material surroundings. As we have seen, human bodies mediate the material and natural world. Bodies sense, encounter, and manipulate the props and settings; but the materiality itself matters too. Studying lived religion means paying attention to where religious practices take place, so in this chapter we will turn to the material surroundings and concrete objects. From the mundane to the spectacular, lived religious practice involves things we can see. How might we think about how the material cultural world does its work? And how might we observe the practices that define and happen within spaces that carry religious significance?

The materiality we are looking for comes in several important forms, and we will have a wealth of lived religion research to guide our thinking about them. Material *objects*—religious stuff—may be the first thing that comes to mind, whether explicitly religious items like a prayer rug or statue of the Buddha or objects made religious by how they are used. Think yellow ribbons or teddy bears made sacred by inclusion in a roadside shrine. In each case, practices depend on those material expressions. In addition to the stuff we use, practices also depend on *spaces*. They may take place inside a physical building that has been constructed to facilitate religious activities, or they may cross spatial boundaries in ways that sacralize or contest the meanings of otherwise-ordinary space. Both material objects and built spaces are among the things that students of lived religion pay attention to.

There are at least two other kinds of places, as well. The first of them is the oldest kind of space: *nature*. The other is the newest: *cyberspace*. One is apparently multisensory and untouched by the modern world. The other is apparently "virtual" and oriented toward impersonal technology. But as we will see, those characterizations hardly capture the reality of things; and each of these spaces can be the site for lived religious practice. Observing the religious things people do may take you into the woods or on a virtual pilgrimage at your computer. What all of these material objects and spaces have in common is that they become part of the practices we hope to understand.

Lived religion research has shown that spiritual experience can be embedded in everything from mementos on a desk to a gazebo by the shore to plaques on the wall or a favorite chair by a window.[1] Objects, that is, can participate in producing and encountering the sacred. In religious studies terms, they can be icons—something material through which the sacred is seen (Winchester 2017). These are objects that signal and encapsulate who we are and our relatedness to something beyond ourselves.[2] As we look at what people are doing, we remember the multidimensionality of practice—the interplay of material things and stories about what they mean, the interaction of bodies, aesthetic senses, and spiritual experience.

The material culture of religious practice has been the focus of a multidisciplinary cloud of researchers. Anthropologists have long analyzed material culture alongside the rituals and meanings present in a community. What amulets are employed, and how are sacred spaces marked? More recently, historians and religious studies scholars led the way in drawing attention to the stuff of religious life and the way it constructs the worlds people live in. From devotional art to mass-produced T-shirts, they have reminded us that faith is often declared in material form. In addition, geographers have been instrumental in helping us analyze the way space works. How do cities, cultures, and states tell us what sort of space we are in and how we should properly use it? Sociologists and other social scientists of religion were somewhat slower in making links to the burgeoning studies of consumer culture, media, art, and fashion, but that work is among the exciting new frontiers of research. How might the social structures and processes of the material cultural world inform our understanding of religion? From across these disciplines, we have guides for turning toward the material side of religious practice.

All of these students of materiality had to resist two nonproductive detours. First were the older notions that giving credence to the material world is to succumb to material*ism*. We are not saying here that religion is *merely* material. Nor are we saying that it is utterly captive to the forces of consumer capitalism. We will want to know something about who produced the things we study and how some people may profit by them, but we also want to know how they are used and given meaning by practitioners. As we see throughout this book, the material is one dimension of practice, not the whole. There are circumstances in which the material and its conditions of production tell us a great deal and other circumstances in which it is less critical, even as it is always there.

The second nonproductive detour led through the world of the religious experts and their pronouncements. They might insist that the point of studying religious objects and spaces is to understand the proper dogma attached to them—to learn the museum-catalog description or theological treatise about what an image or object *really* means. Material culture, however, plays a far larger role in the world of everyday religious practice than just the expert meanings and rules. It may include some or all of those official interpretations, but that is not the whole picture. Colleen McDannell was eloquent about this in her agenda-setting book *Material Christianity*. Both Protestant (especially Puritan) theologies and American historians of religion too often equated "pure" religion with intellect and words, either condemning material and sensual dimensions of practice or simply ignoring them. People who employ objects and images were taken to be the "women, children, and other illiterates" who are "not properly trained in religion" (McDannell 1995, 8–10). For the student of lived religious practice, the official theologies and the officially sanctioned spaces matter, but our task is to understand how material things are used in practice. To do that, we simply need to acknowledge that human life—including religion—takes place in physical spaces, places that are shaped by our collective activity and act back on what we do.

To make that a bit easier to see, let's go to South London to observe how an ancient cemetery became a different kind of space. Religious studies scholar Steph Berns (2016) used participant observation, in-depth interviews, and archival research to tell the story. Her work gives us a vivid tale of the way a street in London and a derelict construction site were contested spaces, with evolving and competing representations defining what this space was and how it should be used. There were existing categories of space at work—paupers' burying ground, consecrated ground—describing what the cemetery was and wasn't. There were also legal, cultural, and technical categories for defining the land—abandoned lot, development site, contaminated soil. Each of those categories shaped what members of the community expected to see and do in that place. But what they did mattered. New ritual actions began to redefine the space as one of remembrance and resistance against injustice. And what they did employed material objects like ribbons and candles that would be widely recognized as signaling that new commemorative meaning.

A Place for the Outcast Dead in London

Along a quiet residential street near London Bridge stand a large set of rusting ironwork gates. Yet, these are no ordinary gates, as from every railing hang ribbons, photographs, soft toys, amulets and dream catchers.... Prior to 2015, those who peered through the railings saw an unremarkable concrete car park. However, at the far right of this concrete void stood a curious array of objects: a small weathered statue of the Virgin Mary, ceramic geese, and tea lights. A circular plaque, affixed to the rails, states that the site was "Cross Bones," an unconsecrated graveyard for medieval prostitutes (once colloquially known as the "Winchester Geese") and later a paupers' burial ground during the eighteenth and nineteenth centuries. And now, the plaque reads, the gates are a "memorial shrine" for the "Outcast Dead." ... The vigils, shrine and garden conversion transformed Crossbones into a place of healing where vigil attendees could bring stories and news of injustices (sometimes accompanied with an object to tie) as a way to honor their lives. (Berns 2016, 167, 183)

After having long sat unnoticed, Crossbones began its life as a new space on Halloween in 1998, beginning an annual ritual of collectively tying ribbons and amulets to the gates. Then in 2004, a local pagan shaman introduced vigils on the twenty-third of every month, when a growing group of "Friends" shared songs and readings and announcements, burned incense, beat drums, and trickled gin on the ground. All the while, the space beyond the gates, including the cemetery itself, was owned by Transport for London. An electrical substation had already been constructed, and the space was considered prime for commercial and residential development. The Friends, however, eventually gained permission to construct a community garden of remembrance, and the gates were ceremoniously moved and installed as both a boundary and a focal point for rituals. The space and the rituals proclaimed that what had been "bad deaths," not consecrated by the Church, now are occasions of witness to ongoing injustices. By continually altering the material shape of the space, the Friends effectively contested the old meanings and eventually won at least partial legal recognition. But just as important, they established routines and relationships that reinforced those meanings. The space itself materially changed, but so did the collective action surrounding it.

Materiality Is Social

In other words, what we make, how we make it, how it is understood and used—all are lodged within the cultures and interactions of which we are a part and, in turn, shape those cultures. Religious practice does not stand apart in this regard. Things and places are not neutral blank slates, but neither are their meanings and uses "written in stone." Practices are socially constructed ways of acting that are both structured by their history and subject to the collective work of people enacting them. Recall that Theodore Schatzki defines practices as "embodied, materially mediated arrays of human activity centrally organized around shared practical understanding" (2001, 11). Understanding how to behave in a given time and place is something we share with the others around us, an understanding that includes our shared definitions of those material surroundings.

Think about how we even recognize a place as a place. We look around and say, "This is a kitchen," but people in other cultures might be befuddled or expect a "kitchen" to look quite different. Much of what we take for granted as we navigate the physical world is much more malleable than it may first appear. French critical theorist Henri Lefevbre (1991) was one of the foundational thinkers on "the production of space," and pointed to a trio of social processes at work in defining and structuring interaction in a place. Drawing on Lefevbre's work, geographer Kim Knott (2005) suggests we should pay attention to "representations of space," that is, the abstract concepts and names that describe our categories and ordering of space; "spaces of representation," that is, the lived space in which there is interaction and struggle to define it; and "spatial practice," the more settled routines that are enacted in relation to a space. In other words, there are shared understandings that are part and parcel of the places where they are enacted and the objects with which we work.

The construction of shrines and memorials is one of the most vivid reminders of the social processes involved in material religion. No one person constructed the Cross Bones site, for example, nor did they invent the markers and rituals completely from scratch. Similarly, no one person constructs the spontaneous shrines that appear in the places where there has been a tragic death (Grider 2006). Once created, the things themselves can evoke actions—stopping, reflecting, storytelling, perhaps praying.

Photos and other visual images are among the most powerful and pervasive of material objects that populate the world of religious practice. Buddhist and Daoist temples house a panoply of images, and churches throughout the Christian world have housed some of the world's most revered Western art. But much more mundane images play a role, as well. Devoted Catholics may carry prayer cards depicting their patron saint, and Protestants might carry similar inspirational cards but without the saint. Devotional embroidered samplers hang on the wall in homes, alongside images of Jesus and Mary. Internet memes are used to convey spiritual messages. As David Morgan (1998) has documented, the image of Jesus (the "Head of Christ") created by Walter Sallman attained sacred status as a kind of icon for many mid-twentieth-century Protestants in the United States. Whether carried in a wallet alongside pictures of the family or hung on the living-room wall, this picture was intended to remind viewers of their spiritual relationship with God.

All of these images and objects, of course, were made by someone, and the work of creating a religious object can be a religious practice itself. For members of Eastern Orthodox Christian traditions, painting icons is experienced as a spiritual practice, not just an artistic one. Centuries of history have gone into the details and style (Kenna 1985). In Hinduism, "it is believed that the tying of flowers into garlands requires both internal and external purity; it is also defined as an act of devotion and is to be undertaken with a reflective stance, the person chanting appropriate mantras and meditating on god" (Sinha 2008, 179). At an English village church, sociologist Abby Day discovered that setting out the cups and saucers for Sunday after-service refreshments was an equally significant material religious practice (2017, 126–127).

In Europe and the United States, in recent years, knitters have touted the contemplative benefits of their craft. Religious studies scholar Anna Fisk (2018) has written about the therapeutic and expressive "implicit spirituality" of knitting, while others have created more explicitly religious meanings from similar material practices. Pastor Susan Izard (2003) wrote about the beginnings of a knitting circle, located in her church and dedicated to producing "prayer shawls." Both Fisk and Izard learned about these practices by being there, participating along with the other knitters. What they saw was the way a material practice—knitting—became something more. They were attentive to the social relationships, the material surroundings, the meaningful stories, and the spiritual sense of being part of something beyond oneself.

Knitting in a Prayer Circle

Ten women attended our first knitting circle one cold January morning in 2000. We gathered around a candle in rockers and wood chairs with our knitting needles and yarn. . . . [The room] was abuzz with activity and excitement as we helped each other cast on, discussed the variety of colors being knitted, and experienced the joy of being together. Our opening prayer wrapped us in the compassion and love of the Holy One and grounded us in the purpose of our work—to knit God's love, care, and warmth into shawls for those who needed them. (Izard 2003, 12)

Not all material religious practice is so intimate, however. In fact, most of the objects that accompany and embody religious practice have been mass produced and sold for profit. As David Chidester and Edward Linenthal wrote about their research on sacred places, "we immediately had to recognize that these places were intimately entangled in such 'profane' enterprises as tourism, economic exchange and development, and the intense conflict of contending nationalisms" (1995, 1). Historians of religion have documented how publishers and manufacturers rushed to produce the Bibles and decorative items that nineteenth-century middle-class Americans wanted (McDannell 1995). Religious holidays, especially, became commercial bonanzas (Schmidt 1995). Displaying one's class and style and giving the right gifts became entangled with reminding oneself and others of connections to God, to religious tradition, and to the others who will recognize and appreciate the material gesture.

This isn't just American or contemporary, of course. Archaeologists are often able to reconstruct the religious practices of ancient people by studying the buildings and objects they created. Across the humanities, there are now digital archives that open up new possibilities for students of lived religion, documenting images and objects from around the world that we might not otherwise have access to. One such project is a collection of posters produced by Christians in China before 1951. They were cheaply manufactured and hung in public places, intended for the masses. "The bright-colored posters briefly attracted attention before they tore, were covered by a more current notice, or dissolved in the rain. . . . Propaganda posters portray the gospel, not as Chinese theologians wrote about it, but as artists pictured it for the common people" (Center for Global Christianity and Mission 2020). Images of these fragile objects provide a window on the lived religion of that time and place.

Students of Asian religions, across disciplines, have provided rich descriptions of the temples, ritual spaces, foods, and prayer items that make religious practice possible across Asian religious traditions. Singaporean sociologist Vineeta Sinha takes us through the religious/commercial world of "Little India," a neighborhood developed as a Hindu enclave under British colonial rule. She notes that everyday Hindu practice "requires an extraordinary range of religious specialists and ritual paraphernalia" (Sinha 2008, 169). In the diaspora, however, the caste-based systems for creating religious items may not be available, so entrepreneurial commercial providers have stepped in. There are shops of all sizes scattered along main commercial streets and into the public-housing neighborhoods. Sinha goes on to note the complex trade practices that surround the Singapore flower market and how flowers go through a life cycle of sacred and secular meanings. They may start off as a secular commodity but then be transformed by how they are used, returning to mere profane trash to be disposed of in the urban environment. Sinha's walking tour and keen eye were supplemented by attention to economic records and interviews. She asks about the growers, workers, trade routes, and sources of capital, but she is also present on the streets, even noticing what is in the garbage bin. All are part of exploring the religious material world where business and the spirit intersect.

Selling Flowers in Singapore

[They] sell a mixture of "Indian" items—including not only "prayer items," but also Indian groceries and spices. It is interesting that these spaces also service the non-Hindu and non-Indian communities. For instance, the Chinese religionists and Buddhists, who also require oil, loose flowers (jasmines, roses, orchids, Lotus, etc.) and flower garlands for their religious rituals and festivals. . . . The collection of products in the market is diverse and ranges from mass produced items (which can be rough in their finished form) to custom-made and individualised pieces—displaying fine workmanship. . . . Some large retail outlets in Singapore have by now, also successfully branded specific items so that home prayer altars, gold plated prayer utensils and hand-made *kavandis* are seen as the speciality of these businesses and attract customers from all over the island and also from parts of Malaysia. . . . Shop owners see themselves first as businessmen, even if they were motivated into starting this trade for personal, meaningful, spiritual reasons. (Sinha 2008, 173–174)

Each culture defines the characteristics that will mark material objects as part of religious practice, but it often takes very ordinary social processes to bring those objects into being. Once constructed and defined as religious, material objects do, in fact, take on a kind of settled existence. Manufacturers depend on this (as do tattoo artists, as we saw in chapter 4). They want their audiences to recognize their products and put them to proper use. Whether it is jasmine or jewelry, people make and display things that they think will be socially recognized as religious. Like a building with recognizably religious architecture, some things seem so definitively religious that we forget the social processes that made them so.[3]

But things do change, and various sites of disruption can be especially interesting places to learn about lived religious practice. Churches are "deconsecrated" and become community centers or condos, for example. They may still look like religious places, so does that affect how people interact with them? Do they still shape the character of a neighborhood? Or what about when storefronts or factories or movie theaters become churches or mosques? Like roadside memorials, sometimes such things are only temporarily and contingently religious—marked as such only until the flowers fade. How do they make the transition from ordinary to sacred and back again?[4]

That interplay between emerging definitions and traditional forms is also seen in the spaces we call "nature." There is perhaps nothing inherently religious about a sunset or a forest, but they can, and often do, participate in lived religious practices. Many Indigenous peoples mark the four cardinal directions of the Earth with daily prayers and by the way they orient their homes. Aspects of the natural world may be inhabited by spirits, stashes of sacred plants, or rocks stored or carried. Being in right relationship with the natural world is being in right relationship with the spirit world.

Otherwise-secular people who reject religion may similarly seek out landscapes where they can encounter "the sublime." From interviews with "nature lovers" in Sweden, Denmark, and Estonia, David Thurfjell and his colleagues describe the transcendent experiences of people who walk the sand dunes at water's edge in Denmark, often encountering a reality beyond the everyday. "Our interlocutors make statements like, 'It's almost magical,' 'It's almost holy,' or 'It's regenerating,' or they use terms such as 'invigorating' and 'life-giving'" (Thurfjell et al. 2019, 201). One man pointed to the way the open horizon gave him a sense of hope. Like some of the people I studied, their spirituality is one characterized by "awe" (Ammerman 2013a). These very individualized experiences seem to stretch our notion of the social dimensions of religious practice, but we might do well to remember that only some places in nature evoke such experiences. The natural things we think of as potentially sublime become so through our cultural and social experiences, and the places we look are driven by social trends, as well as by the characteristics of the places themselves. Given the religious and political history of Scandinavia, with its empty churches and strong ecological ethic, it is no accident that nature is the location for so much quasi-religious practice.[5] It seems that the absence of religious practice in one place has opened up space for religious practice in other places.

Nature and the outdoors are often seen as special places because they encourage people to leave behind the noise of everyday life. But silence as a lived religious practice can also happen in humanly constructed physical structures. Even people who are not otherwise religiously active may value the experience of walking into a religious building; taking in its sights, sounds, and smells; and perhaps just sitting in silence. From grand mosques in Istanbul to the Sagrada Família cathedral in Barcelona to the decimated Notre Dame in Paris, buildings are not simply spaces where people do religious things. They make possible and participate in the experiences people have (Fuller and Löw 2017).

But religious buildings do not have to be grand to shape and be shaped by the practices that happen in and around them. Understanding any religious group means understanding the spaces it occupies and the "artifacts" that tell often-hidden stories. A walk through a space with someone from the community can tell an observer a great deal about how the space is used in the religious lives of the members (Ammerman 1998). Done with multiple guides, a walk can also reveal the differing appropriations of the space by women, children, or perhaps multiple cultures (Hoover 2014). Discovering how materiality plays its role requires being there to see and experience it, as well as listening to the stories of the people who inhabit it.

How people appropriate cyberspace for religious practice may seem less obvious, but it is no less important. This has been a lively area of research in recent years. One doesn't have to look very far to discover websites designed to teach doctrine, sites designed to connect people to brick-and-mortar congregations, sites that seek to simulate pujas and other rituals, sites that stream images of other people doing religious things, and—in a pandemic—people "gathering" for worship.[6] But what kind of places are these? In spite of being rife with place-oriented metaphors—traveling a highway, exploring, shopping—the experience of being online is still anchored by a screen, perhaps some speakers or earbuds, and (usually) a chair in a very physical space. One might light a physical candle as part of a ritual, but the space is still the family room at home. As Douglas Cowan notes, "Marianist Catholics who frequent websites devoted to the apparitions at Lourdes, Fatima, Medjugorje, or Clearwater seek the experience (or a simulation of the experience) of being at what they regard as supremely holy places" (2005, 261). Still they know the difference between the experience of physically being there and the experience of watching online. No matter what kind of place it is, however, religious places are "places" because a group of people have made them so, even via Zoom.

What Materiality Does

Like all social practices, religious practices do work for the groups that enact them. By establishing patterns, they define the groups that share them. They set expectations that empower some people and disempower others. They enact declarations of right and wrong, what is to be admired or condemned. And objects and spaces are integral to how lived religious practice participates in those processes.

Most basically, however, materiality is an actor in the drama of everyday life. Material objects and environments help to define a situation and shape how we act (Pink 2012). Consider, for example, the nineteenth-century Protestant practice of "camp meetings." People gathered—not just on the frontier but across the country—to sing and pray and listen to preaching that stretched from morning to night for days on end. Withdrawing to a place in nature and setting up a campground allowed religious interactions that could not have happened in settled individual churches and amid the rhythms of everyday work (Messenger 1999). Something of the same dynamic is at work in the Wiccan communities that sociologist Mary Jo Neitz has studied, but for them, meeting in a secluded place also helps to avoid prying eyes. In this account, note that Neitz's own response to the landscape is very much part of her analysis. Once she arrived on-site, her observations of the size and layout of the camp and of the appearances of the participants became integral to her analysis of the group's changing norms of gender and sexuality. Attending over several years brought those changes into focus for her and made clear how places provide both opportunities and constraints.

Driving to the Dragonfest

As we bumped along gravel roads, we attended carefully to the xeroxed map we had been sent along with a list of items for camping, rituals, the community "stone soup" supper, and confirmation of our registration. That year [1987] attendance at the four-day festival neared 200, and the organizers began to look for a bigger site. Now [1996] I drive through the towns of

> the foothills—Evergreen, Conifer, Pine—and turning off onto the inevitable gravel roads, and into the mountains. The road follows the creek. My eyes light on the willows that border it, the meadows, the Ponderosa Pine forests, the face of the mountain. A born-and-bred westerner, this landscape is sacred and holds magic for me on any occasion. (Neitz 2000, 375–376)

Just as we observed the physical signs conveyed by clothing, jewelry, hair, and tattoos, so the physical spaces we inhabit and the objects we use mark our membership in a community of shared religious knowledge and practice. We are the people who know how to kneel on the kneelers, how to touch the fringe of the Torah scroll, what food to bring for the god—or the potluck. Membership in a religious community orients a person toward inhabiting the physical places where that community gathers. One "goes to" church or temple—both a physical act and a religious practice. Religious space and community membership are intertwined, but those relationships can change over time.

Postcolonial Africa is the kind of unsettled place where such changes are visible. After twenty years of study in Ilé Ifè Nigeria, religious studies scholar Jacob Olupona (2011) produced an exhaustive account of both the history and contemporary practices of this sacred city that is at the heart of Yoruba history and practice. Under traditional Indigenous systems, the links between place and identity were strong and clear. Today they are more complicated, nowhere more visibly than in the palace that is at the center of the city's religious and political power. There traditional practices are intermingled with those of Pentecostal newcomers. Olupona's account of that complexity is possible partly because of his own history and his long period of observation but also because he sought out interviewees who could help him understand the events he observed.

Sacred Spaces in Ilé Ifè

The indigenous social structure of Ife, under which the aboriginal inhabitants lived, was based on blood relations (mòlébí). It was made up of lineages whose members regarded themselves as descending from a common ancestor. Each lineage shared a common compound regarded as the ancestral home bequeathed to them through time and without end. Most importantly, however, the power and influence of these lineages were consolidated in myriad myths and rituals of the ancestral deity and in the ceremonial centers: shrines, temples, and lineage halls (àkòdi) that belonged to them. . . . As Ilè-Ifé has changed from traditional to modern structures through the intervention of the colonial authority and the new Ifé intelligentsia, Ifé indigenous religions have responded to the changes in different ways. Religious symbols, beliefs, and practices continue to serve as strong markers for kinship groups, despite their conversion to Islam and Christianity. . . . In the modern era, even after these lineages had ceded large chunks of their territories as land grants to the Nigerian state government to establish schools, community hospitals, and other development projects, the lineages and clans still make symbolic claims to these government-controlled institutions, many of which, by virtue of the names they bear, attest to their [religious] identity. (Olupona 2011, 94, 283)

Such links between territory and identity are, of course, at the heart of nationalism. To be a nation-state is to have borders and territory, and often that territory itself is idealized through religious practice, sometimes with violent consequences. Michael Sells (2003) writes about the confluence of myth-making, ritual, and territorial claims that accompanied the 1990s revival of Serbian nationalism and led to genocide in Kosovo. New or revived sacred spaces were celebrated, as people told stories of past victimhood that must be avenged. At the same time, Croat Catholics were crusading against Serbian Orthodox. And both sought to wipe out every vestige of Muslim presence. Integral to the campaigns was the destruction of religious buildings, art, and literature—iconoclasm. Each group sought to destroy anything that would testify to the legitimate presence of a religious group they wished to cleanse from the nation. Elsewhere, campaigns of secularization have happened in similar ways. Physical evidence of religious practice is destroyed or appropriated by the secular state.[7]

Thankfully, not all religion-based occupation of territory is so destructive, but it is always an exercise of power, whether political, economic, or cultural. Setting territorial boundaries and filling the space requires the authority to do so. In contemporary times, we might look, as urban geographer Sarah Moser (2013) did, at entire new cities being planned in Malaysia, Chechen Republic, and the UAE, cities intentionally designed to reflect Islamic style and identity. On a smaller scale, it is often neighborhoods that are the stage on which religious identity is played out. Sometimes those spaces are the result of legal acts of segregation, creating compounds or ghettos. Remember the Hindu neighborhoods in Singapore that owe their creation to imperial rulers who wanted each religious group in its place. When we see these kinds of religiously defined spaces, historical and political work is called for to find their origins.

That is the kind of work social historian Etan Diamond (2000) did to understand the Jewish neighborhood he studied. A combination of economic contingencies and Jewish practices helped to explain the movement of Jews into the northern suburbs of Toronto. Using official census documents, Diamond noted that by the early 1970s, Jews were the largest ethnic or religious group in the neighborhood surrounding Bathurst Street, a central artery around which there had been much postwar suburban development. Using newspaper reports, government planning documents, neighborhood histories, synagogue records, and other archival records, he gives us a description with careful attention to spaces and patterns of interaction that made this a distinctly Jewish neighborhood.

> ### Making a Jewish Neighborhood in Toronto
>
> In the 1980s, a Jewish developer built housing in the Bathurst neighborhood and included "a large Orthodox Jewish synagogue-cum-community center, a shopping plaza with kosher food stores, and a Jewish book and gift store. By the late 1980s, forty-five Orthodox Jewish congregations were located on or adjacent to Bathurst Street, . . . a first step in creating a sacred space. . . . But homes and congregations alone did not create sacred space. For that to occur, other religious institutions were needed, institutions that would add to the visible religious activity of the district and to the sense that this was a Jewish neighborhood" (Diamond 2000, 41). Those institutions included a Jewish old-age home, a Hebrew Day School, a mikveh (ritual bath), and a kosher restaurant. That sense of sacred Jewish space, Diamond writes, was further enhanced by the clustering of Jewish establishments and by parking arrangements that necessitated a good deal of walking about among the clusters. That activity in the space gave the street the appearance of an urban neighborhood despite its suburban context. That it was a distinctly Jewish space was also clear from the recognizably Orthodox Jewish hairstyles

and clothing. "A passerby on Bathurst could not help but see Jews of all types," marking it as a Jewish place long before there was an official eruv to mark out the ritually sacred territory (41).

Religious territory is often interwoven with the secular urban territory around it. In Toronto, a distinct Jewish territory was created when economic resources and government planning combined with the Jewish religious practice of walking to Sabbath services, the need for kosher food, and the desire for communal gathering places. Similarly, when Catholic authorities encouraged immigrants in the United States to build schools, and Church membership was based in geographic parishes, neighborhoods were often defined by the particular ethnic Catholic population that inhabited them and all the institutions that supported their ethnic Catholic way of life.[8] Lived religious practice in these contexts is likely to happen on the streets and in the shops, as well as in the churches and synagogues.

What about the sounds and smells? They are part of the physical landscape too, and students of lived religion should keep their ears—and noses—open as we explore the places where religious practices are happening. Think about the smell of incense, for example (Kenna 2005), or the ringing of bells or the sound of the Muslim call to prayer. Sounds and smells mark religious territory as much as do the buildings, and like buildings, they can become the source of contention when neighborhoods become more diverse. Tong Soon Lee (1999), an ethnomusicologist, listened for the transformation of religious practice that followed rural Muslims as they were incorporated into the urban area of Singapore. Rural community mosques had broadcast the sound of the call to prayer from the minaret, but now those calls were "noise pollution" in a multireligious city.

The link to territory can be lost in a variety of ways, but when it is, religious objects are often the means through which people continue to identify with a distant place. Once migrants arrive and settle in, the things they brought from home keep the connections alive. Faida Abu-Ghazaleh (2011), an archive specialist, studied a small network of Palestinian families in Maryland, paying special attention to what he saw in their homes. He took digital images while visiting them but also invited them to share pictures. "For the Palestinian families, material artifacts serve as the concrete expression of the lost land. It is the bridge between life in diaspora and Palestinian lands" (Abu-Ghazaleh 2011, 113). The artifacts the families showed him were national and social but also religious. They were reminders, ways of constructing and preserving identity, and important in teaching their children. Speaking of families who had completed the Hajj, Abu-Ghazaleh noted, "They brought several artifacts back with them, and placed these around the house for everyone, including their children, to remember their trip and their religious obligation towards Islam. Also, many of the artifacts in their homes are gifts from family and friends who had visited Mecca" (122). Note that objects provoked the telling of stories that were central to ethnic and religious identity. Children see and ask; parents and extended family tell the stories. Similarly, lived religion researchers see and ask, opening the door to stories that provide the links between objects and lived religious practice.

That objects provoke stories of identity is closely related to their function as conveyors of morality. It is often something visual and physical that embodies a moral ideal. Statues and images of saints express the identity of the community that venerates them, but they also speak of the virtues that the saints' lives exemplified—courage, purity, compassion, and the like. And as times change, so can the meaning of those virtues. Confederate monuments in the United States, for example, extoll the virtues of those who fought to preserve a way of life, a way of life built on slavery and the continued subjugation of African Americans. Conflicting moral messages have made them sites of intense debate. Monuments to the horrors of the Holocaust have often had mixed moral messages, as well. Religious studies scholar Janet Jacobs (2010) traveled among the many sites of memorialization with her camera in hand, looking at the stories they told—and didn't tell. What sorts of rituals of mourning did they invite or discourage? Soviet-era memorials, she noted, tended to frame the Holocaust in larger antifascist and anticapitalist rhetorics, rather than giving specific attention to the Jewishness of the genocide. Since the 1980s, Jewish voices and narratives have begun to be added, but especially at Ravensbrück, Jacobs used her photographs to show the "marginalization of Jewish memory within a motif of national remembrance"

(2010, 75). She vividly demonstrated the Christianization of images of women's suffering, as they rendered Jewish mothers in images that evoke a Christian pietà. Memorials speak a vivid moral story, but which morals and whose virtues? Observers need to ask what isn't there, as well as what is.

What these examples suggest, of course, is that religious material objects have power and are used to demonstrate and enhance the power of those who use them. We can sometimes observe this power in physical characteristics like height or loudness or size or central location. What draws attention and has features that a given culture has come to associate with sacred power? How is space allocated to groups with more and less social power?[9] What role do states play in supporting or forbidding the presence of religious images or the use of common space? Inside religious spaces, ritual leaders exercise power by how they arrange the space, as well. One might think of the contrast between the Catholic liturgy before and after the Second Vatican Council, when parishes removed the communion rail separating laity from the space where the sacred elements were consecrated. Or of the status recognized (and conferred) on a Jew who is "called to the bimah" to read a Torah portion. Gaining access to sacred spaces and touching sacred objects conveys power in the here and now.

We will return to those questions of exclusion shortly, but it is also useful to think about the way religious objects participate in ritual practices that leave participants feeling empowered. Believers apply holy waters or oils to their bodies and feel as if they are more well. The person in possession of a sacred amulet may undertake tasks or journeys that otherwise seem impossible. For Mexicans in Chicago, in the face of an everyday world in which they often feel powerless, enacting the Christian passion narrative (the Via Crucis) on the streets of Pilsen can become a ritual of empowerment. Participants visibly express their lament for the way their world is, even as they are physically occupying the streets. Karen Mary Davalos is a Chicano/a studies scholar who studied the history and present realities of Pilsen in the 1990s. Domination, she argues, is an ever present reality in the lives of the community, but as one ritual participant told her, "We must be Christlike. He fought [against] injustices. We should also fight [against] injustices, to make our life and our world a better place to live" (Davalos 2002, 60).

In quite the opposite fashion, the religious practices of communities along the Mississippi River—in what is known as "cancer alley"—seem intentionally aimed at hiding the material, earthly, sources of suffering. Sociologist Arlie Hochschild quotes a "grief-stricken parishioner, the mother of an ill child living in the highly polluted town of Mossville": "I don't know how I could have gotten through this without my church." But, Hochschild observes, "as for altering the pollution, poverty, ill health, and other things that had to be endured, for many that lay beyond the doors of the church" (2016b, 124). Religious practice can mask reality and disempower participants.

Paying Attention to Material Boundaries and Difference

When we pay attention to the materiality of religious practice, then, we see how it helps to create the identities of those who inhabit certain spaces and use sacred objects. What they understand to be good and bad is given visible form in monuments and images. People know who they are partly by where they belong. Space and the things in it can also bestow or withhold power. Studying each of those properties, we immediately see that materiality participates in exclusion at the same time that it defines inclusion. We have already noted how religious officials use space to project their power and exclude laity from privileged forms of participation. We have seen how religious nationalisms can foment virulent forms of exclusion that can lead to cleansing of unwanted religious groups. Less overtly, the religious objects and places that make one group feel at home are simply alien to others.

All the forms of difference that characterize social life can also be seen in the material dimensions of lived religious practice. As you begin exploring what people do when they do religion, keep key sources of material difference in mind.

You will almost certainly notice that gender matters. Even though women outnumber men in most religious settings (Pew Research Center 2016), there is a long history of religious exclusion based on gender. As a result, many women, especially in liberal Western contexts, have come to see religion as an unfriendly space.[10] They assume that one cannot be religious and feminist at the same time and that their calls for equal treatment will fall on deaf ears among religious officials. That assumption is reinforced by male language, male images, and male leaders who leave no space for women, except on the margins. Giselle Vincett (2013), a British religion scholar, set out to understand how such women nevertheless sometimes manage to create their own religious "safe space." She conducted interviews with feminist women, about half of whom were Christians from a variety of liberal denominations. In addition, she observed an independent Christian feminist ritual group, kept up with email lists, and explored other computer-mediated spaces such as web forums. She also asked people to write reflections for her. That is, she looked at both virtual and physical spaces where women were engaged in lived religious practice. These were places where women reconstructed images of God that were embodied, inclusive, and freeing. They also "recolonized" church spaces by seeking ordination and standing behind the altar to lead in worship. They softened hard lines of architecture with fabric and candles and new colors. These women gathered for religious practice in cyber and physical spaces, creating a social space of their own on the margins of the religious communities that often excluded them.

Differences in social class and social location may not be as immediately obvious as differences in gender, but any careful observation of religious materiality will quickly reveal how inequality and differing tastes shape the material religious environment. We will return to matters of taste in chapter 7, but for now it is sufficient to note that differences in economic, social, and legal resources shape how religious spaces are created and maintained. Is this a showpiece mosque paid for by a government on the rise? Or do legal sanctions mean that religious practices need to be out of sight? From zoning laws to religious bans, governments are very much a part of allocating space, and it is worth paying attention to what they do and do not allow (Woods 2018). It is also worth noticing who is competing for space and how the nature of the space itself is part of its attraction or repulsion for religious practitioners (McRoberts 2003). Fenggang Yang's (2005) observation of Chinese Christian groups who meet in McDonald's is an excellent example of how religious practice, state restrictions on where religion can be located, and the social appeal of a Western commodity combine to send roving Bible-study groups to the tables of a fast-food restaurant.

Often religious practice happens in unexpected niches that are dictated by resources, as well as tradition. Meeting in an open-air space is both habit and necessity for many African practices. Meeting in an overcrowded apartment where families can sing and pray is a necessity when churches make no space for people who speak an immigrant's language (Berrelleza 2020). Attending the only mosque with a wheelchair ramp can be a matter of necessity. Social differences can be seen in all sorts of material ways. Is the *mikveh* dingy and well worn or a shiny new spa? Is the artwork tagged with the names of famous artists and wealthy donors, or are there homemade objects in makeshift displays? Is the worship space at the center of the city or on the outskirts? Or is this a religious building in a rural area that matches the simplicity and DIY habits of hardworking farmers (Neitz 2005)? The social places people occupy in the economic and occupational world can be seen in the physical spaces to which they have access for their religious practices.

Materiality as Part of the Whole

The study of immigrant religion has been especially fruitful in showing the role of materiality as a dimension of practice. Across the world, religious spaces play constantly evolving roles as populations come and go (Vasquez and Marquardt 2003). Often physical spaces are knit together through cyberspace as migrants communicate and even worship together across borders. Since the 1990s, migration researchers have provided students of lived religion a rich body of research documenting what people are doing in these extraordinary circumstances. Among the best of those studies comes from Jacqueline Hagan (2008), who assembled a research team based at the University of Houston to interview over two hundred undocumented Mexican, Guatemalan, Salvadoran, and Honduran migrants who had crossed multiple miles and borders to reach the United States. She and her team also paid attention to the religious organizations and leaders active in responding to migrants' needs and spent time at the border and in Guatemala. They listened to stories, observed rituals and acts of solidarity, and experienced firsthand the places in which lived religion was happening.

Material Religion across Borders

During their long treks across nations, over mountains and rivers, through towns and deserts, in the remote reaches of the migrant trail, nine out of ten migrants in the study practiced religion to help them cope with the journey north and, in some cases, to understand their own survival of near-death experiences. Some, including infrequent churchgoers, practiced what they knew from their tradition in their home communities and stopped at churches along the way to attend a religious service, say a prayer, light a candle, or seek spiritual assistance from clergy. Others strayed from their migratory route to visit a shrine to give thanks for making it as far as they had or to beseech further protection for the days ahead. In the absence of holy places sanctioned by the Catholic Church, some migrants visited shrines housing popular saints that had been erected by local residents. In the absence of these shrines, some migrants improvised and spontaneously erected shrines to revered icons from their home communities in order to reproduce those cultural practices with which they are most familiar and most comfortable and to recreate relations with their sacred icons. Still others called on the companionship and protection of revered local saints and icons in their home communities to whom they had prayed for protection before their journey; in transit they wore medals around their necks depicting these saints and carried holy cards in their pockets. Some, like Javier and his fellow travelers, coped with impending death through group prayer and then interpreted their rescue from death in terms of a miracle from God. These migration miracles provided meaning and hope. (Hagan 2008, 116–117)

Central to the story of these practices are the places where they happen and the objects that give expression to them—shrines and churches and holy cards, located in the desert between nations. Legal and economic systems shape the journey, and fragile bodies are at risk. The saints bless the pilgrims with protection that gives them courage, and both saints and communities send them out with a sense of moral necessity to care for family and each other. In the midst of fear, sacred practices evoke comfort, and sometimes there are even miraculous spiritual experiences. The religious communities along the way provide both familiar and unfamiliar words and practices, but the migrants themselves improvise. And in the end, what happens is shaped into a narrative account that provides meaning. The lived religious practices of migration are best understood in all their complexity—embodied work in real material places, shaped by intense emotion, moral imperative, and spiritual experience, and narrated in ways that bring sacred meaning to a very this-worldly journey.

Ideas for Further Study

1. In addition to the other studies cited in this chapter, you may be interested in Mary Ellen Konieczny's (2009) look at domestic spaces, as well as Roman Williams's (2010) use of photo elicitation to analyze spiritual dimensions of a variety of everyday spaces. My own *Sacred Stories, Spiritual Tribes* includes significant attention to materiality, as well (Ammerman 2013a).

2. Social theorist Jeffrey Alexander makes a similar point about icons. His theory can be a bit esoteric, but students of the material dimension can benefit from his work, including the essays he has gathered from others in *Iconic Power: Materiality and Meaning in Social Life* (Alexander, Bartmanski, and Giesen 2012).

3. Robert Brenneman and Brian Miller's book *Building Faith* (2020) is an excellent example of taking the complexity of religious buildings into account. From zoning boards to architects to competing factions within a religious group, creating a religious building is a socially shaped religious practice through and through.

4. A nicely detailed study of religious practice in otherwise-secular space comes from Dann Wigner's (2018) description of a church that meets in a very modern warehouse-style space and uses material objects—candles and Eastern Orthodox icons, for example—to invite experimentation with religious practices.

5. Another fascinating study of lived religion in nature is historian Rebecca Gould's (2005) study of homesteading. Many of those who took the practice up in the 1960s and '70s were disillusioned with organized religions and sought spiritual reconnection in the work of living off the land. If you are interested in the intersection of religious practice with movements of Earth care, a good place to start is the collection of essays in *Ecospirit: Religions and Philosophies for the Earth* (Kearns and Keller 2007).

6. John Turner and Lincoln Mullen (2020) have collected essays, images, and reports on how religion was being practiced during the 2020 COVID-19 pandemic. Social scientist and filmmaker Jenn Lindsay produced "Quarantined Faith: Rome, Religion, and Coronavirus," which captured the dilemmas and innovations of religious communities in that most "material" of cities. The dislocation experienced by much of the world's population created an opportune moment for reflection on how life is physically located.

7. Genevieve Zubrzycki's study of the making of Québécois nationalism traces the movement largely through visual images, including the changing material

shape of the annual St. John's Day festival. Now, she writes, "the ethno-religious genesis of the French-Canadian nation prior to its Québécois redefinition [is excised]. While the holiday is still commonly referred to as 'La Saint-Jean' (and rarely, if ever, colloquially called by its official name), few people under the age of forty-five can explain why it is celebrated on June 24 or referred to by that name" (Zubrzycki 2016, 118).

8. It is important to note that religious practice has an important role to play in shaping how groups relate to urban space. Gerald Gamm (1999) documented the difference between Catholics and Jews in Boston neighborhoods, and Omar McRoberts (2003) describes the way small African American churches related to some of those same urban Boston spaces. The "Journey through NYC Religions" project (www.nycreligion.org) is a fascinating effort to raise awareness about the presence of enormously diverse religious groups in that city. The street-level accounts of what is happening give a vibrant picture of lived religious practice. In London, another group of researchers has been at work documenting what they call the "desecularisation" of the city, with neighborhood-level explorations of how new populations are inhabiting old spaces (Goodhew and Cooper 2019). Similar projects are happening in the United States, in St. Louis, Missouri (https://religioninplace.org); in Rochester, New York (https://digrocreligions.org); in Birmingham, Alabama (https://magiccityreligion.org); and in Boston, Massachusetts (www.hiddensacredspaces.org). These projects often employ visual methods and produce museum-quality displays. Perhaps there is one near you?

9. An instructive example of the way space and style can be used to express power comes to us from archeological anthropologist Lars Fogelin (2003). He studied the architectural plans of thirteen early Buddhist stupa, the stylized burial mounds that contained remains and relics of the Buddha and his followers and were the primary ritual sites in the earliest days of Buddhism. Sites controlled by monks were physically designed to focus on their own activity, not on what laity did.

10. A number of observers have noted the phenomenon of "alternative spaces" created by women inside otherwise-patriarchal religious traditions. Jewish women make the *mikveh* their own (Kaufmann 1991). Conservative Protestant women have a variety of prayer groups (Brasher 1998; Griffith 1997). Muslim women study the Qur'an together (Mahmood 2005). It is important to pay attention to what is happening in these alternative spaces, as well as in the places that are official and public, to note both what is and is not possible there.

6

Lived Religious Emotions

An evangelical convert weeps over her sins. A crusader fights a religious enemy with intense fury. A pilgrim is joyful at reaching her sacred destination. A synagogue volunteer reaches out with care and empathy to a newly arrived refugee. The religious practices of conversion, crusade, pilgrimage, and community service cannot be fully understood without paying attention to the emotional dimensions of those practices. Nor can we understand the more ordinary moments of prayer or religious learning or veneration without knowing about the feelings that bring those practices to life and the patterns of shared knowledge that provide religious emotional know-how. The study of lived religion includes the study of emotions, and learning to pay attention to emotions is the work to which we turn in this chapter.

That is not to say that religion *is* simply an emotion or that there is any single distinctive religious emotion. The enactment of religious practice employs the full range of human feeling. It is as much about anger and jealousy as about love and compassion. As Ole Riis and Linda Woodhead say, "What makes an emotion religious is . . . the fact that it occurs within a religious context and is integral to its social and symbolic relations" (2010, 54). As we have seen in earlier chapters, even the definition of a context as religious is a matter of shared understanding. Within those contexts, religious traditions offer their followers distinctive emotional repertoires—encouraging calm serenity or energetic praise, happiness or contrition. Emotion itself is as foundational to religious practice as to any other social practice. As with all the things we do, feeling, expressing, naming, and regulating emotion is embedded in our bodies and in our social contexts (Scheer 2012). Understanding patterns of shared religious practice requires attention to the emotions they evoke and express, as well as to the social rules that manage that expression.

Emotions Are Social

Studying the emotional dimension of religious practice requires recognizing that emotions are not just a matter of the individual psyche.[1] There are social patterns at work. We may experience an emotion as something that overwhelms us from outside or something that is lodged in our inner body, mind, and heart, but emotion is not untouched by outside influence. The situations that evoke feelings and the interpretations for explaining them come from our past experience, our relationships, and our surroundings. They have become a part of our shared knowledge. We know, without thinking, when it's appropriate to laugh or to cry. When the movie music or the political speaker give us cues, we know when to be excited or to be afraid. We also know when to show overt emotion and how to explain it to ourselves. Just as different cultures expect different expressions of grief at a graveside, different religious communities expect different expressions of emotion in a worship service or at a temple. Sometimes the triggers are very intentionally built in, but mostly we just know. We may think of individual emotions as private and uniquely our own, but sharing an emotional moment in a public ceremony is no less real and authentic.

However, individuals do not always find themselves in emotional harmony with the situations around them. The tie between shared emotion and shared belonging is perhaps most apparent when it is disrupted or absent. When everyone else is acting joyous but you are unmoved or when you are feeling great sorrow but no one else seems touched, you may have the first clue to the possibility that you are out of place. An individual's own past experience or evolving sense of identity may mean that the emotional expectations of a given religious practice are felt as dissonant or even oppressive. Equally likely, simply being in a new cultural setting means learning to tune one's own emotions to the expectations of others. Because that is true, participant observers should not discount their own emotional involvement in what they observe. When we think reflexively about our position within research relationships, our own feelings and those of others are an important starting point in the task (Burkitt 2012). How we know others and how we know ourselves requires emotional awareness no less than any other form of analysis.

Along with the participants themselves, researchers will experience the emotional expectations of religious communities. That is true even if the emotions in question seem "unemotional." Even the most stiff-upper-lip self-control is a "feeling rule" no less than the admonition to praise God with all one's heart.[2] Being an observer in a community that is not one's own can reveal both one's own emotional expectations and the community's. That is one of the things Timothy Nelson (2005) discovered by spending a year deeply enmeshed in the life of the Charleston, South Carolina, congregation he calls Eastside Chapel. We saw in chapter 4 how differing positions of privilege influenced his understanding of their experiences of health and embodiment, but there were more layers of difference to uncover. This is an African American church, and Nelson is white, and he writes openly about the degree to which his first experiences of the congregants' worship were disconcerting. He slowly became a part of the community, though, and formed close relationships with several of its members. Eventually he was able to discern the particular emotional repertoire that characterized their services. Notice how he is able to describe the emotions and how the actions of the worship service and the relationships in the congregation structured them. The words of the pastor, the church mothers leading by example, and the songs that members sing made clear which emotions were being called forth and when. This is not something members might have been able to describe in words, but Nelson's own presence and participation allowed him to map out these patterns.

Emotion Worship at Eastside Chapel

Adoration. Love. Hope. Joy. Gratitude. The worship service at Eastside Chapel is an emotionally charged affair. When I say "emotional" here, I don't simply mean it in the sense of overt action like shouting, dancing, clapping, and loud cries. . . . I mean that these five specific emotions are evoked by and displayed in the service. Putting it sociologically, these emotions are normative—people expect other worshippers (and themselves) to not only display them, but actually feel them. . . . When the Eastside congregation sings the final stanza of "Amazing Grace," "When we've been there ten thousand years, bright shining as the sun; / There's no less days to sing God's praise / Than when we'd first begun," each congregant is reminded of his or her belief in God's provision for the future and the eternal life to follow, evoking hope within. When the choir sings, "A mighty fortress is our God, a bulwark never failing," those present are reminded of the power and majesty of God, an image that evokes feelings of praise and worship. When worshippers sing the words of the old spiritual "I know I've been changed, the angels in the heaven have changed my name," it may call to mind their own spiritual journey out of spiritual darkness and evoke joy and gratitude within. (Nelson 2005, 134–138)

Identifying the emotional realities in religious practice is also critical because we learn about the world through our feelings and those feelings prompt action. Feeling afraid tells us to act cautiously. Feeling anxious may tell us to be especially vigilant. Feeling loved may encourage us to engage in sexual activity or acts of kindness. Emotions deliver information to us, and we convey information with them. They can direct our attention toward some things and away from others. People may engage in some forms of religious practice because it brings them pleasure, avoiding other practices because they are accompanied by unpleasant emotions. Studying lived religion means paying attention to that full range of attraction and repulsion.

It can also work the other way around. Action can motivate feeling. It may even be hard to tell which came first—performing a certain action or feeling a certain way. Religious rituals are often aimed at generating emotional states, and how they do so tells us something about the participants and the group. Saba Mahmood's study of Muslim women in Egypt points to the ability of emotion to lead to religious commitment, rather than the other way around. She describes weeping during prayer as both an expression of an interior state of piety and a behavioral means of acquiring that state. The mosque women she studied adopted an intentional program of practices intended to bring them to an ideal feeling of "tenderness of heart appropriate to the state of being in the presence of God" (Mahmood 2005, 123). Emotional expression was chosen and intentionally taught until it became internalized and spontaneous and desired.

The relationship between visible displays of emotion and inner states is, then, complex, as the religious studies scholar Pamela Klassen (2009) discovered at the wedding of a Hindu friend. Feeling sad when a child leaves the nest to get married may be a common experience, but the ritual structure of the flow of emotion was especially apparent to her as an outsider. She saw how collective action provided a ritual container for emotion, whether or not individuals spontaneously experienced the prescribed feelings.

Crying at a Hindu Wedding

After the long Hindu wedding ritual, and before the North American–style reception, my friend took me aside to warn me that "the time for crying" was about to start. Accordingly, many of her female relatives gathered around her in the hotel lobby to weep publicly as a display of their grief over the loss of their sister/daughter/niece. To my unaccustomed (though tipped-off) eyes, the scene appeared to be entirely ritually provoked—that is, the women were crying because the schedule of the ritual called them to do so as they said a ritualized farewell to their beloved kinswoman whom they would see again at the reception in an hour. Perhaps due to its diasporic setting within a downtown Toronto hotel lobby and its timing in the middle of the wedding celebrations, and because I was warned of it by the bride, the weeping at first appeared to me as entirely contrived—as inauthentic tears that, though they might represent authentic feelings, were called on by ritual and not by the natural course of emotions.

Reflecting on this, of course, it is easy to see how my limited perspective of what counted as "natural" in the course of a ritual shaped my estimation of the authenticity of weeping. The "time for crying" provided a container to let out the grief of separation that comes with the maturing of a child in a way that the Christian weddings I was accustomed to did not. (Klassen 2009, 151–152)

Notice that Klassen was an on-the-scene observer, and she had an informant. That combination of direct observation as the event unfolds and before-and-after conversation with an insider is a common method for exploring the emotional dimension of religious practices. We can observe activity and behavior and setting, but we may have difficulty accessing what the participants are feeling. The scene itself may seem to evoke emotion—lights dim and music slows—but just how prayerful is that moment? A bloody Passion play (depicting Jesus's last hours) may seem revolting to one observer, while it moves another to feelings of gratitude or compassion. Sorting things out means asking directly. It is important not to make assumptions but to find a participant who is willing to talk about what they felt and why. It is important, too, to realize that conversations *about* emotions are as socially structured as the feelings themselves. Talking to more than one person is important, just as reflecting on our own experience is. There is a complex interplay between individual experiences and social expectations.

What Emotions Do

People who study emotion sometimes talk about it as the aspect of human experience that indicates and expresses "involvement" (Barbalet 2002). That is, emotion is our point of connection and commitment. A group's solidarity is not just about its ideological unity but also about its ties of affection. Doing things together and having a common focus combines with shared emotion to create attachment to the group and commitment to doing things together in the future.[3] We don't just calculate the costs and benefits of belonging, we *feel* our relationship to people. We don't just *think* about what we should do, we respond based on our sense of membership and the collective emotions we generate together. Emotions do important social work.

Feelings and relationships are, in fact, inseparable. Mutual attention and affection are at the heart of what it means to be part of a group, and maintaining positive connections requires "emotion work." Hochschild was among the earliest and most important writers about the sociology of emotion. She says that emotions are something we work at, rather than simply an uncontrolled bodily reaction. "We feel. We try to feel. We want to try to feel" (Hochschild 1979, 563). That is, we size up the social situation and figure out the appropriate feelings for that place and time for people "like us." If we do not yet feel enthusiastic enough, we may evoke memories of exciting past moments or engage in physical displays of feeling to get ourselves in the mood. As Hochschild (1983) also showed, getting *out* of the mood is equally important. If everyone aboard the plane is terrified by the turbulence, the determined calm of the flight attendant provides reassurance. In each case, people are working together to achieve and maintain the feelings that will also establish or reestablish a group's sense of well-being. Social psychologist Rowland Miller (2004) has studied the importance of embarrassment, for instance. He points out that realizing one has committed a gaffe, feeling chagrined (maybe even blushing), and expressing an apology give one's compatriots an opportunity to make light of the situation and thereby maintain good relations. Regulating emotions—good and bad—is part of keeping a group together.

How would we observe such things? Both participation and interviews can be important, but other methods can be useful, as well. Social psychologists study emotion work by using questionnaires and even experiments to identify which emotions are triggered by which kinds of situations. While that has not been common among students of lived religion, it is not hard to imagine using surveys to ask about emotional components of religious practices. The National Congregations Study, for example, asks a representative (a "key informant") to report on congregational practices that can have a bearing on participants' emotional experience, and the US Congregational Life Survey asks congregants directly about their experiences during worship. Both surveys can be accessed through the American Religion Data Archive (www.thearda. com). Survey data can make it possible to see larger patterns that might not show up in a single place and time, even as they must be interpreted cautiously. We should remember that different respondents are likely to differ in what they mean by "happiness" or "comfort" or any other feeling word that they are asked about on a survey.

When a group's emotional ties are strong, commitment is strong, but that very bond may also mean negative feelings about other groups.[4] In fact, the two emotions can feed off each other—affection for compatriots can generate antipathy for others, and vice versa. That's one of the things Hyun Jeong Ha (2017) discovered when she spent seven months in the churches, streets, and markets of a mixed-religion neighborhood in Cairo. She wanted to know, among other things, how emotions affected the way Christians interacted with their Muslim neighbors. The overall tension in Egypt and widely publicized incidents of violence against Christian churches made her participants nervous, and they showed it in what she called "subdued behaviors." That is, they were likely to talk "in hushed voices, looking around to make sure their conversations are not overheard" (Ha 2017, 139). They also got annoyed. In everyday interactions, there were often points of irritation, times when Christians felt that they were disadvantaged and put down. Notice all the subtle cues Ha documents—how people talked and what they wore, as much as what they said. Note also that lived religious practice does not stop at the church door. We might not think about shopping as a religious practice, but when it is framed by religious identity markers—a crucifix necklace and the absence of a head covering—it becomes a religious part of everyday life. In a situation where religious life is precarious and contested, the emotional dimension of everyday practice comes to the fore. Fear and anger stand opposite affection and solidarity.

Antipathy on the Streets of Cairo

Sarah was shopping at a store when the "Islamist" owner approached her and ordered her to cover her hair as Muslim women do. She left the store after telling him, "No, I am a Christian." As Sarah recalls the situation during the interview, she frowned and said she was "annoyed." In her belief, the Islamist owner knew that she was Christian from her crucifix necklace that she always wears. Since then, she stopped going to Islamist-run shops because she realized that Islamist owners were "very rude" and "not respectful" to Christians. . . . These microaggressions and the provocation of negative emotions distance Christians from Muslims in general, while shared, collective emotions bind Christians and reinforce solidarity. (Ha 2017, 142–143)

If we want to study religious practices of exclusion and hatred, there are unfortunately many examples in history and contemporary life—Christians and Buddhists against Muslims, Hindus against Sikhs, Muslims against Christians, and more. These conflicts almost always involve land and ethnicity and politics in equal measure with religious difference, but the most violent atrocities can build on ground-level emotional momentum. Religious rituals such as prayers, songs, and chants encourage people to work themselves up to a state that permits violence, but that happens in a context where divisions have long been stoked.[5] Political scientist and anthropologist Timothy Longman has carefully documented the role of the Christian churches in Rwanda's 1993–1994 genocide and concludes,

> It should not be surprising that many Christians believed that the genocide was consistent with Christian belief, that it even had the sanction of

the churches. The case of Ngoma parish in Butare, where Christians went to pray before they went out to kill, was not isolated. The fact that people could desecrate church buildings and kill even at the foot of the altar or in the sacristy is not evidence of a lack of respect for Christianity or a shallowness of Christian faith. Instead it reveals the nature of Christianity in Rwanda as a politicized, conservative, discriminatory faith. (Longman 2009, 197)

Institutions and political power are the backdrop, but emotions of hatred and fear, all sacralized by religious authority, are necessary components. Even after the violence has ended, later rituals may commemorate the group's struggles and thereby continue to build group solidarity. National anthems often state (or at least imply) the godly rightness of vanquishing the nation's enemies, while invoking the blessing of the divine on the citizen singers. Studying the role of emotion in religious practice, then, has to include attention to practices that intensify conflict by generating and remembering sacralized feelings of outrage and hatred.

Undertaking this kind of research may require taking up historical cases, given the difficulty posed by being present in the midst of violent confrontations.[6] Longman's research is remarkable for his close observations and wide-ranging interviews, both immediately before and immediately after the 1994 genocide. Even when one is documenting long-ago events, however, there are many records to tap—visual as well as written—available for analysis and often accessible soon after the fact in web-based formats and social media posts. There are tools for "scraping data" from social media, as well as tools for digital analysis of massive volumes of historical texts. Theologians Timothy Snyder and Ashley Theuring used Twitter posts as a basis for studying the lived religious practices of thousands of people in the wake of the Sandy Hook school shooting tragedy in the United States (T. Snyder 2013). Digital tools allowed them to see patterns of religious practice, paying special attention to both the verbal and visual expression of emotion.

Grieving on Twitter

Our research on Sandy Hook indicates that following a national tragedy, social media creates new possibilities for religious practice, allowing us to directly access firsthand accounts and to express our faith and solidarity in the face of unimaginable suffering from essentially anywhere on the globe. We found that Twitter provides us a place both to offer condolences and compassion to those who have been directly impacted and to make meaning of such events for ourselves. For example, in the wake of Sandy Hook, the hashtag #nowords, which began as a social commentary on the ridiculousness of the Internet, took on a more solemn and profound sensibility. Indeed, many of us did not have the words to make any sense of it. Social media offers a solution to this "speechlessness." Twitter, Instagram and Facebook allow users to express in images what they might struggle to express with words. We discovered that these visual articulations offer a surprisingly powerful tool for prayer.

When we compared tweets about Newtown, we found that tweets designated as prayer used photos and graphics 50 percent more than general condolences. These included photo memorialization of the victims, photos of prayer vigils and other images filled with religious significance. Twitter and smartphones provided an unanticipated and soul-stirring alternative to conventional words of prayer, inviting us to forgo language altogether and bring the poetry of silence to our contemporary religious practices. . . . After the Newtown shootings, many Twitter users documented their participation in a crowd-sourced memorialization by sharing photos of candles lit inside white paper bags they'd placed in their driveways, a symbolic gesture to guide "home" the innocent souls of the victims. In this case, participation via Twitter didn't replace traditional religious practice; it improvised it. (T. Snyder 2013)

As we see in Snyder's example, emotion can build bridges. Ecumenical and interfaith groups know this and often design gatherings they hope will promote positive feelings among the participants and thereby counter tendencies toward conflict. They emphasize what all have in common and tell stories of kindness and compassion. A rational argument about ideas and interests might make all the same points, but the shared emotion and shared ritual are likely to build more formidable bonds. One extensive study of faith-based community organizing emphasized just that by analyzing what the authors called "bridging cultural practices" (Braunstein, Fulton, and Wood 2014). These are practices that define inclusive social categories to which everyone can potentially belong and then enact rituals that allow people to inhabit common emotional space. Again, being there to observe was critical for these researchers, as was an imaginative analysis of how words are connected to feelings. Notice how their observation of an opening ritual benefited from their familiarity with the diverse religious and racial contours of the audience. They also paid attention to the multiple dimensions of the religious practice that a progressive rabbi invited her listeners into. Emotions, evoked by and embodied in religious ritual practice, do important social work, especially in establishing—and transcending—social boundaries.

Emotional Bridges in Interfaith Organizing

[The rabbi] spoke of the challenges faced by the [ancient] Jews after they were sent to wander the desert. Before offering her prayer, she recounted how the Jews built relationships as free members of a new society:

"One of the things that really strikes me about this journey is the instructions for the priests, who are the leaders . . . responsible for carrying the communal center—the Tabernacle—through the desert. So when the priests are being prepared for their role, they put oil—do this with me [she acts out putting oil on her ear and encourages others to follow along]—they put oil on their ear. Yeah, put it on. And on their thumb. And on the toe, the big toe of their foot. [Everyone laughs as she lifts up her foot and touches her toe.]

"It's an amazing set of reminders for us, too, as we gather in relationship building. Because it meant that these leaders—and all of us are leaders tonight—had to listen well first. The first thing was the ear. . . . Second, they had to reach out their hand—right?—to connect to someone, and to use that human connection. What makes us human? It's our thumbs. . . . And then to make those connections, they couldn't just stand there and reach out their hand. They had to walk over and connect with somebody—right?—which made an active possibility of connection all over the six hundred thousand and more people. . . .

"Let's turn our attention to prayer for a minute, and be thinking about your ear, and your thumb, and your toe. Let's turn to God. We ask you, oh God, who creates human beings in your image, and teaches us the way to walk through our life, that you give us knowledge,

knowledge that we need to go back to our communities to create relationships, to organize there, so that eventually we can reach out into our entire city and improve the lives of so many. And in that way, we'll be listening, and we'll be reaching out, and we'll be taking the steps to make that happen. Amen." (event transcript)

By engaging participants' bodies in collective rituals surrounding spoken prayer or encouraging transgressions of personal space, practices like these draw the group together into shared embodied experiences. These rituals create opportunities for individuals to enact the relationships they seek to create or strengthen. (Braunstein, Fulton, and Wood 2014, 714–15)

Emotional Boundaries and Differences

If emotions are socially structured, that means that they are also subject to the dynamics of culture, power, and exclusion that are part of the social world. We have seen that in the way emotions define membership. To know one's "place" in society is to know the emotional repertoire that accompanies the practices typical of one's group (Stets and Turner 2014). Each culture and subgroup values a particular range of emotion—and often devalues the way other people act. It is both a matter of simple difference and a stratified, hierarchical order. If the people at the top value restrained public affect, the more expressive habits of other groups may be part and parcel of why those groups are denigrated as lesser people. Whether the division is ethnic, racial, or class based, it will shape how the emotional dimensions of religious practice are experienced and perceived. Just who is seen as "too emotional"? The long history of colonial dominance by the "restrained" and "rational" cultures of the North Atlantic has, in fact, meant that it is more often lower classes and the cultures of the Global South that are criticized for being emotionally out of control (Fanon [1963] 1968). As Nelson (2005) points out in his study of Eastside Chapel, however, *all* cultures have emotion rules, and the job of the observer is to look for those patterns. Inevitably that will also mean observing how the emotional dimension of religious practice plays a role in setting up social hierarchies.

We are likely to notice, for example, that gender and age structure the emotional dimension of religious practice. In many instances, women are expected to be the visible bearers of the community's emotion, while men are the quiet ones.[7] But that can be deceiving. More to the point, we should pay attention to *which* emotions are expected of different groups. How are anger, ecstasy, affection, joy, remorse, courage, and excitement distributed among the participants?

As with so many things in the study of religious practice, we often recognize the rules when they are broken. A 2019 concert of Boston's Handel and Haydn Society made news for exactly that reason (Annear 2019). A young boy, attending his first classical music concert, loudly exclaimed "Wow!" at the end of a piece of music, and the audience of more staid adults had to decide how to respond. They laughed—often a sign that a rule has been broken—and then applauded. They had been reminded of the emotion rules—and perhaps of their own suppressed emotional response.[8] Not only does gender dictate who does what, but youth is often a license for modes of expression that adults have learned to leave aside for more approved responses such as polite applause.

Discovering divisions and hierarchies can sometimes be hard. Careful direct observation, accompanied by formal and informal interviews, is the standard tactic for good methodological reasons. But many people resist talking about divisions in their group and insist that everyone is equal. Getting past that barrier requires very gentle questioning, often with concrete "what if" questions that allow seemingly hypothetical responses. Paper-and-pencil surveys also allow enough distance for people to say something about what they really expect and value and what they don't. Innovative web-based experiments can also present scenarios that show variations on practices that feature different kinds of people behaving in different ways, allowing participants to assign evaluative scores based on their responses. Whatever tools we choose, it is important to consider the ways lived religious practice follows the emotional contours of the status hierarchies in which it takes place.

Emotions as Part of the Whole

Lived religious practice has multiple dimensions, and they are experienced as parts of a whole. The perception of being in the presence of the divine signals the spiritual dimension of practice, but that perception is sometimes inseparable from the emotion of crying, as among the

Muslim women whom Mahmood studied. What people understand as a spiritual experience may be defined by its emotional content. Likewise, in discovering the power of emotion to set (or transcend) boundaries between groups, we have seen the interaction between emotional and moral dimensions of practice. What we think is right action is recognized by its emotional resonance and not just its theological justification. It *feels* right. Theological combatants can call for emotionally charged practices of moral exclusion, but religious leaders can also seek inclusion through equally emotionally charged practices of unity. The person or practice that is anathema or blessed is defined as such by the emotion. That, too, is a lived religious practice.

Note especially that emotions intersect with embodiment and materiality. They are made visible in tears or laughter and are integral with movement and postures. Lifting hands in praise both expresses an inner feeling and actually embodies and evokes that feeling. Bowing to the ground in *salat* prayer expresses an inner feeling of submission, but it also reminds the Muslim participants—arrayed side by side and physically facing Mecca—of the community to which they belong. Similarly, clasped hands and the eye-to-eye greeting "The Peace of Christ" expresses the warmth of relationship of shared Christian belonging. All the questions we asked about the material and embodied dimensions of practice are at play here. Material surroundings evoke emotion, as do touch and aroma and movement. They are all intertwined parts of lived religious practice.

Emotions are, that is, situated. Lived religious practice involves material surroundings, and those surroundings are part of what constitutes the emotional dimension of the practice. Being surrounded by a multitude of other participants intensifies the feelings. Being in a large quiet space may do the same, but with different feelings. In chapter 7, we will turn our attention to the aesthetic dimension of practice, which is closely tied to these physical and material realities, but for now, we will focus on the observation that spaces and places have a power to evoke feelings (Löw 2008). They have what some theorists call "atmospheres." The space itself participates in the experience of the emotions. Geographer Caitlin Cihak Finlayson (2012) offers an example. She was interested in how people respond to worship spaces, and she interviewed participants in two very different religious communities: Saint Paul's United Methodist Church and the Taoist Tai Chi Society, both in Tallahassee, Florida. She chose in-depth interviewing as her method so as to get at the interior emotions that are not necessarily expressed outwardly. She speaks of these emotions as highly personal, but she nevertheless found striking parallels and patterns in the feelings people described. Lived religious practice—whether American Protestant worship or tai chi movement—was characterized by emotions of serenity that were tied to the physical spaces in which the practice took place. This student of lived religious practice was able to discover and assess those patterns in the emotional dimension of practice by both her own observations of the space and the interviews she conducted.

Emotions in the Buildings

"Saint Paul's was described by one of its members as 'a classic church up on a hill.' . . . The Taoist Tai Chi Society's location, on the other hand, reflects a strong Taoist emphasis on harmony with nature" (Finlayson 2012, 1770–1771). Participants in both groups, Finlayson observed, consistently talked about feelings of calm and serenity they experienced in these very different locations. Using initials to denote her interviewees, she reports, "Participants consistently noted that they felt differently upon entering these spaces and, at the Taoist Tai Chi Society in particular, these feelings of serenity began even before walking into the physical building, as YR noted: 'Because as you enter from the street, you right away begin to see the gardens, you see the gazebo, and you see actually the gravel driveway, and already this is putting you in touch with something different from life in the city'" (1771). That wasn't just a matter of Taoist practice and space, however. Finlayson continues, "'I think I get a serenity and a peace from the space' (interview, RK, United Methodist Church). But what brought about these feelings of serenity and contentment? . . . Another member, like many others, was struck by the open and airy design of the sanctuary as a whole: 'The openness [of the sanctuary] really is, for me, it's a combination of calming [and] it's actually welcoming. And it really just, it makes me feel comfortable. It makes me feel more comfortable' (interview, NH, United Methodist Church). For another member, the simplicity of Saint Paul's cross, which is unadorned and back-lit, brought about feelings of peace: 'You can have something very simple and the austerity of it can bring forth peace' (interview, JP, United Methodist Church). Yet another

> member's emotions were shaped by the windows in the church, which are clear, leaded glass—as opposed to the stained glass found in many other houses of worship" (1772).

Emotions also, of course, take form in words and stories. We tell people how we feel (or how we think we should feel), and we recount religious experiences in full emotional detail. Emotions themselves are powerful triggers of memory and sometimes prompt participants to try to find words and stories to explain the experience. Emotional memories thrust themselves on our consciousness and seem to demand explanation (Whitehouse 2009). We may also supplement the religious words with visual images, as the Twitter users did. We use emoticons and memes in our emails and tweets, since words on the page sometimes miss what we hear when the words are spoken or read. The sheer range of those electronic images is testimony both to the range of emotions that need to be described and also to the way we often need visual cues to go along with the words.

However the emotions are communicated, religious communities bless some of those emotion words with theological importance—"awe," "repentance," "joy," "love." Religious leaders learn to say those words with special, approving fervor, just as they learn to express religious disapproval for an equally wide range of other feeling words—"rage," "lust," "jealousy," and the like. Each language and community has its own array of words, reflecting the culture's expected range of feelings and the moral and theological significance attached to them.

Religious words, that is, can also narrate what should happen, including how one should feel. Observers need to listen to the theologies, sermons, and other narrative practices of a religious group for what they say about emotions. Is God angry or loving? Are good disciples stern or comforting? How does a good religious life feel? Religious narrative practices of emotion can be observed in the literature being read and the other cultural products people consume. For example, Jason Bivens (2008) has described the pervasiveness of fear in evangelical comic books, "Hell Houses" (Halloween creations designed to depict the terrors of sin), and the famous "Left Behind" books that imagine the world at the end of time. In contrast, it is gratitude that begins the typical worship service in many African American traditions. The mood in the sanctuary shifts as the deacons move to the front of the congregation and pray, "Thank you, Lord, for waking me up this morning clothed in my right mind." Religious words express and elicit feelings. A spiritual story of inner awakening is also present for Buddhist converts, but for them, it is one structured around accounts of discovering contentment. Each community has both cosmic, official stories and everyday ones that recount the emotions of sacred experiences.

Indeed, theology itself may be deeply focused on emotions. That is exactly the argument Tanya Luhrmann (2012) makes in her study of what she calls "renewalist evangelicals," that is, those like members of the Vineyard church she studied in Chicago. They are influenced by Pentecostal practices, but the movement's shifting theological focus can be found in what is and isn't heard in members' testimonies—that is, the particular emotional depths they recall.

Transforming Emotions at The Vineyard

The Vineyard took the basic Christian narrative about the distance between a limited human and a boundless mighty God and shifted the plotline from our inadequacy to God's extraordinary capacity. Gone is the fear of snapping the connection. Gone is the torment of the abyss. The story becomes the delight in drawing closer. Its protagonists fear lifelessness—not death. In this new Christian narrative, the problem is human emotional pain, . . . and the resolution of that pain is God's infinite and personal love that can be had now, today. . . . [These feelings are embodied in practices, from] crying in the presence of God [to] practicing love, peace, and joy [to] rare, powerful instants of happy emotional collapse that demonstrate to the congregant (and to whoever was listening to the testimony) that they had personally experienced the absolute certainty of God's love. (Luhrmann 2012, 104, 126)

Not surprisingly, the kinds of churches Luhrmann studied rely heavily on music to set the emotional tone. She notes that the church where she spent two years observing and interviewing sets aside thirty minutes at the beginning of each service for what congregants call "worship"—a musical space in which individuals commune with God (Luhrmann 2012, 4). Bodies, emotions, settings, and spirituality come together in musical practice. Mark Jennings (2008) also wanted to understand the religious experiences of Pentecostals, and his description of their worship makes note of all the dimensions of the lived religious practice he observed. The role of music has been one of the most lively areas of research on lived religious practice. Recall the account of Sacred Harp singing in chapter 4. Singing together involves emotions, bodies, material settings, aesthetics, morality, spirituality, and narrative all at work together. Paying attention to the emotional dimension sharpens our understanding of all the rest.

Emotion in an Australian Pentecostal Church

> Would you believe me,
> would you listen if I told you that
> There is a love that makes a way and never holds you back
> So won't you break free
> Won't you break free
> Get up and dance in this love . . .
> (Hillsong United—Break Free)

It is Sunday morning, and I am standing in the darkened performance hall of the local high school. It is early on the classic Australian sleep-in day, but I am not alone. Standing in front of rows of hard plastic chairs, people all around me are bouncing, quivering, shouting, singing, raising their hands and swaying, most with their eyes closed and faces raised upwards. The expressions of those around me are astonishing. They display intense passion and perhaps even ecstasy, often with tears or laughter. On a pushed together block stage in front of us, a group of musicians and singers pound out a loud, heavy musical sound that builds and disperses in waves of volume and rhythm. The white screen, stark in this dim environment, displays the words of the current song, but most do not seem to need them. They sing from memory, or do not sing at all, allowing the sound to wash over them as they stand with arms outstretched to heaven. This is worship time at Breakfree Church, a Pentecostal congregation in the suburbs of Perth, Western Australia. (Jennings 2008, 161–162)

Ideas for Further Study

1. Sociologists of culture pioneered this understanding of emotion. Sara Ahmed's (2014) work in feminist theory was especially important in bringing the reality of power into how we understand the structuring of emotion.

2. "Feeling rule" is a term borrowed from Arlie Russell Hochschild (1979), whose work is discussed a little later in this chapter and is well worth exploring further. As we will see in chapter 9, her account of the Louisiana Tea Party is a powerful analysis of the way emotions structure members' view of the world (Hochschild 2016).

3. Recall Emile Durkheim's ([1912] 1964) ideas about the way ritual creates identity and solidarity. He described the heightened emotions of ritual as "collective effervescence" (250). More recently, Randall Collins (2004) has written about "entrainment"—emotionally charged mutual attention—in his work on "interaction rituals." Earlier, Rosabeth Kanter (1972) wrote about the necessity of "affective ties" for group commitment in the communes she studied. She outlined the social mechanisms they employed for achieving those ties. Each of these theories puts emotional experience at the center of their understanding of how society works.

4. Those who have studied group emotions point to the complexity and danger in how we react to outsiders. Actions by a potential rival can easily evoke anger (Mackie, Silver, and Smith 2004). Or a fear of losing something beloved can produce what Ahmed calls a "shared 'communal' visceral response of hate. Because we love, we hate, and this hate is what brings us together" (2014, 43).

5. The link between religion and violence is something we need to study carefully, without leaping to conclusions. All the world's religions have employed violence either symbolically or physically, so we should not assume that any one religion promotes violence more than another. A nuanced quantitative accounting of the recent entanglements of religion, politics, and violence can be found in research done by Jonathan Fox (2004), as well as by Monica Toft and her colleagues (Toft, Philpott, and Shah 2011). Analysis of the *practice* of violence is more clearly in view in qualitative studies closer to the ground. Here, too, there are examples from around the world. A sampling includes Ian Baird's (2009) work on Cambodia, Richard Parks's (2012) work on Jews in Tunisia, and Michael Sells's (2003) research on the violence in Bosnia-Hercegovina.

6. Anthropologists have had long experience navigating research in difficult places. Ruben Andersson's (2016) reflection is a helpful reminder of the way definitions of "the other" (including our own) intersect with fear of danger.

7. The relationship between gender and emotion is not just about women. It also plays out in how men enact their religiousness. John Bartkowski's (2000) research on the evangelical group Promise Keepers noted a move toward emotional intimacy among the men he observed in the 1990s. Others have insisted that exaggerated displays of "Christian manhood" have been encouraged across evangelicalism, especially after World War II (DuMez 2020).

8. The little boy's status on the autism spectrum added an additional element to his position as an outsider to the event's feeling rules. Hierarchies and cultural differences also affect the intersection of emotion with aesthetics, so we will look at a similar example, from Tex Sample (1996), in chapter 7.

7

Lived Religious Aesthetics

Over and over, when people are asked what they think of when they think about spirituality, they say they think about beauty. There is something in the experience of a beautiful sight or sound that seems to uplift us, take us out of mundane realities. That connection between beauty and spirituality tells us that there is probably an aesthetic component to lived religious practice that bears note. The aesthetics we are concerned with, however, are not the refined, high-art connoisseurship of the elite. Nor are we speaking of a philosophical stance that seeks to define essential qualities of art and beauty. Rather, we are looking for an everyday dimension of social practice, one that encompasses our shared attempts to arrange the material world in ways that are satisfying, pleasing, comfortable. It is a sensuous dimension of experience that is concerned with the flavors, sights, sounds, and smells of life and how we perceive them as either attractive or repulsive, beautiful or alien.

Embodiment, materiality, and emotion are dimensions of experience that lay the groundwork for an examination of aesthetics. A focus on the aesthetics of religious practice takes those dimensions and adds attention to how the sensory experience is organized to convey a sense of the sublime (as religious studies scholar Birgit Meyer [2008] puts it). Aesthetics is a way of talking about sensual contact with the world— through bodies and emotions and perception—as well as how we judge what it is we perceive.[1] It is a dimension of all social practices, so-called high culture and low, sacred and profane. Sociologist Bernice Martin argues that every religious group has an aesthetic, what she describes as "a repertoire of appearances, artefacts, representations, self-presentations and performances" (2006). We might add that every religious practice has an aesthetic, as well.

Portions of the material, sensual world are, of course, labeled as "art," a category as definitionally fraught as religion or spirituality. Still it would seem only natural for students of lived religion to examine the intersection of art and religion, since so much that we recognize as a culture's art has been produced by religious practices and institutions. Whether the art takes the form of simple carved images or elaborate icons, paintings hanging in a museum, or architecture and landscaping setting aside sacred spaces, religious communities have long produced objects that are intended to inspire and to create or facilitate connection to transcendent, divine realities. The search for moments of beauty can itself be akin to a religious ritual. A transcendent musical performance or an awe-inspiring piece of art can be the vehicle for a shared moment of touching something beyond ourselves, acting as what Peter Berger (1970) called "signals of transcendence." Religious practice and aesthetics are often intentionally intertwined.

Sometimes an artistic object or production is itself the focus of religious practice. In Eastern Orthodox traditions, gazing on an icon is an act of worship, for example. In Islam, Qur'anic calligraphy is thought to reflect the sacred character of the holy book itself. The letters act as a talisman (Nasr 1987). Music and chants may be religious practices and artistic productions at the same time. Alvin Ailey dancers perform "Revelations" at the end of each concert, and the beauty and pathos and joy of the movement is transcendently linked to the prayers voiced in the spirituals to which it is set. Similarly, an architect might say that designing a church is a spiritual exercise (Brenneman and Miller 2020), just as Johann Sebastian Bach signed his work "Soli deo gloria." And a Zen practitioner may find a well-designed garden to be a space that focuses her meditation. When artists create something they hope will be compelling, masterful, focusing and transcending the senses, they are also often creating something spiritual, often evoking a recognizably religious tradition.[2]

Religious events themselves are marked by the efforts that go into creating something that participants will experience as a feast of the senses. All over the world, religious festivals are a riot of color and sound and smells into which participants pour boundless hours and energy for the sake of what may be a momentary experience of excited engagement. Most of these festivals are a complicated mix of sacred and secular practices, but careful study can reveal just what that mix looks like and the importance of the aesthetic dimension.[3] In China, for example, the newly revived Qingming ("grave sweeping") festival takes place in early April each year. After a century in which both the Republic and the Communist regimes attempted to suppress such traditional "superstitious" rituals, there has been a slow opening in recent decades (Pang 2012). Studying the way Qingming is practiced, especially in these years of cultural transition, reveals the tentative presence of spiritual elements alongside the thriving aesthetic dimensions. It also reveals the roles of status and resources—who can afford which flowers? As in cemeteries around the world, grave decorations very much reflect both social status and local cultural tradition (Kipnis 2017).

Beautifying the Ancestors' Graves

Today, millions in China's cities journey to the graves of their ancestors (both locally and in the countryside), bringing food and flowers (Zhou 2017). They tidy the graves and often do obeisance, perhaps burning incense, paper money, or pictures of items the ancestors might like to have in their afterlife. There is the sight of kites with lanterns lighting the night sky, the pleasant smell of the incense and the less pleasant smells of burning paper money or firecrackers; but more than anything, the practice is marked by selecting flowers that are chosen for their beauty. News accounts note that flower vendors do a booming business as Qingming approaches. "The bouquets are delicate and beautiful. White roses, yellow and white chrysanthemums, and white calla lilies, together with forget-me-nots and some light-colored carnations make for a beautiful token of appreciation for those who left this world without really leaving us" (Qian 2019).

In the United States, one of the pioneering explorations of lived religion's aesthetic dimension comes from historian David Morgan's writing about "visual piety." He is interested in how images express and remind people of what they believe and the divine powers they are related to, or "the reassuring harmony of the believer's disposition toward the sacred with its visualization" (Morgan 1998, 33). His book traces such visual piety through a long history of images, but one of the most intriguing proved to be Walter Sallman's "Head of Christ." Along with a collaborative of other religious historians, Morgan explored the many facets of that image, describing it as "one of the most iconographically distinctive, and certainly the most ubiquitous, bodies of images deployed in Protestant communities (also widely used among Roman Catholics as well, though on a smaller scale)" (1996, 18). By researching the economics of the image's production and consumption, he helps us recognize the mundane practices behind the scenes, and by paying attention to an entire network of cultural practices, he shows how this aesthetic object works. In addition to combing through historical records, Morgan and his colleagues solicited letters from contemporary believers. They placed ads in seventy-three diverse religious periodicals, asking people to describe their uses of the Sallman images. The 531 responses they got allowed an even deeper understanding of how this image was used in practice.

Religious Images and the Experience of Piety

Sallman's publishers provided an image for every occasion in the daily lives of the devout: pictures by Sallman adorned bookmarks, calendars, prayer cards, tracts, Bibles, lamps, clocks, plates, buttons, stickers, and stationery. . . . [The market for the use of the images was shaped by] the practice of observing holidays and rites of passage with commemorative religious gifts. . . . Created in a studio, manufactured in a printing factory, sold in stores, installed in homes and churches, exchanged as gifts, and cherished as mementos, Sallman's mass-produced images belong to a cultural economy in which the inexpensive image is charged with crucial significance [as an object of] visual piety. (Morgan 1996, 21–22)

When a believer judges Sallman's Head of Christ "beautiful," my research suggests that the picture's beauty consists in the satisfying experience of perceiving a particular understanding of Jesus adequately visualized. The image, in other words, fits a viewer's ideal. . . . As one woman put it, "As a Christian [I think] this picture is a beautiful portrayal of Jesus. . . . The picture is full of love, compassion, empathy, peace, kindness, gentleness. And it is very welcoming!! How very lovely—And isn't that what Christianity is supposed to be all about!" (Morgan 1998, 32)

Ordinary religious practices, like all other everyday social practices, are inherently expressive of the particular way we have arranged the material and embodied world to make it pleasing. Sometimes we are aware and deliberate about those aesthetic qualities, but just as often they register without us consciously thinking about why we do or don't like something, why we are attracted or repulsed. That is, attention to aesthetic dimensions of religious practice means attention to what sociologist Omar McRoberts calls "intuitive, precognitive aspects of religion" that nevertheless have the capacity to elicit action, to draw people toward some things and away from others. Reflecting on his experience studying Black churches in Dorchester, Massachusetts, McRoberts says, "I came to understand beauty as a key part of religious experience and religious communities partly as spaces where people generate and appreciate certain kinds of beauty" (2004, 198).

This chapter explores what it means for a practice to express a group's way of presenting itself—its aesthetic style—and what the "pleasing" qualities of a practice tell us about people's place in the world. Some practices—like admiring Sallman's depiction of Jesus—put aesthetic dimensions of practice right at the fore. Other religious practices foreground other dimensions, with aesthetics only implicit. Whether aesthetics is obvious or in the background, it is nevertheless part of the experience and therefore part of what we need to be studying.

Aesthetics Is Social

Matters of aesthetic taste and style, the things that make something pleasing or compelling, are inevitably defined by the people making the judgments. Whether food preferences or attractive colors, our cultures have shaped what we find delightful or nasty. Speaking about art, social theorist John Levi Martin puts it well: "When 'we get it'—when we experience the artistic beauty of a painting, say—we focus on the 'it,' the object in question, and the beauty as a quality of this object. But, when we get the 'it,' we get the 'we' as well, in the sense of establishing a presumption of like-mindedness with those of similar taste" (2011, 203). Finding an object or a body or a place beautiful and pleasing is embedded in the intricacies of our social location, a location that includes our social class and educational positions, our religious traditions, and the larger culture of which we are a part.[4] Tastes and experiences of beauty identify us.

The very places we identify as "religious" are recognized as such by our cultural experiences of what religious space should look like. It's not a static definition but one that evolves over time as part of what actually happens in and around a place. Cultural historian Gretchen

Buggeln has written extensively about church buildings, and her recounting of a tragic fire at West Presbyterian Church in Wilmington, Delaware, can give us a vivid window on how both the church members and the community articulated ideas about beauty they had previously taken for granted. She tapped the lived experience of the congregation and community through church minutes and yearbooks, neighborhood tour guidebooks, and news reports, as well as her own interviews. She argues that church buildings, especially large and historic ones, often "invite a sense of general proprietorship from a community. They . . . work their way into the cognitive maps of those who are in and around them" (Buggeln 2001, 88). Note how her description gives attention to the aesthetic sensibilities of both congregation and community and how those changed over time.

A Beautiful Church—Then and Now

West Church's original building, dedicated in 1871, was "handsome" and Gothic in style, Buggeln writes. It "revealed the desire to create something 'substantial' with vague historical and romantic associations" (Buggeln 2001, 91). After the building burned in 1993, the struggling congregation was faced with a dilemma. Some wanted to save the historic façade as a part of the neighborhood's architectural heritage. Indeed, the city's historic preservation agency got involved in the decisions. The neighbors themselves, however, were simply invested in there being a worshiping community there, even if they never attended themselves. But they did care what it looked like. "One interviewee, who had lived in Quaker Hill for nine years and was active in its neighborhood association, asked specifically that the church be beautiful, not simply another social service center like the YMCA or the Scout buildings. She urged the congregation to 'remember that it was still a church,' the interviewer recorded, 'and should have the appearance of a church'" (95). In the final reconstruction, they managed to preserve portions of the original façade but coupled it with a smaller, more functional interior space, with lots of light, and various artistic furnishings created by well-known craftspeople. Buggeln concludes, "Although the building's exterior and most of the interior is far from awe-inspiring, the new sanctuary arguably has the same numinous quality of the plain-style, Protestant meeting houses that have charmed and even transported generations of admirers" (101).

If fire was the catalyst for reimagining the aesthetics of one religious space, the Second Vatican Council (1962–1965) was no less dramatic a catalyst for transforming hundreds of Roman Catholic churches. Before the Council, churches were often ornate and stuffed full of statuary. There were ranks of candles and a plethora of colors, textures, styles, and images adorning the space. The altar was elaborately draped, inhabited by men who were equally elaborately adorned, and separated from the congregation by a rail. After the Council, the rail came down, and in some places, so did just about everything else. New churches were encouraged to adopt a more austere style. Over time (and often after much conflict), the renovations tended to reflect the varied lives and desires of local parishes. Religious practice, theological claims, and aesthetic style came to reinforce each other (McDannell 2011). Such times and places of aesthetic transformation are potentially fertile for examination of lived religious practice by theologians and others. What insight emerges in this remaking of aesthetics and practice?

That work can build on the research of sociologists and historians who have spent time observing what happens in religious spaces. Sociologist Mary Ellen Konieczny described a neotraditional parish where she spent many months doing ethnographic field work.

> A dome decorated with 12 stained glass windows picturing the apostles rises at the intersection of the nave and transepts. Above the main altar, a half-domed ceiling mural pictures the Blessed Virgin Mary. Murals and stained-glass windows throughout depict images of saints. Behind the marble main altar, a gold baldachino, or sacred canopy, encompasses the tabernacle, and in the nave *l'art Saint-Sulpice* statues of the Blessed Mother, St. Joseph, and St. Therese of Lisieux are enshrined. A picture of Our Lady of Perpetual Help hangs near the left side altar, and a portrait of Saint Josemaria Escriva hangs in the right transept with a prie-dieu and candles below it. These accoutrements of worship create an ambiance for a particular practice of the sacred. (2009, 426)

By keeping but adapting a pre–Vatican II aesthetic, this parish's building facilitated a "neotraditional" theology and style of worship.

Historian Colleen McDannell charted the broad changes in Catholic style and practice from the 1950s to the present. She begins the story with her own First Communion in 1962 and traces the changes through the life of her mother (Margaret). Her autobiographical approach also draws on the historical and sociological and news accounts of the times, and the result is an intimate sense of the spaces and practices she describes. Again, note how she captures the aesthetic dimension of attendance at Mass and how shifting patterns of participation have existed in dialogue with the physical changes.

Sights and Sounds in a Changing Catholic Parish

Across the country, parishes have modified the Second Vatican Council's preference for noble simplicity with a post-Council fondness for traditional Catholic symbols. Now when Margaret and Ken slip into one of the back pews at Blessed Trinity for Sunday Mass, they experience a "post–Vatican II" church. A renovation in 2005 made precious space available in the sanctuary while erasing the hard edges of Vatican II modernism. The new visual centerpiece was a dramatic life-size crucifix hanging behind the altar in a blue-painted niche that is stenciled with gold relief. Columns and arches in dark wood draw attention to the white body on the cross. The Risen Christ bronze has been moved from the center and placed near a new baptistery, where running water flows from a small basin for babies into a larger one that can be entered for immersion Baptisms. On each side of the sanctuary are two ranks of pipes for the new organ and colorful statues of the Virgin Mary and St. Patrick. Along the walls of the church are the fourteen Stations of the Cross with descriptive plaques. The days of folk masses, vacant white walls, and orange carpeting are over at Blessed Trinity. (McDannell 2011, 211)

Aesthetic experience and religious experience are intertwined, and definitions of beauty interact with the theologies and religious practices of a community. Those practices and their associated aesthetic are part of what identify the group itself, which is perhaps one reason aesthetic changes can precipitate such intense internal conflict. Whenever we look at a particular aesthetic practice, we are also looking at the community in which it resonates.

Religious practices happen both inside religious communities and in the everyday world, of course, so attention to their aesthetic dimensions will allow us to more fully see how religious identities are lived beyond times of worship. Listen to Bernice Martin's description of households in Latin America: "Methodist Pentecostals whose homes we visited in Chile in 1990 were especially keen to show us their dining tables covered with white cloths and to emphasize their ability to feed their children adequately. Women who said of their homes and tiny gardens, 'It's so pretty!' were referring primarily to the cleanliness and order that had become possible, once hard-drinking, hard-spending husbands had come into the faith and embraced its disciplines" (2006, 153). Religious identity was practiced in everyday spaces that were experienced as pretty. Spreading a white tablecloth on a modest dining table is a lived religious practice whose aesthetic dimension is at its heart. Even in modest circumstances, a visual reminder of spiritual connection did its work.

Aesthetic practices, that is, embody and express identities, something that is true across cultures and eras. Anthropologist Harvey Markowitz's (2001) description of Sioux Sun Dance painting is an excellent example. He draws on early twentieth-century anthropological accounts that included interviews with elders about pre-reservation life, and he engages in his own analysis of more recent art. He traces this artistic practice from its original form within the community to its "representational" form in the work of professional artists. Markowitz's account of this evolving lived religious practice attempts to capture the full sensuous experience that is integral to it and therefore constitutes a key element in the group's identity.

Sun Dance Aesthetics

It was the chief objective of ceremonial painting to present or manifest the *wakan*. Such painting was always performed as part of the process of *yuwakan* that included sacred songs and prayers that served to activate the *tonwan* of the specified colors or designs. . . . [Through steam and sage smoke] the candidates' bodies [were transformed] into suitably pure canvasses to be painted with the sacred designs and colors required for the dance. . . .

[Later, Lakota artist Oscar Howe painted] *The Sun Dancers* . . . at the peak of his artistic powers. Its bold colors and sharp lines dramatically evoke the carnal force and spiritual ecstasy of the moment when the dancer breaks free from the ropes that have tethered him to the sacred pole. (Markowitz 2001, 166–173)

Bold colors and designs might also describe the "hijabi fashionistas" documented in cultural historian Reina Lewis's study of changing Muslim fashion in the United Kingdom. The 1990s saw both a renewed sense of religious identification for Muslims there and an Asian-inspired aesthetics in mainstream fashion. But "the advent of hijab wearing redefined the wearer as Muslim rather than Asian," she writes (Lewis 2015, 186). A change in fashion aesthetic and a change in identity went together. The fashionistas needed to replace the midriff-baring Asian sari with more modest clothing. The result was an expanded market for modest fashion, built on the earlier styles from the diaspora Asian fashion industry. Today the young cohort of hijabi fashionistas buy clothes that express their style but also identify them as Muslim. What they find beautiful and stylish has evolved in a complex mix of ethnic, religious, and economic possibilities.

To the extent that aesthetic experience is also religious, there is important work for theologians to do. Far from the fashionable streets of England, Rebecca Spurrier has undertaken a remarkable theological ethnography of a Christian community in Atlanta. The congregation she calls Sacred Family has a membership that is largely made up of people with various forms of disability, primarily psychiatric challenges. Spending three years worshiping and playing and talking and creating with them, she describes their community life as sometimes (seemingly) chaotic but joyful. Their worship involves "a performance art" of creativity in how differences in perception and ability form a "liturgical choreography" (Spurrier 2020, 22). Using the theological concept of liturgy as communal work of and for the people of God, she looks for all the ways that aesthetic work is done around the edges and across the week. She learns to see the pleasures they create together, including the art they make and use. She learns to see and name beauty as it shapes the life of this community, even as the challenges remain. The complex aesthetic of this church expresses the complex world they inhabit.

Creating Pleasure in an Atlanta "Disabled Church"

A short time into my ethnographic research, I become aware of my own embodiment as a source of interest for the people I worship with and the pleasure of shared embodiment as a way to pass time. In a pew a woman praises the colors of my manicure and invites me to admire her own. Another comments on the color of a dress I am wearing, stroking it, and expresses curiosity over my choice of shoes. When I discuss haircuts with another gentleman, he examines my hair. . . . I find that congregants rarely desire to go in depth about their day or week; instead, we admire together new items from the clothes closet, or sniff the bottle of lotion won at bingo. . . . We discuss the color of the sky, the cold air, or the plants in the church garden. . . . Sensory pleasures, such as the ones I experience [there], occur around the peripheries of the sanctuary, accumulating as we pass time, waiting for events to begin or end. They occur inside the sanctuary, during the time of a service, along the peripheries of the official liturgy. . . . Such textures often distract from the centers of instruction or proclamation. They also appear inconsequential in light of the suffering some congregants bear. What difference can any textures of pleasure make when those who gather have been asked to carry so much? . . . [Sacred Family] is a place where some take a break from the daily routines of personal care homes and rest for a time. (Spurrier 2020, 109–111)

Aesthetic Practices of Difference

If an aesthetic expresses identity, it will also express difference.[5] Bernice Martin's extensive experience in Latin American Pentecostal communities introduced her not only to styles of household decor but especially to the music of Pentecostal worship. By listening to the instruments used and the degree of pop influence, she could hear how musical styles served as "markers of identity indicating the boundary between the group and 'the world' and/or the lines of demarcation and distinction within the movement" (2006, 145). Similarly, reflecting on the Black churches in Dorchester, Massachusetts, McRoberts (2004) noted that even when they shared similar doctrinal positions, they might have very different aesthetic styles in decor and music. Creating identity often involves seemingly small distinctions that nevertheless loom large within a community.

Other distinctions cross boundaries of community and permeate social institutions of all kinds. Wherever people are, they reflect the differences that a society has created around race, class, education, and gender. Resources make it more and less possible for people to have access to things they desire to produce beauty and pleasure (Swidler

2010a), even as they improvise with what they have. More basically, it is important to ask who has the ability to create "art," to define it as such, and to get it to the people who will appreciate it. As Colleen McDannell (1995) so provocatively asks, exactly what separates "kitsch" from art if not the gender and social position of the consumer? Kitsch is not just different from high art but something to be looked down on and avoided. Michèle Lamont's research has also been useful in showing how a sense of style is linked to moral boundaries (Lamont and Fournier 1992). A sense of style is likely to provoke judgment about the value of both the art in question and the people who like it. Societies declare some cultural productions to be worthwhile and others to be trash and declare some people to be the valued experts who can educate the rest of us. At the same time, those whose art is being devalued may establish their own discourse about "elite" art, describing it as worthless splashes of paint that any child could do.[6]

Social divisions of style and taste can be seen in all the religious things people construct and surround themselves with, even the intangible ones. For example, the intersection of religious practice and aesthetics can be seen in Black Gospel music as it defines and expresses the experience of race in the United States. Music historian and performer Pearl Williams-Jones opened her influential article about Black Gospel by saying, "If a basic theoretical concept of a black aesthetic can be drawn from the history of the black experience in America, the crystallization of this concept is embodied in Afro-American gospel music" (1975, 373). The experience of living and worshiping in a segregated society meant that there was cultural space for the development of a distinctive style, a style that expressed the deep pain of living with oppression, as well as joy in visions of liberation.[7]

As we saw in chapter 4, musical style proves central in the efforts of some churches to "cross the racial divide." Gerardo Marti (2012) found that a favorite strategy of such churches is to feature a gospel choir and to expect Black singers to model "true worship" by performing an expressive, embodied style of praying and singing. While the church's professed ideal might have been a universal experience of worship that could transcend race, the reality was that race was being essentialized. Sociologist Korie Edwards's (2008) detailed ethnographic study of an interracial church in the Midwest was even more explicit about the way a white aesthetic defined the culture, even if there were Black people present. She was there for worship and committee meetings and conversations in the halls, so she could observe how people interacted. She also did formal interviews and found that while Black and white members were participating in the same events, they brought different aesthetic sensibilities with them. Whites were far more likely to express satisfaction with the church's mixing of traditional hymns and praise songs, for example, since it was consistent with what they knew. "For whites, worship at Crosstown was upbeat, but for African Americans, that was far from true" (Edwards 2008, 27). Differences in cultural style were apparent throughout the church, and those differences marked who had power and who didn't.

Cultural differences in style were also apparent in the mosque that John O'Brien (2017) studied. He spent three and a half years interacting with a group of immigrant Muslim teenage boys at a mosque in a West Coast city in the United States. He was a bit older and not an immigrant, but he shared their religious identity and practice, which eased his entry into the community. He saw how they experienced the cultural expectations that came from urban American teenage life, as well as the expectations that came from their tight-knit religious community. It was important for them to be religious but not too religious, to be cool but not too cool. They dealt with those tensions in a variety of ways, not least through their use of hip hop performance. They would poke fun at performers who created strictly Islamic lyrics that seemed "cheesy," but they would also go to elaborate lengths to avoid or alter the obscene lyrics of the mainstream hip hop they heard. This aesthetic tug-of-war expressed their recognition of the cultural boundaries they were attempting to navigate.

Clashes of taste and style are nowhere more apparent than in differences based on social class. Many people have written about this but perhaps none so vividly as theologian Tex Sample. He wants people to see how everyday experiences of social-class positioning often alienate working-class people from church life. With a deep dive into country music ("white soul," in his words), he highlights its critique of the church's failures, the tendency of church people to "close off people who need it, to serve the rich and neglect the poor and needy, and to be highhanded and hypocritical" (Sample 1996, 150). But to get to that theological point, he needed to illustrate the divide he is decrying, so his opening example was designed to get the reader's attention. Here he is describing his own working-class response to something usually thought of as an elite pastime, namely, opera. In this story, the opera was *La bohème*, and he was attending with his wife and a couple he describes as having come from wealthy families. This is very much a first-person account, told with a preacher's flair, with the intent of teaching church people something about how differences in taste and expression divide people.

Working-Class Style at the Opera

In the opera, a duet is sung by Mimi and Rodolfo . . . [that] I believe to be one of the most rapturous moments in the history of Western music. . . . When it comes to opera and symphonies, I am a classical music Pentecostal. I could not sit still. . . . I was twitching and jerking, holding my breath one moment and bursting out with sighs and glossolalia-like expressions the next. . . . I was having an aesthetic conniption, a "hyperventilated" ecstatic orgasm, a mystical, spiritual apprehension of "the eternal." Had I put it in a country music idiom, I might have said that I was so carried away that "my eyes were all bugged out like a stomped on toad frog." . . . By the time they came to the final "Ah!" I was emotionally a line of wrung-out washed clothes hanging in a windstorm of musical power. As the audience came to its feet, I was shouting, whistling, and clapping as loudly and as vigorously as I could. I looked over at Joe. His face was a picture of emotionless calm. . . . "Joe, didn't you like it?" I asked, stunned by his absence of cathectic involvement. "I thought it was extremely well done," he answered. . . . "Did you really like it?" I asked, trying again, because his affect had all the repose of death. "Oh, I thought the voice control and the blend of the soprano and the tenor were exquisitely done. The last progressions were especially effective. It was a superlative performance." All these things he said without overt feeling, the way someone might read a phone book. (Sample 1996, 27–28)

Social-class markers are carried in every aspect of life, especially in how we dress, and even that is a site where religious practice and practices of aesthetic distinction come together, as Lewis's hijabi fashionistas showed us. In the pages of high-fashion magazines, readers can be instructed not only how to dress but also how to be "fashionably" religious. Lynn Neal (2019) analyzed seventy years of *Vogue* magazine

(1944–2014), plus selected issues of *Harper's Bazaar* and *W*, analyzing articles, ads, accessories, and apparel. She describes a "haute couture" vision of US Christianity, one that was increasingly focused on cultivating individual experiences of transcendence. The religious elites who wrote articles were liberal and sophisticated, like the assumed audience. They pictured a religion that was to be personally experienced, with bits and pieces to be appropriated like accessories—a stylized angel here, an ornate cross there. Both fashion and religion were something to be consumed by those who could afford it. Think about how that stands in contrast to the "Sunday Best" practices in a Black church, where dressing up for church blurs the class distinctions among the members and also enacts a visible resistance to the everyday world of uniforms and work clothes where such sartorial pleasure might be impossible (O'Neal 1999).

Whether it is clothing or food, architecture or music, styles organize our experiences, including religious ones, and they are likely to identify religiously inflected cultural boundaries. Throughout the religious landscape, the kinds of literature consumed and the kinds of visual art found to be moving and evocative reflect social and cultural class positions. That is, religious practice, status position, and aesthetic style are likely to coincide. Whether one is drawn to the polished choral music and visual pomp of an Episcopal cathedral or the simple country style of a piano and guitar leading congregational harmony, class-based aesthetic style is a part of the lived religious experience.

Aesthetics as Part of the Whole

To bring all of this together, we can turn to historian Robert Orsi's (1985) classic description of the festa of Our Lady of Mt. Carmel in Italian Harlem. He wanted to capture the lives and the "theology of the streets" in that lively neighborhood, so he drew on parish records and contemporaneous histories of the neighborhood, as well as his own interviews with those who still remembered what it was like there before World War II. The result is a book full of insight about religious and family life that begins with a description of the day of the festa, July 16 each year. His observations include attention to the sensuous delights (and pains) of the day. He notes the sonorous ringing of the church bell just after midnight that signaled the beginning of the celebration and the lights and decorations that adorned the route of the procession. He speaks of the new outfits purchased so that "the family should make *bella figura* in the community and show proper *rispetto* of the Virgin on her feast day" (Orsi 1985, 2). The shape of that respect and the promises made to the Virgin reflect the *moral* dimensions of this festive practice. Its *embodied* reality is full of the pain and hope of families making a way for themselves, and the *material* world of the streets and the church is the canvas on which the feast's drama is sketched. Orsi vividly draws the reader's attention to the *emotions* of the day, as well, as worldly burdens are brought to the Virgin, with whom they feel a *spiritual* connection. And as Orsi also tells us, this celebration that brings the Madonna through the streets to her honored place in the church also *narrates* the story of the immigrant community itself.

Orsi ends the description with the figure of the Madonna. Note his attention to decoration, clothing, hair, and embodiment and how they reflected the lives and aspirations of the parishioners. His goal is not to say whether these things are *really* beautiful or to analyze their artistic worth. Rather, his goal is to describe the religious practices within which these scenes were experienced and to attend to the importance of the *aesthetic* dimension of the practice for those who were there.

The Beautiful Madonna del Carmine

The statue that still stands high above the main altar is a lifelike representation of a young Mediterranean woman holding a small child. The Madonna's first gown, which she wore until her coronation in 1904, was decorated with rings, watches, earrings, and chains, all given to her by men and women who believed she had helped them in a moment of terrible difficulty or pain. . . . Both mother and child have real hair, long, thick, and very beautiful; la Madonna's hair flows down over her shoulders. The woman's figure is full. She has broad hips and an ample bosom. Her face is round, though not heavy, and her neck is delicate. She wears pendant earrings. The child she holds is the Infant Jesus. His hair resembles his mother's, thick and very long, as Italian women would often keep their sons' hair until they were four or five years old. (Orsi 1985, 12)

Ideas for Further Study

1. If you would like to learn more about the various scholarly traditions in the study of aesthetics, you might start with Ben Highmore's (2010) brief article on "social aesthetics."

2. S. Brent Plate (2002) has assembled a thick collection of writings about religion and visual culture from around the world. This is an excellent place to start if you are interested in how art figures in the practices of different religious traditions. The connection between spirituality and the creativity of artists is also documented by Robert Wuthnow (2001).

3. There are dozens of studies of such festivals, usually treated as "folk" or "popular" religion. Hispanic studies scholar Frank Graziano (2007), for example studied practices across Latin America. Jennifer Hughes (2010) focused her study on the practices surrounding a particular three-foot-tall Mexican crucifix (*Cristo Aparecido*). The festival celebrations around Día de los Muertos are no less aesthetically interesting and are ripe for attention from students of lived religious practice. If you are particularly interested in the tug-of-war between religious and secular interpretations, recall Genevieve Zubrzycki's (2016) study of Quebec's St. John's Day festival. Having been in Porto, Portugal, on St. John's Day, I can report that the stunning launch of hundreds of lanterns into the night sky capped a day filled with the pervasive smell of grilled sardines, colorful plastic banners, toy hammers for bonking passersby, and raucous crowds into the night. I found it only partially "sublime."

4. Cultural sociology has given ample attention to the way our aesthetic sensibilities are shaped and organized by cultural, political, and economic forces. Janet Wolff summarized the sociological argument this way: "The very products which aesthetics and art history posit as 'works of art' cannot be uncritically taken as somehow distinguished by certain intrinsic features, but must be seen as produced in that history by specific practices in given conditions. The evaluations of works which form the artistic tradition are performed by people who are themselves institutionally and structurally located" (1983, 105). A foundational article in this line of work is Paul DiMaggio and John Mohr's (1985) study of "cultural capital."

5. Theoretical discussions of how art embodies difference usually begin with Pierre Bourdieu (1993) and his notion of distinction in the art world. He argues that a field of cultural production—say "Gothic architecture"—can control and differently value the styles and manner that will be recognized within that field. An appreciative critique of Bourdieu's thinking about aesthetics can be found in the work of Richard Shusterman (2000), who takes up a pragmatist's assessment of how to think about a philosophy of aesthetics. What Bourdieu's insights miss, however, is the depth of emotion and spiritual connection present in aesthetic religious practices. These theoretical debates are not the subject of our work here, but some students of lived religion may be interested in digging deeper.

6. This low opinion of modern art—that any child could do it—is expressed by roughly one-third of Americans when asked by the General Social Survey (https://gssdataexplorer.norc.org). It is often useful to check general polls and surveys to put what we see in a larger cultural context.

7. If you are interested in knowing more about the African American gospel music tradition, James Abbington (2001) and Glenn Hinson (2000) have each written appreciative accounts. Melva Costen (1999) is a leading liturgical scholar, and Carolynne Brown's (2009) dissertation provides a fascinating history. The intersection of Black Gospel with "Southern Gospel" is detailed in Douglas Harrison's (2012) history, along with the way sexuality has played its own role. There has always been cultural borrowing, as well as distinction.

8

Morality in Religious Practice

The assessments we make about style and beauty are not the only ways in which social practice involves acts of judging. Even when we are not consciously aware of it, we make moral judgments, as well. The way we perceive and react to the everyday world around us is shaped by our deeply held intuitions about what is right and wrong, good and evil. This is more than just "following norms" and doing what people expect us to do. Those are moral practices, too, but some cultural expectations for behavior carry even more weight because they are situated in emotionally laden stories and practices marking them as good. As sociologist Christian Smith (2003a) argues, we are "moral, believing animals." Even when we aren't consciously thinking about rules, our behavior is guided by what we have learned to expect of ourselves and others.

Sociologists Steven Hitlin and Stephen Vaisey have helped to bring the study of morality back into focus in the social sciences, arguing that morality "encompasses any way that individuals or social groups understand which behaviors are better than others, which goals are the most worthy, and what people should believe, feel, and do. . . . [Moral assessments are] thick understandings about what kind of person (or society) it is good to be" (2013, 55). They go on to say, "Morality is not just about personal beliefs or intuitions but also involves a combination of psychological processes, social identities, and institutionalized meanings and practices" (60). That is, we bring our own ingrained moral sense with us, but there are also moral meanings embedded in the setting. Both can be at work shaping our behavior, even if we have difficulty explaining what those meanings are or why we are doing what we are doing. These and other writers in the social sciences are increasingly looking at how our minds, our bodies, our emotions, and our cultures come together to produce the moral frameworks that guide our action. As we make moral judgments and evaluations, we are not necessarily engaging in reasoned deliberation. Rather, we are acting based in the informal theories we have in our minds (and hearts) about what is to be desired. Every social practice, that is, includes a moral dimension in its assessment of the situation as well as in its pattern of expected behaviors.

The same is true for lived religious practices. When people pray, for example, they presume a moral judgment that endorses some desired futures and not others, that lauds some actions and asks forgiveness for others. Prayers may call down divine wrath on evildoers or express gratitude for blessings. Their very form may enact compassion and solidarity through joined hands for the "Our Father" or the shoulder-to-shoulder touch of Muslim Ju'mah prayer. Not all moral practices are religious, but religious practice, like all human action, has moral dimensions.

Moral judgment combines with the emotional and aesthetic dimensions of religious practice to stir people toward action. Practices are not just rote, habitual behaviors but "projects" that contain within them movement toward beauty, virtue, happiness, and other states we have learned to value. Our interactions are animated by a sense of "what is good to strive for" (J. Martin 2003, 37). This is not to posit that there are a priori values that consciously and directly lead to actions but that practices contain values within them. Those same judgments may also lead us to avoid immoral things by triggering emotions of shame or disgust. That is, attention to emotional, moral, and aesthetic qualities of religious practice can provide a window on both the patterned, taken-for-granted reactions and the emergent energies that motivate action—both the established structure of the situation and the struggles of the actors. The emotional, aesthetic, and moral qualities we have packaged into our cognitive interpretations of the world pull us toward some practices and away from others.

Sometimes they pull us away out of fear of contamination, of being soiled or profaned. It is not just that "cleanliness is next to godliness." The very notion of contamination has moral implications. As much as we may think we are avoiding dirt or germs out of purely scientific and medical necessity, our judgments about where the danger lies are always tinged with our assessments of the moral character of the people and places we shun.[1] As anthropologist Mary Douglas put it, "certain moral values are upheld and certain social rules defined by beliefs in dangerous contagion" (1966, 3). In response, religious rituals of all sorts symbolically use water to wash away the contamination of sin. Christian baptism, immersion in the Jewish *mikveh* or in the river Ganges, the

Muslim practice of Wudū—all require a bodily enactment of cleansing that inevitably also reminds the participants of the moral contamination being washed away. In countless ways, religious practices remind us of the ways we are supposed to live and the moral communities to which we do and do not belong. Turning attention to this moral dimension of lived religion is the task of this chapter.

But first, because understanding morality is something many disciplines have tackled, we should be clear about what this particular exploration will set to the side for others to study. Studying religious practice is not an exercise in moral philosophy, for example. We are not seeking a reasoned argument for what is right and wrong and why. It is also not an exposition of how any particular moral virtue—altruism, for example—is cultivated or set in motion (as a cognitive psychologist might wish to explore) or how moral virtues evolved in human beings (as evolutionary biologists would do). Similarly, we will leave aside any attempt to identify a set of universal human moral emotions (disgust, desire, and the like), even as we pay attention to how emotion works alongside moral judgment. We will also not assume a predetermined set of moral virtues and vices to be studied or a single continuum of more and less moral behavior (as moral psychologists might do).

The moral dimension of lived religious practice is also not (just) about the moral precepts taught by religious groups. We are interested in understanding how the people we are observing employ moral categories, how morality is lived. So we will not declare in advance which moral virtues should be studied or which ones are best. While we will pay attention to the larger cultural patterns that are at play, this is also not an attempt to identify a definitive set of "moral schemas" that are used by any cultural group to make their judgments. Any of those enterprises may be worth pursuing, and there are ample resources for doing so.[2]

The task for students of lived religion, however, is to see the moral dimensions of religious practice in action, and that requires attention to the full range of enacted moral practices and the social settings through which practices take shape. In the end, those observations may very well lead the student of lived religion to engage in their own moral reflection. What do these practices suggest about how human life might better be served? There is good reason to develop recommendations for change, but that is not where we will start.

The Social in Religious Moral Practice

As we have noted throughout this book, socially recognized patterns of activity are most often habitual and do not require participants to stop and make an explicit explanation. People who share a common culture can, without a lot of conscious thought, recognize and participate in the routine practices of their everyday lives; and that is no less true when we turn our focus to the moral dimension of those practices. The moral implications are carried in the assumptions and expectations of everyday practices, whether or not the practice itself is aimed at an explicitly moral goal. To draw attention to the moral aspects of religious practice is not, then, about discovering a coherent moral system that provides a logical justification, but it is about recognizing the social dynamics that make underlying moral assumptions seem sensible to the participants.

Sometimes we can see the underlying moral assumptions best in times and places of flux. Contemporary China, for example, offers a dramatic mix of moral and religious traditions (Yang 2012), so youths growing up there draw on a wide array of religious and nonreligious possibilities. They can find, among other things, revivals of ancient traditions that are embodying and teaching virtues in new ways. Sociologist Anna Sun (2013) has been observing the evolving Chinese religious scene for over ten years. She observed and did interviews at a dozen temples on the mainland and in Taiwan, supplementing that with additional fieldwork at three temples in Taiwan and four in Japan, where she also collected material objects such as prayer cards—all this aimed at understanding religious practices as they are being adapted to current realities. She found not only a proliferation of new rituals but also explicit teaching of virtues, done in an institutional context where those virtues are also modeled in practice. No longer built in as an assumed way of living, rules have to be taught, but the way they are taught carries the moral lessons, as well.

Teaching Confucian Ways

[Temple prayers to Confucius are part of] the thousand-year-old legacy of the civil examination system in imperial China, which consisted of a particular institutional and cultural structure in which ascendant social mobility was gained through Confucian learning and rigorous examination. . . .

> [Today, there are new after-school courses—Confucian academies—where] there are specific social rituals related to Confucian teacher-student relations, which emphasize the utmost respect for the teacher through manners and speech, as well as the veneration of Confucius. The classical text Rules for Students and Children (*dizi gui*), written by a seventeenth-century scholar as a simple manual for cultivating Confucian virtues such as filial piety, moderation, and benevolence in children, has been gaining a startling amount of popularity in China today. (Sun 2013, 167–170)

There are indeed moral systems that are bigger than any one situation or any one person, like the elements of Confucian teaching that linger in the culture. But the link between stated logic and individual action is not always as straightforward as learning the precepts. Religious communities and traditions have explicit moral rules, and they do attempt to pass those principles along to their followers. Studying the moral dimension of lived religious practice means paying attention to those explicit morally focused religious practices. But it also requires the hard work of paying attention to the less explicit everyday routines that carry moral logics, as well.

The implicit moral logic of everyday routines can sometimes be illuminated by attention to the larger moral narratives—both the institutional ideals and the larger cultural goals—but generalizations can be tricky. It is probably a mistake to imagine that any society can be characterized by one or even just a few ways of thinking about morality. Nevertheless, explorations such as those of Robert Bellah and his associates in *Habits of the Heart* (1985) often suggest moral questions to ask as we observe. The authors listened to a broad sample of Americans, seeking evidence of the moral projects guiding the culture. They were able to identify "utilitarian individualism" and "expressive individualism" as the dominant ways people justify their actions. Their historical and philosophical reading then led them to contrast these moral projects with the United States' earlier "biblical republicanism." But that long view sometimes missed important realities on the ground. The young nurse they call Sheila Larson, for example, was their epitome of expressive individualism, but as Meredith McGuire points out, their preoccupation with the larger cultural narratives led them to pay little attention to any spiritual depth or collective significance in Larson's everyday practices of care (2008, 151–152).

While the larger cultural narratives may give us clues about the moral dimensions of everyday practice, they may also lead us astray. This is especially apparent in efforts like the "World Values Survey." Aimed at broad cultural characterizations, this multinational survey lacks any base in local conversations. Its generalizations presume a universalizable list of beliefs and values that can be compared across countries, and researchers use it then to divide up the world into moral categories (e.g., Norris and Inglehart 2004). Despite its "world values" claim, there is little for a student of lived religious practice to glean from the results. A more solidly grounded study, by the sociologists Michèle Lamont and Laurent Thévenot (2000), used in-depth interviews to compare the "repertoires of evaluation" found in France and the United States. They suggest that each society provides its members with a variety of ways of thinking about what matters and what is of value. Those repertoires are by no means uniform across the society, but they are recognizably different from one country to the next.[3] Just as a given religious tradition provides distinct moral repertoires, so does the larger culture in which it is located. Both will help to set the terms for how a religious social practice is enacted.

Thus, the moral dimensions of any practice are enmeshed in how people think about what it means to be a member of a group. Certain actions and attitudes are simply part of what it means to belong. In different religious traditions and different practices, the moral dimension may come more and less to the fore, but each will incorporate moral virtues and taboos that become part of a religious identity. In studying Christians across a variety of denominations in the 1990s, I was surprised how many answered, "Do unto others as you would have them do unto you," when we asked what it means to be a Christian. I dubbed these people "Golden Rule Christians" because their everyday ethics seemed to be more definitive of their religious identity than doctrine or religious observance (Ammerman 1997b). More recently, the Jewish historian and theologian Jack Wertheimer has argued that "Golden Rule Judaism" has become similarly prevalent. Jews who are otherwise not very observant say that "being a good person is the essence of being a good Jew" (Wertheimer 2018, 64).

Wertheimer's argument would seem to be borne out in sociologist Philip Schwadel's (2006) analysis of the data on Jewish teens from the

National Study of Youth and Religion (NYSR). Schwadel drew on the study's nationally representative telephone survey, along with what was learned from in-depth face-to-face interviews. Indeed, all of the reports from the NYSR are excellent evidence for the utility of combining survey and interview methods.[4] Because the survey team asked a wide range of excellent questions about religious practices, the results provided a representative baseline. Because they oversampled smaller religious groups like Jews, they were also able to make interesting comparisons. Following the survey with interviews then allowed them to capture a great deal about lived religious practice and how it is infused with moral expectation.

Golden Rule Judaism among Teens

One Jewish girl explained that she volunteers because she is "a lot more fortunate . . . than like the lower class." She clarified that she does not volunteer out of a sense of religious obligation. Nevertheless, her primary form of community service is to volunteer in her synagogue's gift shop. . . . Other Jewish teens were more direct about the connection between volunteerism and their Jewish identities. For some, helping others clearly takes on religious significance. Rather than praying or attending synagogue, they focus on performing *mitzvot* (acts of loving-kindness) and *tikkun olam* (repair of the world) as an outlet for their religious beliefs and values. One girl asserted that people have an obligation to volunteer. "I guess it's what I've been taught. . . . Volunteering and helping people," she explained, is "one of the main aspects" of Judaism. She spoke about "acts of loving-kindness" and described helping others as "one of the pillars" of Judaism. (Schwadel 2006, 142–143)

Religious moral practice can also take the form of explicit ethical reflection, especially in times of crisis. Anthropologist Jarrett Zigon (2010) describes what he calls "moral assemblages," arguing (not unlike Swidler [1986]) that it is useful to think about "ethical moments" as times when there is a moral breakdown (an "unsettled time") and a person or community is forced to work on what sort of life they should lead. Whether it is a community forum in the church fellowship hall or a book discussion group at temple or a Confucian after-school program or an academic treatise on ethics, there are religiously based practices designed to do moral work when the situation calls for it.

The practices of collective moral learning and teaching are one way religious practitioners acquire practical knowledge about moral expectations and adopt a religious identity. Children and newcomers learn that to be a member, there are moral rules to follow. People facing an ethical challenge work out new ways of acting. But, expectations about a good life are conveyed more implicitly in other religious practices, as well. From scriptural injunctions to heroic stories to *mitzvah* challenges and volunteer service, communal religious life often embodies moral lessons (Lichterman 2005; Allahyari 2001). People learn their community's "golden rules" by observing and doing.

Students of lived religion can also learn which moral practices are most central to the community's identity by looking for boundary work. That was what sociologist Jeffrey Guhin learned in his ethnographic study of four high schools—two conservative Christian and two Muslim. In spite of what seemed like similar beliefs about the importance of scripture and of conservative gender norms, gender was a key moral practice for the Muslim schools, while opposition to evolution was the key defining practice for the conservative Protestants. Guhin heard much more about evolution at the Christian schools, "because evolution was dissonant with Christian key practices (reading the Bible literally) and boundaries (also reading the Bible literally)" (2016, 152). He continues, "The problem is not only that evolution goes against the Bible but that if it is true, evolution would render the way Conservative Protestants understand the Bible ridiculous. For an intellectual community that prides itself on the plain truth of the Bible and the priesthood of all believers, this threat is particularly grave" (163). His careful listening to classroom and hallway discussions, along with his interviews, revealed that Muslim key practices (prayer) and boundaries (gender performance) were not challenged by evolution. "Whereas Muslims worried about being called sexist and violent, Christians feared being deemed ignorant and intolerant" (167). A community's moral center is often revealed by the practices that maintain the boundaries.

As Guhin shows us, moral practice can be discerned in ways of talking, but the moral dimension of practice is also found in embodied religious disciplines. Saba Mahmood's study of Egyptian Muslim women has drawn attention to the way religious practice itself embodies understandings of morality. Morality as "habitus," she says, is a product "of human endeavor, rather than revelatory experience or natural temperament [and is] acquired through the repeated performance of actions that entail a particular virtue or vice" (Mahmood 2005, 137). Religious practice is often aimed at forming persons who will then embody and exemplify the virtues of the community.

Daniel Winchester's research has already provided us with rich examples of the dimensions of lived religious practice. Here, too, he can show us what we can learn through careful observation. He has written about how converts to Islam, in Missouri, "created new moral selves through the regular utilization of embodied religious practices" (Winchester 2008, 1754). He observed their community for seventeen months and did eleven in-depth interviews with converts, but he also participated along with them, even though he is not himself a Muslim. He engaged in fasting during Ramadan and occasionally did Qur'anic recitation and ritual prayer. He says, "These participatory methods were extremely beneficial as they allowed me to be more reflexive in my research, pushing me to compare my normal experience of research and everyday life to the shifts in subjectivity experienced when engaging in particular religious practices" (1760). Learning the moral habits of a new community is an embodied experience, and seeing the patterns is aided by this sort of involved observation.

Converts Embodying Islam in Missouri

Embodied religious practices such as ritual prayer (*salat*), fasting (*sawm*), and covering (*hijab*) effectively produced within converts the moral dispositions associated with becoming a "good Muslim"— dispositions such as mindfulness, humility, discernment, moderation and modesty.... For these converts, coming to Islam was largely about the development of a new type of moral subjectivity—a new set of dispositions (e.g., thoughts, feelings, desires, sentiments and sensibilities) about what is good and bad, right and wrong, permissible and taboo, sacred and profane, beautiful and unsightly in both one's self and the larger world. As a convert named Robert aptly put this change, "Converting really affected a lot of things for me. As far as my behavior goes, the way I feel and act, it was like developing a new moral compass" ... [The] practical reorganization of bodily memory is also interrelated with cultural schemes of authority. The sense of mindfulness affected in *salat* is also related to a sense of humility, an embodied disposition toward respecting and responding to God's time on a regular basis. To be mindful of daily prayers is to necessarily practice some form of humility. It is to let a higher authority take precedence in one's daily life, to temporarily suspend all other activities for the expressed purpose of worshipping Allah. ... [The discipline of fasting] was thought indispensable for developing the spiritual strength and moral discipline necessary for resisting that which is sinful or forbidden (*haram*) in daily life. (Winchester 2008, 1755, 1761–1769)

What the Moral Dimension of Practice Does

There are, then, specific moral practices that can come to identify a person as part of a community. Whether Jewish teens volunteering or adult Muslim converts fasting, identity and morality are intertwined. But the moral dimension of everyday practice goes even deeper than that. One of the insights of sociologists, as far back as Emile Durkheim ([1898] 1975), has been that maintaining the social order is itself a moral imperative. Disrupting everyday expectations and acting "out of place" or being "disruptive" can be seen as an immoral act. Ethnomethodologists like Harold Garfinkel (1967) and Erving Goffman (1967) have demonstrated that keeping things on something of an even keel can be a "sacred" project that everyone works hard to maintain. If these theorists are right in linking a stable moral order with everyday ritualized forms of interaction, then one place to look for the moral dimension of religious practice is in practices that reinforce the status quo and punish disruption. We should ask how any given religious practice articulates, embodies, and exemplifies the moral good of maintaining an existing social order. Studying religious practice means paying attention to the way connections to sacred power and authority may amplify the constraining power of social roles and rules. When people are warned that their god might get angry, whose interests will be protected by heeding the warning?

Not all religious practice reinforces the status quo, however. Sometimes the moral imperative being enacted is just the opposite of compliant. Religious practices are often aimed at inciting and supporting *resistance* to the status quo. Such practices build on a sense of a higher set of obligations that demand moral action. This can be seen when the fervor of a political rally is intermingled with the enthusiasm of a religious revival, calling for disruptive action in pursuit of moral goals. From abolition of slavery to civil rights to antipoverty crusades, social movements in the United States have harnessed religious practices for disruptive moral ends.[5] Observers have pointed to the use of prayer and song and testimony as practices that can have simultaneous political and religious import. As sociologist Ziad Munson (2007) writes, a funeral for a fetus is both a religious ritual and a political rallying cry for those who oppose abortion. Similarly, lifting voices in "Guide My Feet" or "This Little Light of Mine," other groups pursue economic and racial justice, simultaneously engaging in a religious practice with a moral imperative.

Calls to activism often articulate clear ideologies of religious and moral values; taking political action means learning new practices that may follow from or require new explanations. But Munson (2008) discovered that belief was more likely to follow belonging than the other way around. That is, people were invited to participate in a pro-life event, went with people they knew, and only gradually came to accept a pro-life ideology. Even when there is a clear moral narrative present in a collective practice, the links between belief and action can be indirect. What we observe is the starting point, but it will always be important to include interviews with participants to hear their own stories about what it means to be a good person. Whether resisting the status quo or supporting it, religious moral practices have both embodied and narrative dimensions.

All these ambiguities are even more at play when the social situation itself is undergoing change and the moral rules are being renegotiated. As we saw with the Chinese Confucian students, there are times when explicit moral work and collective moral action are in play. Such was the situation studied by medical sociologist Tola Olu Pearce in Ibadan and Lagos, Nigeria. She observed newly formed Charismatic groups that embrace the spiritual gifts of classical Pentecostalism but are actively adapting to the modern demands of contemporary urban life. She spent a ten-month period, along with two female research assistants, and drew on taped sermons, seminars, and fellowship meetings from four churches, as well as semistructured interviews and conversations with leaders and members of the congregations in two churches, one in Ibadan and the other in Lagos. What she observed was real-time deliberation about "which aspects of the culture need to be dropped, which reinterpreted, and which accepted in light of Christianity and increasing technical/secular knowledge" (T. Pearce 2002, 35). Note the many ways these congregations create social spaces for this active moral work around sexuality and reproduction, where questions of how to live are central to creating a new social order.

Sexuality and Reproduction in Nigerian Cities

Church members receive constant advice from counselors at prayer meetings and at fellowships geared to specific segments of the congregation. For instance, there are weekly married women's fellowships, seminars for those engaged to be married, annual revivals, camp meetings, and so forth. In addition, congregations invite guest speakers to speak (and pray) on important topics—infertility, raising Christian children, being a Christian wife, good health, etc. The individual is immersed in a supportive group. . . . A pastor speaking to a women's fellowship group: . . . "We [parents/adults, etc.] have cut ourselves from knowledge. We don't give our children sex education and we ourselves are ignorant of many things, so we don't teach our children. See I Timothy, chapter 4, verses 6 and 1: 'but refuse profane and old wives' fables' . . . Usually when a young lady is about to get married, members of the family say she should go and see an old woman somewhere to get advice. This should not be." . . . [Rather], support for the couple comes from the congregation, fellowship members, and church leaders. A network is set up and surrogate family ties develop. These are the ideals, and people are improvising as problems arise. During fellowship meetings there is often an exchange of ideas about those solutions that work and those that do not. (T. Pearce 2002, 28–42)

Sometimes, the moral dimension of religious practice is right on the surface, as in these Nigerian Charismatic fellowship groups thinking about sexuality and family roles. At other times, the moral dimension is ambiguous, with both beliefs and relationships providing guidance for action. Sometimes the pull of moral evaluation keeps the status quo in place, but it is also possible for religious practice to embody active resistance to that same status quo or to be part of constructing a new social order. Some kinds of religious practices make these moral dimensions apparent, but often we have to observe "between the lines" to see what moral goods are being fostered by the practices we are studying.

Religious Moral Practices Setting Boundaries

As we saw in the high schools that Jeffrey Guhin studied, the moral dimension is situationally and communally constructed, with communal boundaries playing a key role. But there are also boundaries embedded in a society's structures of power and status that can show up in religious moral practices. Moral evaluations cannot avoid the evaluations of worth that are present in a society—evaluations that are shaped by gender, race, class, ability, and more. Michèle Lamont's work on moral repertoires of evaluation in France and the United States shows how competition for recognition and respect shape class-based judgments about virtues of honesty, hard work, friendliness, and character. In the United States, she observed, religion played a role, as well. "Being involved in church activities sends out a signal about respectability, moral character, and trustworthiness," especially where religious participation is relatively pervasive in a community (Lamont 1992, 57).

That precise pattern was noted three-quarters of a century earlier by ethicist H. Richard Niebuhr. In his book *Social Sources of Denominationalism*, he wrote about how Christian practices and ethics divided along lines of social class, nationalism, race, and region. In the middle-class churches, he observed, "the sanction of religion is invoked upon the peculiar virtues of the group itself: honesty, industry, sobriety, thrift, and prudence, on which the economic structure of business as well as the economic and social status of the individual depend, receive high veneration, while the virtues of solidarity, sympathy, and fraternity [more prevalent in the churches of "the disinherited"] are correspondingly ignored" (Niebuhr 1929, 86). Students of lived religion should pay close attention to how practices—from sermons and prayers to congratulatory announcements and gestures of honor—express the moral order, as well as the social hierarchy, of a group.

Employing religious practice to exclude is something many LGBTQ people know all too well. Sociologist Bernadette Barton's study of "Bible Belt gays" documented how they experienced explicit shunning by family and friends who quoted scripture as they disowned those who came out as gay. They indirectly experienced the same moral judgment in the "cross rings, fish key chains, Christian T-shirts, bumper stickers, tote bags, and verbal references to one's Christian identity" that Barton calls a "Bible Belt panopticon" (2012, 24–25). Ordinary religious practices of material display signaled moral evaluations that then shaped social interaction and sometimes exclusion.

Religious studies scholar Lynne Gerber has taken up similar questions, noting that "the moralization of homosexuality has been a major stake in symbolic struggles both within religious traditions and between religion and secular society" (2011, 24). Her book examines the history of "ex-gay" ministries like Exodus International and includes observations at conferences, along with interviews with members, leaders, and ex-members. What makes her study stand out, however, is the inclusion of a strategic comparison—to the way religious practices (along with much of US culture) also moralize fat. That comparison allows us to see the social mechanisms at work beyond the specifics of a given issue. Already by the turn of the twentieth century, Gerber writes, fat had become synonymous with gluttony and sin: "Questions of eating, body size, and weight loss are infused with the gravity of the moral and the power of the sacred" (25). From her observations and interviews with First Place, a Christian weight-loss program, she describes the bodily disciplines that are part of the lifestyle change they promote—calorie exchanges, exercise, bodily measurement, weigh-ins. But the distinguishing feature of the program is its disciplines of mind and spirit. Each weekly meeting includes a Bible study and a verse to memorize. Gerber's careful attention to what participants were doing enabled her to show how religious practice reinforced moral evaluations of body size.

Weight Loss and Religious Practice at First Place

Storing scripture in our minds, the argument goes, puts the most important tool of Christian life more readily at hand for situations where it could prove essential. Jill explained it this way: "I tell them all at the beginning of every session that you are a success in First Place if you are more like Christ at the end of thirteen weeks than you were when you walked in." ... Scripture memorization has some pragmatic benefits as well. For Florence, scripture memorization prevents transgression: "The word says, 'Thy word I have hidden in mine heart that I may not sin against thee.' It is a sin when we abuse the body that God gave us. It's a sin. And so as we memorize and learn God's word and get it inside us, then we are going to start sinning less all the

time." . . . Shaping the Christian mind along scripture's contours is also behind commitments to Bible reading and Bible study. . . . The assignments . . .
are implicitly or explicitly related to weight loss; some tackle food and eating
head-on, while others address self-esteem, sin, and other issues thought to
cause excessive eating or body weight. (Gerber 2011, 130–131)

Religious practice has long been implicated in exclusions of all sorts,
not just shaming of fat people. Protestants exclude Catholics, Christians
exclude Muslims, secular people exclude visibly religious ones, most
Americans exclude atheists, "respectable" people exclude "lazy unde-
serving bums," men exclude women, traditionalists exclude heretics—
the list could go on.[6] In every case, the exclusions are both religious
and moral. The "other" is not only wrong or different but deviant, dirty,
and shameful. These exclusions don't just happen in official edicts; they
happen in everyday practices that signal and reinforce the lines between
worthy and unworthy people. The study of lived religious practice has
to include even these difficult and unwelcome aspects of what people
are doing when they engage in shared religious patterns of interaction.

Morality as Part of the Whole

Everyday experience of connection to a religious community or tradition may play a critical role in judgments of right and wrong, what is
possible and taboo, to be desired or shunned. Religious practices of all
sorts carry moral judgment within them. That moral dimension can
help to constrain action, reinforce the status quo, or enforce boundaries
between people. Since religious practice is also moral practice, shared
collective religious action can also pursue change and disturb the status
quo. Observing religious action means paying attention to what it says
about how the world ought to be. Sometimes that will be very explicit,
as in moral and ethical teaching, and sometimes it will be implicit in the
community's stories and hopes—the narrative dimension of practice to
which we will turn next.

A fascinating place to observe the multiple dimensions of religious
practice is in the "edge places," the borders where differences come together. People whose religions are very different may find themselves
nevertheless pursuing common goals, and that can lead to creative new

practices. Liberal religious advocacy groups often occupy just such liminal social places, and sociologists Grace Yukich and Ruth Braunstein (2014), both of whom study these groups, combined their research projects to gain even deeper insight. Braunstein interviewed national leaders in a variety of liberal advocacy organizations and supplemented those interviews with ethnographic observations and public records. Yukich combined in-depth interviews with New Sanctuary movement activists and allies with content analysis of movement documents. They were both interested in how actual interactional settings had an effect on the practices that developed, so they needed to observe the practices; but they also needed to talk to the participants about their perceptions. The result is a fine-grained analysis of interfaith practices like the rabbi's prayer we examined in chapter 6. Both Yukich and Braunstein pay attention to the material settings and patterns of communication, as well as to the embodied and emotional expressions of touch and presence. Attention to these multiple dimensions of religious practice enables them to understand how new patterns emerged and how new practices worked in redefining boundaries and identities.

Religious Practices and Moral Argument in Interfaith Organizing

[Interfaith activists develop] practices that publicly draw on the recognizable symbols, language, and practices of their varied faith traditions in order to express the claims they make as part of interfaith coalitions. For religious advocates, the most common form this takes involves signing onto joint public statements or letters. . . . This complicated negotiation occurs around meeting tables (or on conference calls or email chains), where representatives of each faith community offer their own scriptural or historical justifications for the policy position shared by the group. One lobbyist from a Jewish organization explains this process, referencing a recent statement on international human rights: "We're speaking with a moral voice on this. . . . It's that moral part of it that's the real key. So how do you best demonstrate the moral? Do we take something from the Torah? Well that's fine for Judeo-Christians maybe, with the caveat that most of the Christian groups would maybe prefer something from the New Testament. But it's certainly not going to work for the Muslim community. And what about Hindus or other religions? So in this case, we pulled one quote from the Old Testament, which we referred to as the Hebrew Bible in this case. We pulled one quote from the New Testament and we pulled one quote from the Qur'an. . . .

[Other activists developed] more integrative practices. In the New Sanctuary Movement, activists developed practices that went beyond aggregating distinct, existing religious rituals and language, instead merging their symbols to create something new that was shared by all groups and belonged exclusively to none. One way they did this was through the use of inclusive prayers that tied the oneness of God to the oneness of humanity. For example, at the end of a private New Sanctuary steering committee meeting where there had been some interfaith tension, the mainline Protestant pastor leading the meeting closed with a prayer. The pastor asks everyone to stand in a circle, to hold hands, and to pray with their eyes open, looking at everyone. In a calm, clear voice, he prays using images of birthing: God giving birth to us, God giving birth to justice through this movement. . . . "We are all children of God, brother and sister." As he concludes, an enthusiastic "Amen" echoes around the room. (Yukich and Braunstein 2014, 802–803)

Ideas for Further Study

1. As I write this, the US president is persistently and intentionally calling COVID-19 the "Chinese" virus—a vivid example of using a fear of contamination for purposes of moral exclusion. There is an extensive literature that builds on the concept of "stigma" first fully developed in sociology by Erving Goffman (1963). As Gabriel Ignatow (2010) points out, morality is always tied to bodily experience. Mind and body can't be disentangled in how we perceive and evaluate the social world.

2. The sociology and psychology of morality are now rapidly growing fields, after having fallen largely out of favor in the mid-twentieth century. Steven Hitlin and Stephen Vaisey's (2010) edited *Handbook of Sociology of Morality* is a good place to start. A comprehensive overview of work in social psychology of morality can be found in the article by Naomi Ellemers and associates (2019). One of the people attempting to define the psychological contours of personal moral identity is Jan Stets (2010). Among the most popular writers on moral psychology is Jonathan Haidt (2012; Graham et al. 2011), who also seeks to identify consistent personal styles that shape moral intuitions. For cognitive linguistics, the work of George Lakoff (1996) has been foundational. Bringing those things together are Jason Turowitz and Douglas Maynard (2010), who build on ethnomethodology and conversation analysis to look at the interactional processes involved in forms

of "moral work," that is, how we assign blame or make a credible complaint in the course of a simple conversation.

3. The question of cultural moral repertoires has been especially important to researchers exploring the intersection of religion and politics. Here, it is important to listen for the ways religious ideas can be adapted to secularized, "public" ways of talking. Jack Delahanty, Penny Edgell, and Evan Stewart (2018) have identified what they call "secularized evangelical discourse," and they argue that one does not have to be a member of an evangelical community to engage in ways of talking about politics that draw on evangelical presumptions. This is another reminder that the moral dimensions of social practice may not be defined exclusively by a given religious community, but those communities can be highly influential nevertheless.

4. The initial book from the first wave of the NYSR (when the teens were fourteen to seventeen) is Christian Smith and Melinda Lundquist Denton's *Soul Searching* (2005). Smith and Patricia Snell Herzog (2009) followed with *Souls in Transition*, based on follow-up interviews as their subjects became "emerging adults." There are many other publications based on the data from this study, all drawing on a rich combination of survey and interview methods.

5. We have already encountered the religious practices of social movements, but here we might add sociologist Richard Wood's (2002) analysis of faith-based community organizing. The collection edited by Ruth Braunstein, Todd Fuist, and Rhys Williams (2017) is a fascinating introduction to a range of good research that takes everyday movement practices seriously.

6. If you are interested in following up on these various modes of exclusion, there are many, many studies to draw on across multiple disciplines. Here are a few places to start: Ruth Braunstein's (2019) analysis of US politics provides an excellent overview of how various religious groups have challenged white Protestant views of "good citizens" and thereby been painted as outsiders to be excluded. On the American propensity to define atheists as "other," see the study by Penny Edgell, Joseph Gerteis and Douglas Hartmann (2006). The opposite dynamic— religious expression itself as "other"—is at work in Quebec, in France, and elsewhere, where religious clothing is banned in public (Elver 2012). On the way ideas about "the deserving poor" shape welfare policy, Brian Steensland's (2006) work is insightful. Practices of religious exclusion are almost always intertwined with political and ethnic histories, which is clear in John Brewer and Gareth Higgins's (1999) study of the history of anti-Catholicism in Ireland. A fascinating case study of tradition, heresy, and political change analyzes a post-Soviet community where the traditional "priestless" Old Believers confronted the willingness of some of their members to adapt to new realities by having priests and a nice new building. Each group had different ideas about how people should relate to each other and what virtues define a proper community (Rogers 2008).

9

Narratives in Religious Practice

We have so far explored the way lived religious practice is spiritual but also embodied, material, emotional, aesthetic, and moral. Each of those qualities of social practice takes us beyond the usual focus on religious words and ideas, but that does not mean that words are unimportant. A study of religious practice needs to include attention to the way people communicate with each other. While there are many ways to approach communicative action, we will use the metaphor of narrative to think about this shared activity—with two meanings of "narrative" at play. The more obvious meaning is that there are religious practices of storytelling, both specific stories to be told and shared ways of telling them. That is the primary focus of this chapter.

The other meaning is more subtle but no less important. Practices themselves have a shared narrative dimension that is as much a part of the experience as the other dimensions we have studied. That is, practices are shaped by implicit stories about what is happening and why, and those temporal and relational narrative structures are as important as the more overt practices of religious storytelling. Every time a person engages in assessing a situation and deciding how to act, they are working with a kind of structured story in their heads, even as they may be called on to improvise. There may not be a clear plotline from start to finish (in fact, there probably isn't), but our perceptions of what is happening draw on the "characters" we recognize (including the role into which we ourselves are cast) and the "events" we can recall or imagine. How we then take up our role plays out in an ensemble effort of interaction that happens in a particular place on a particular stage.[1] We are never acting alone or without context and script.

Margaret Somers (1994) is a political theorist who argues that narratives make events understandable by connecting them to a set of relationships and practices. We act in terms of our place in the social world (relationships) and the habits we have formed (practices). Those actions sit within a temporal arc; they are layered with expectations that come from the past and imaginations of possible futures.

Narratives also have multiple social layers that both constrain and enable our action. One kind of narrative, Somers argues, is a kind of internal story we tell ourselves about "who *I* am." While this autobiographical narrative may seem like a psychological and idiosyncratic creation, it is very much a collaborative effort, since we have looked to others throughout life for feedback and reinforcement.[2] It is also constantly being disrupted and rewritten when new situations and relationships appear. Nevertheless, the identities and personal stories we claim for ourselves are ever present in our practices. Those identities are also lodged in the second kind of story—what Somers calls "public narratives." These are part of the institutions and contexts themselves. They are about "who *we* are," the memberships and identifications that we claim and that are thrust on us. And the "we" is, in turn, lodged in bigger cultural stories, ways of talking about the world that we share with others far beyond our immediate situation.

Throughout this chapter, we will look for both the temporal and the social layers in the narrative religious practices we study. As throughout this book, the focus is on everyday action and the shared practical understanding that guides it. In turning to this narrative dimension, we continue to look at the religious practices that happen among ordinary laypeople, as well as the practices of specialists and elites. We continue to remind ourselves that practices are both structured and habitual, that they often reinforce inequality and division but are also open to disruption and improvisation. And we continue to keep the full multidimensional nature of lived religious practice in view. Even when a narrative religious practice takes the form of a written text, there are questions to be asked about materiality (its form), embodiment (its accessibility and use), emotion (its desired attitude), aesthetics (its fit and pleasingness), morality (what it teaches), and the spiritual character of the world it describes.

There are a variety of disciplinary partners who have taken up work like this and on which many students of lived religion may want to draw. While communication certainly goes beyond mere words, it is good to pay attention to the words themselves, to vocabulary and jargon. That can help to identify the boundaries of the group we are observing. Hearing specialized words can also invite us to ask about the experiences that called for new language. Drawing on other disciplinary partners, we might pay attention to style and genre in what we read and hear. Linguistic analyses can fill in important historical context, for example, just as semiotics alerts us to the work done by signs and symbols in the social world. In addition, when we ask about the use of language in the exercise of power, critical discourse analysis is a useful way of thinking. By looking for the way language is used, by whom, and in which contexts, we can ask questions about the relationships and structures of power that are revealed.[3] Scholars have studied language and communication in a variety of ways, but as always, our work will start with people using words rather than the words themselves. Using the metaphor of narrative, we will look for what is communicated about past and future, about relationships and boundaries, as they are present in everyday lived religious practices.

In this book about studying lived religion, you may have been surprised to see so little so far about beliefs and meaning systems. Scholars and ordinary people alike often think of belief as central to what it means to be religious, and they turn to definitive texts (scriptures, sermons, treatises—words) as a way of studying such beliefs. Survey researchers, in turn, ask people if they believe in God or if they think the Bible is literally true. Social theorists echo that theme in their own way by talking about religion as a "meaning system" or a "sacred canopy."[4] As we look at the narrative dimension of lived religious practice, the role of beliefs and meanings will come more directly into view. We will see that people use words and stories to construct the meanings that guide their actions. We will see that they talk about beliefs, and in doing so, they are saying something about who they are and where they belong. But the beliefs and meanings that show up in everyday narratives are usually more modest than world-defining interpretations of life, death, and tragedy. Nor are they usually formed into a coherent system. There may be many different stories about life in a person's cognitive library, with vignettes sometimes jumbled and discarded in any given interaction. Analyzing the narrative dimension of practice takes us beyond dogmatic formulae, but without leaving belief aside.

Instead, we will train our attention on the way divine beings and spiritual moments and religious institutions populate the stories people tell about everyday life and the way their lived religious practices tell stories about what is right and true and possible. That does not mean theology is irrelevant to this task. Not only will we listen for how people use existing theological language and categories, but we can also ask how theologians themselves are working with the stories of everyday life to think about what they can learn. Religious studies scholar Charles Marsh has pioneered a turn toward "lived theology." He argues that "crafting a more direct and communicative rendering of the divine-human encounter requires us to place new demands on [theology]. . . . Restoring the power of the individual encounter with God in the concrete situation and in its community to words, into language—this is the task and responsibility given to each generation of theologians" (Marsh 2017, 10–11). If that divine-human encounter can happen anywhere, the theologian's task may include asking people to tell a story about what happened *after* church on Sunday or what they are praying about or what makes them angry about the world as it is. These stories may even be more revealing than asking them directly about life's meaning or about their beliefs.

Narratives Are Social: Audiences and Cultural Resources

Understanding the social layers of a story means recognizing that narratives are coconstructed by narrator and audience, and when the researcher herself is the audience, that is an important part of what we need to analyze. Interviews are probably the most common method for hearing stories, but firsthand observation is extremely useful, as well. In each case, it is important to keep in mind that process of co-construction. Stories told to you are told *to you*, in all your particularity. Likewise, the history of relationship between "people like you" and the people you are interviewing becomes part of the story. Sociologist Lynn Davidman, herself a formerly Orthodox Jew, describes this reflexivity well: "Respondents did not simply 'have' a narrative that I, as a researcher, could 'get.' Rather . . . my informants interacted with me as a woman, and as a co-defector" (2015, 8).

As students of lived religion, we bring to an event our own individual stock of stories that interact with and shape the stories we hear. In addition, there are collective stories (what Somers calls "public narratives") that have the power to tell us how things should go in "this kind of event." That is, the immediate social rules, material places, and institutions matter. Places we observe have rituals and histories. The stories people tell and the way they tell them are situated, both in social spaces and in relation to the legends and plots available to us in our cultural and religious traditions. Studying lived religion means paying attention to the social patterning in all three levels—interacting individuals, structuring institutions, and overarching cultural resources.

Think about the narratives that structure an individual life as it is lived in the cultural and legal contexts we have called *institutional*. There are separate public narratives that describe life's progression through educational institutions (up through the grades) and occupational ones (entry level to the top), through citizen involvement, through families and relationships, through stages of health, illness, and aging. Each person's story will be different, but each will be structured by familiar markers that place us in recognizable roles and at recognizable places along the way. There are also religious ways of telling the story. A child may be marked at birth by sacred words whispered in their ear or holy oil and water on their head. Those rituals define that child's place in a family and a community. The story continues with key markers such as bar mitzvahs or quinceñeras and marriage rituals. Similarly, at death, stories are told by the families and communities who wish to keep the ancestor alive in memory. The telling and the doing are intertwined, each shaped by the community that is the audience and the institution in which it is told.

Because there are multiple institutions offering public narratives in this kind of context, creating a spiritually defined version of a life story requires work. Anthropologist Michael Brown's ethnography of New Age human "channels" (spirit mediums) can give us a window on how that work happens. The wide range of practices that are clustered under the "New Age" umbrella share a common emphasis on self-exploration and improvement. Brown says, "The New Age seems largely constituted by narratives: life histories, tales of spiritual adventure and 'self-empowerment,' moments of 'personal sharing,' and accounts of affliction and recovery. The movement's networks and collective gatherings are designed to provide opportunities for storytelling" (2002, 103). That is, there is a social context in which this individualized spirituality takes shape. New Age practice often involves workshops that bring together a spiritual counselor and an interested audience in conference centers and meditation rooms and organic gardens. There is a great deal of emphasis on finding one's own path, free of external constraints, but this is a particular kind of biographical narrative that exists in a cultural context and with the support of communities where it can emerge and be affirmed.[5]

Religious communities and traditions of all kinds contribute patterned stories that can shape how people enact a practice or narrate a life. Religious organizations establish narrative templates that encourage participants to tell the stories of their lives in sacred terms. As children grow up, they learn the important stories about the gods, about the community's history, and about how spiritual dimensions of life are experienced. Those stories depend, however, on the communities that tell them, and they exist alongside all the other stories children are learning outside the community. The stories and practices may, in fact, be forgotten in later life as other commitments and relationships take center stage. Professor of education Khyati Joshi (2006) studied the ethnic and religious identities of the children of immigrants to see how those identities were constructed and sustained and when they were forgotten. She interviewed forty-one second-generation Indian Americans—the majority Hindu but the rest representing the broad range of India's other religious traditions. They all grew up somewhat distant from any of the Indian enclaves in the United States that would have strengthened the ethnic and religious influences of their childhood. Still, many, from all the traditions, reported going to "Sunday schools," where they were taught the stories and how to do the rituals. That laid a foundation, but later in life, unless they lived near their parents and their home community, these young adults were unlikely to continue participating in religious communal practices. Stories told at one time in life may be a kind of reservoir, but they require an ongoing set of relationships to remain alive. It is worth asking our participants, then, about the stories they have heard and the celebrations they have had, but those earlier stories may be distant memories rather than living narrative frames for their lives.

Religious organizations themselves want to see such storytelling succeed, of course. Birthright Israel tours, for example, are designed to connect communal religious stories to individual lives, instilling Jewish identity and love of Israel in their young participants. Shaul Kelner (2010) studied these tours for several years, first as a program evaluator and then as an independent researcher. His original role meant that he was predisposed to seeing how the programs succeeded, a critical recognition for anyone who is doing research from within an organization. To check what he had learned, he returned later with the specific goal of looking for things he had missed. His primary method in all instances was simply being there—on the bus, in the discussion circles, and listening to the presentations. His interviewing of participants seems mostly to have been informal, although his book provides less specific information about his methods than ethnographies usually do. What he was able to document was the intentional linking of Jewish stories to individual life stories, and he was able to show how the context of the liminal, in-between space provided by a group tour made this possible. The setting and the relationships prove central to understanding how narrative practices do their work, and both watching and listening are the tools we need.

Jewish Stories and Jewish Identity on Birthright Israel Tours

What the social context of the group homeland tour makes possible, tour organizers' efforts make common. One of the primary ways trip sponsors encourage and impose structure on public exchanges about private Jewish lives is by instituting group discussion circles as a regular feature of the Israel experience curriculum. These institutionalize a process in which tourists explicitly link their own stories to the collective Jewish and Zionist stories that are being used to frame Israel. . . . Irrespective of their content, the discussions are structured to encourage tourists to look to their own pasts. . . . In speaking to their personal histories, tourists also discuss aspects of family history that predate their birth. It is common in the discussions surrounding the visit to Yad Vashem, for instance, for grandchildren of survivors to talk about their grandparents' experiences in and after the Shoah. . . . [The students] find themselves in a separate social environment whose structure and discourse work hand in hand to both enable and encourage them to overlook the complexities of identity and, instead, construct radically simplified conceptions of self. The travelers are in their very essence and more than anything else, the tours suggest, Jews. (Kelner 2010, 173, 179)

Practices of religious narration happen both in intentional religious activities and in everyday conversation, in individual life stories and in the spaces where collective stories are generated and retold. The stories people tell about their everyday lives may be told as blessings or curses, as times of divine presence or absence. Listening for narrative practices that include religious and spiritual elements means recognizing that not everything we hear comes from authoritative religious sources. In *entangled* social contexts, relationships of all sorts convey spiritual knowledge. Where there are officially *established* or widely *institutionalized* religious organizations, there are theological authorities and programs that convey religious ideas. But in *interstitial* contexts, the stories may come from many sources, and the elements of explanatory stories must be pieced together. As media studies scholar Lynn Schofield Clark (2007b) puts it, this can be "religion, twice removed." Popular music, television programs, and movies can borrow religious images and stories from existing traditions, and those images then find their way back into the way people describe their lives.[6]

The range of such media is now vast. Writers and artists, bloggers, vloggers, and tweeters tell stories about love and life that sometimes invoke sacred actors and images, as well as seeking to define often-contested religious identities. Their audience is cultivated through comment spaces, and their authority is authenticated by the way their stories resonate with followers and establish the popularity of their "brand" (Lövheim and Lundmark 2019). These sites of online religious practice allow new dispersed communities to form and new pastiche practices to emerge, but they often intersect with and borrow from offline religious practice. The study of religion and media has blossomed in recent decades so that the student of lived religious practice has abundant sources at hand. There are practices to observe online and practices portrayed in film and television (which are often consumed online, as well). All are worth studying on their own, but we can also study how those media images and practices make their way into life stories.[7]

Clark's (2003) research is pioneering in this regard. She writes about the media producers and their products but also how they are consumed. She analyzed the popular 1990s TV shows *Touched by an Angel* and *Buffy the Vampire Slayer*, including how images from the programs showed up in teens' talk about their lives. She analyzed interviews with one hundred teens who were part of a larger, multimethod project called "Symbolism, Meaning, and the Lifecourse," begun in the late 1990s. Her book includes a detailed and helpful discussion of the methods the team used. The team followed up initial individual interviews with conversations that involved whole families and circles of friends. The broad socioeconomic and ethnic diversity of the sample, along with its religious diversity, makes for a rich picture of the spiritual and religious lives of teens in the United States and especially the way they weave together their own stories and those available in popular media.

For example, Clark describes Jake, a teen with little knowledge of religion, who nevertheless told a story about a miraculous appearance of an angel. "When I asked Jake to further describe what he thought angels were like, he noted, 'Well, there's a lot of movies that have angels in them, so that's always what I thought they were like'" (Clark 2003, 101). In fact, she continues, in teens' stories "an angel could be a ghost and vice versa, or a ghost could be an ancestor. Stories and symbols might be drawn from religious sources or from places like family stories of good fortune, 'legend trips,' the entertainment media, or popularized African traditions of ancestors" (112). The cultures we live in have always been repositories for a pastiche of stories. As we listen to people narrate their lives, we may find that occupational lore, neighborhood myths, congregational histories, and family legends are woven together with whatever religious stories to which they have had access, even through mass media.

Some of those stories can rise to widely shared myths and aphorisms, but as they do, competing voices may be silenced. The "civil religion" that presumably tells the moral story of a nation, for example, is likely to ignore its conquest of Indigenous people or the subjugation of racial minorities.[8] As we hear religious words and stories, it is worth paying attention to their sources. Whose symbols are mass produced and widely heard, and whose are forbidden? While individuals may seem to be stitching together a personal narrative, there are both audiences and producers at work. Some cultural sources are more readily available to them than others, some symbols and roles more respected than others, some voices louder than others.

Stories about everyday life take place in complex social layers, but they also have real material and embodied settings and evoke moral and aesthetic judgments, as well as complex emotions. All the dimensions of experience and all the social layers, from personal to institutional to cultural, are present in the telling, as are the listeners (including interviewers) whose response keeps the story alive.

How Narrative Practices Unite and Divide

The stories that frame a social practice are shared practical knowledge, and as such, they draw lines between those who know the practice and those who don't. As we have seen, spiritual narratives create and sustain memories of events in one's own life, linking them with the history of one's community and one's people. In other words, they reinforce identity and membership. Stories create—and negotiate—boundaries. Telling stories reminds hearers of where they belong, but it also creates moments when belonging can be redefined. People on the margins can sometimes renegotiate the boundaries by playing with the stories. Recall the Muslim teenage boys whom John O'Brien (2017) studied—boys struggling to establish a place for themselves somewhere between US teen culture and halal religious expectations. One expression of this struggle was their humorous invocation of the "extreme Muslim," a character whose "forceful, harsh, and loud manner," O'Brien notes, signals that his strict admonitions are "not our way." To illustrate, O'Brien relates an incident at the mosque. Walking through one day, he heard a high-pitched voice lecturing on the Qur'an and mistakenly assumed it was a woman:

> When I reach Muhammad at the front desk, I tell him, "I thought that was a woman speaking." Muhammad puts on a heavy "Arab" accent and an expression of mock horror, and says, "Astaghfirullah [God forgive you], bruzzer! A woman addressing the masjid [mosque]? Zis is not right! What do you want to have next? A stripper in ze mosque? Would you want to put a stripper over zere instead of the bookstore? [he points to the bookstore]. Maybe you think zis would be a good way to raise money, because no one is buying ze books? Maybe you are right." (O'Brien 2017, 66)

Humorous stories are often the medium for just this sort of boundary setting and negotiation. Peter Berger's delightful book about humor outlines the many uses to which it is put—rebelling against authority (as these Muslim boys were doing), expressing fears or resentments, or diffusing uncomfortable situations. He goes on to argue that comic moments are often like sacred ones in their "non-ordinary" quality, breaking through routine expectations to open up other possibilities. But ordinary in-group jokes, he points out, are also effective boundary markers. Berger quips, "What happens if you cross a Unitarian with a Jehovah's Witness? A person who goes from house to house, and doesn't know why. Try telling [that] joke to someone with no knowledge of American religion" (1997, 57). A funny story may do a great deal of work in marking or challenging who belongs.

Timothy Longman, on the other hand, writes about very unfunny stories. Physical memorials always invite narratives, often heroic or poignant but also sometimes horrific. Over the past half century, it has become common to construct spaces that challenge viewers to remember genocides and other tragedies, hopefully vowing "never again." These spaces are material artifacts intended to provoke emotional and moral responses by implicitly telling a story.[9] Sometimes private and religious groups construct memorials and shape the message; sometimes it is governments or just random passersby. Longman (2009) has written extensively about the role of the churches in Rwanda's 1994 genocide, as well as the way the story of that genocide is now being told, especially through physical memorials. He and coauthor Théoneste Rutagengwa visited dozens of such memorials, conducted a survey of over two thousand residents in three differing communities, and convened focus groups to learn how memorials were telling the story of what happened.

Honoring a Painful Past in Rwanda

In nearly every province . . . at least one church building—sometimes a school, sometimes a monastery, often a church sanctuary—was set aside as a memorial. The form these memorials take varies substantially. In only a few places were bodies left where they fell. In a number of churches, bodies were arranged carefully, with the bones of children in one room, intact skeletons in another, skulls and bone fragments in another. . . . In Nyamata, a Catholic parish south of Kigali, a large complex of open catacombs has been built behind the church, where bodies are buried yet still visible and the parish building itself is cleared but still bears stains of blood and fire. A guide takes visitors through the church, telling the story of the genocide. (Longman and Rutagengwa 2006, 141)

While guides tell official stories, the people in the communities tell their own. Some echo the story of necessary remembrance ("never again"), while others reject this focus on the past, and still others incorporate these places into long-standing ways of remembering ancestors. Like all stories, memorial stories are dynamic, being shaped by the moment, the tellers, and the audience. Outside observers who did not experience the event need to listen carefully. Who is being constructed as victim and who as perpetrator? What about the event is to be remembered and what forgotten? Who now belongs, and who must therefore be excluded? Paying attention to the places themselves, to embodied responses to them, to the emotions they generate, and to the moral message can help students of lived religious practice to hear the story more clearly.

Stories, that is, can perpetuate differences within a society or a community. Some stories explain why one group deserves to be privileged and another not. Karl Marx famously posited that a religious life narrative with a "sweet by and by" was a convenient salve for this life's economic wounds and might therefore serve the interests of people in charge ([1844] 1963). Similarly, every patriarchal tradition has stories to explain the inferiority of women and the legitimacy of male power. Such institutionalized patterns of inequality also impose constraints on who can tell which story (Barr 2021). Conservative Christian organizations may, for example, establish a familiar story about how a person is "called" to be a leader, but that story can only be told about a male member of the group. In many traditions, stories that combine being a faithful person and being LGBTQ are illegitimate (or just impossible). In many places in the world, telling a story about one's conversion to a new religion is a practice discouraged by law or custom (Hackett 2008; Yang 2012). Spiritual narratives, that is, are situated in particular legal and cultural contexts and can be part of the repertoire that is used to mark distinctions of status, privilege, and exclusion. The constrained conditions that make some stories hard to tell pose particular challenges for an observer of lived religious practice. Sometimes the narratives of a group hide as much as they reveal so that seeking out marginal members and moments of disruption becomes especially critical.

The Work Narratives Do

Narrative work, like all social action, is both situationally emergent and institutionally patterned, constrained by shared convention and amenable to the creativity and agency of the narrators. That mix of openness and structure is at least partly a function of the fact that narratives, by their very nature, contain a temporal dimension. They begin at one time and end at another. Prayers themselves are often framed as narratives about what the divine has done in the past and what is hoped for in the future. In the moment, new things might happen, in part because the story of the past is being retold. There are practices reframing the past, practices that reinterpret the present, and practices that suggest a new future.

In thinking about observing such practices, Daniel Winchester's work is once again helpful. With Kyle Green, he has given us a study that shows how stories of the past are reframed in the present. Winchester and Green's collaboration is another example of taking advantage of two separate ethnographic studies to draw out larger lessons. They combine Winchester's study of converts to Eastern Orthodoxy with Green's study of people who take up mixed martial arts. As we have seen in earlier examples from Winchester's study, he is attuned to the embodied, material, and moral dimensions of religious practice, but here we turn to the evolution of converts' narrative accounts of their growing attachment to new practices. "Although initially post hoc justifications, over time, these accounts became reworked and internalized by actors as part of their own self-interpretations" (Winchester and Green 2019, 262). Winchester and Green show that in each of these very different communities, narrative "hooks" are proffered by community members and take hold precisely when new people are feeling ambivalent and unsure. Once the hooks do take hold, accounts of what happened in the past can motivate action in the present and future. "Practices undertaken in the here and now were ultimately leading them to some version of a more enlightened and desirable self" (273).

Becoming an Eastern Orthodox Self

Before becoming an Eastern Orthodox Christian at the age of 48, Danielle had spent most of her adult years involved in New Age Spirituality and then later as a committed Buddhist. In her early 40s, however, Danielle became what she described as "burned out" on Buddhism and religion altogether. Only after discovering the Orthodox Church . . . did Danielle "find my spiritual home, where I really belonged" and "who God was leading me to be all this time." Danielle's explanation of her conversion as a moment of profound self-discovery, of finding out where she really belonged and who she was always meant to be, was an extremely common theme within the conversion narratives of Eastern Orthodox Christian converts. . . . [In the beginning, she was curious, but not comfortable, definitely ambivalent. A conversation with the priest helped. Then,] Father Peter and others drew a plotline between Danielle's religious past as a Buddhist and her current quasi-interest in the Orthodox Church. This narrative alignment between past experience and present action effectively hooked Danielle's interest and seemed to motivate her to return—"I had to come back and learn more," as she put it. . . . [Gradually the story became her own. Danielle] explained how she had been practicing the Jesus Prayer and that it had "opened up something in me that I haven't experienced in years, . . . a very transcendent, spiritual feeling." Danielle told [me] she used to get this type of feeling with Buddhist meditation but now "also with this strong feeling of great love and acceptance." At this point, Danielle said, "there is a reason that I found the Church; I think this is where God has been leading me all along." (Winchester and Green 2019, 266–270)

Like others who have studied conversion,[10] Winchester and Green show how past events are reframed as prelude to the present. Lynn Davidman describes a similar gradual process of trying on new life accounts when one leaves a significant relationship or community. Her book *Becoming Un-Orthodox* highlights the multiple dimensions of practice involved in leaving behind an ultra-Orthodox way of life. She especially notes the way bodies participate in telling the story of who we are and are not. Those who leave the Hasidic community have to "disinscribe their internalized routines of the body" (Davidman 2015, 20). They often began the process in private, experimenting with leaving certain bodily rituals aside. They broke a commandment and discovered that they didn't incite divine punishment, so that the story they had internalized began to fall apart. At some point, they began a phase of "passing," in which they were presenting themselves as Orthodox when they were inside the community but freely breaking Orthodox norms when they were not. Finally, they "stepped out," risking loss of family, community, and way of life. They became "scriptless," in Davidman's words (142). Relationships, habits, and their very bodies were changed, but in the end, she notes, "You can't turn off your past" (181). This research is a good reminder that narratives are not just words. The religious practices of constructing and reconstructing a life story are just as embodied and material and emotional as every other religious practice is.

The negotiated character of that reframing is even more apparent when the effort fails. Among evangelicals, a central religious practice is witnessing to one's faith and attempting to win new converts. Not nearly all evangelicals actively engage in this practice (Pew Research Center 2015, 84), but we can see a vivid example in an encounter recorded by sociologist David Smilde. He was taking a break from an event at one of the Pentecostal churches he was studying in Caracas, Venezuela, chatting in the parking lot with one of the church leaders. Enrique (the leader) spotted a kid nearby smoking crack and took the opportunity to confront him. As Smilde records the conversation, we hear an unsuccessful attempt to reframe the present and the future for this young man. Ultimately, Juan Carlos walks away, smoking his crack. The evangelical life is not a story he can imagine, in spite of the intervention of Enrique. For Enrique, on the other hand, engaging in this kind of evangelizing conversation is part of the narrative religious practice of his life.

Is This the Future You Want? Witnessing in a Caracas Parking Lot

ENRIQUE: Why are you smoking rock? You have to quit. You're going to destroy your life, man. [pause] That's bread for today, hunger for tomorrow. Right now you're going to feel good. But tomorrow you're going to be in bad shape.

JUAN CARLOS: It's a curse, hermano.

ENRIQUE: It's a curse and you know it. So why don't you look to Jesus Christ then? [Juan Carlos finishes packing his pipe and puts it up to his mouth.] . . .

JUAN CARLOS: What's the question?

ENRIQUE: Whether you want to continue this lifestyle destroying yourself little by little.

JUAN CARLOS: I haven't destroyed my life yet.

ENRIQUE: Whatta ya mean you haven't destroyed your life yet? ... You can't keep on like this, man! You're going to destroy yourself. Satan wants to destroy you. And there's a way to escape it. You don't think there is a way to escape it?

JUAN CARLOS: [pause] Escape ... yeah, I think so.

ENRIQUE: Why don't you come to the church and toss that [the crack] ... [After an interruption, the conversation continues.]

ENRIQUE: Christ loves you, man. [pause] Christ loves you. [pause] Christ wants to free you from your vice. You're a young man, good looking. Satan wants to possess you.

JUAN CARLOS: I hadn't consumed rock for four months until today.

ENRIQUE: Look what the Bible says [pages through the Bible until he finds a verse]: "The Devil came to kill you, steal your life and your peace, and destroy you" [John 10:10]. That's what Satan came for. But Jesus Christ came to destroy the work of the Devil. Get up from the stupor you're in, man. You're causing your mom and kids problems. Your brothers and sisters are seeing your example. Do you want them to be tomorrow like you are today? You're not a good example for society, son. And Christ knows it, he's putting his hand out to you and saying, "Hey, my son, I love you. Stop that foolishness, man." You're desperate to do drugs and Christ doesn't want to see you that way. (Smilde 2003, 317–319)

Other religious traditions put no such premium on dramatic life changes; past and present are already contained within the stories of the community and the storytelling habits community members have learned. They may have learned to talk about everyday events as visitations from the gods or to see life challenges as times of spiritual trial. Where shared religious assumptions are present in a situation, spiritual stories may simply evolve in routine conversation. We can also hear the story in requests for prayer, for example. In one of Kwabena Asamoah-Gyadu's many visits to Ghanaian Christian communities in various parts of the world, he heard accounts that linked present difficulty with hoped-for future.

During a visit to one Ghanaian congregation in Amsterdam in December 2008, a middle-aged female member walked up to me and asked for prayer. . . . Literally she was saying in Twi, "Pastor, I am getting stuck abroad [meaning she cannot visit Ghana] because I have lived here for ten years, and I still do not have proper documentation or papers. Please pray for me." In the religious life of African immigrants, prayers for *nkrataa*, "papers" (that is, proper resident documents), rank next only to healing in requests made at prayer services. (2010, 90)

These immigrants, gathered at a regular prayer service, tell the story of their migration as a matter for prayer. Studying such lived religious practice may best be done by being there to listen, but attention to published and online sources may be fruitful, as well. Thousands, if not millions, of tweets and Facebook posts are daily repositories of stories about what divine powers are believed to be doing in the world.

Theologians and ethicists and other religious leaders also invoke the power of stories as they do their work. Traci West is a womanist ethicist who has taken seriously the everyday stories of African-descent women as sources for her ethical reflection. She has traveled to Ghana, Brazil, and South Africa to listen to the stories of women working for change, women who told her about their own use of stories as ways to link past, present, and future. Like other students of lived religious practice, these religion scholars and activists are digging into what stories reveal about the lives and religious understandings of ordinary people. In turn, like the South African woman whom West describes, they are using narrative methods of teaching and writing.

Stories of Rape: Doing Ethics in South Africa

When we met for a one-on-one discussion Sarojini spoke about the challenge she found in the fact that South Africa had one of the most progressive constitutions in the world "and we still can't overcome gender violence. Because legislation alone will never achieve it, you must engage the worldviews of people in the villages and their cultures. And the Bible does this." Sarojini described her work on Bible study methods. . . . She stressed how "the communities with which I work, with which I want to work, take the Bible very seriously, which means that we have to take it seriously." Sarojini and the other leaders of Ujamaa Centre (faculty and local community partners) nurtured an approach to interpretation that invited analysis of community consciousness, starting with the community in the biblical text. In their study sessions she would ask the members of the women's groups if any of them knew a woman who had been raped like the woman in Judges [who was given up by her husband to be gang-raped by strangers]. "And then the stories begin," Sarojini said. "Oh, my goodness. You never have enough time" to get through all of the stories the women have to tell or to explore all of the insights that emerge. (West 2019, 173)

By speaking across time, stories are also intended to call forth imagination about how the world might be.[11] Stories are constructed to evoke possible futures, to speak of dreams and visions. The story of the Exodus, from the Hebrew scriptures, inspired African American slaves to dream of freedom, and that same story is claimed by Zionists in Israel, as well as by immigrants elsewhere who are seeking a better life. Martin Luther King Jr. famously proclaimed, "I have a dream" and "I've been to the mountaintop." He invited listeners to imagine a future when the content of character matters more than the color of skin. It is precisely that imaginative function that has made storytelling, including religious storytelling, so central to social movement activism.[12] We have already benefited from Ruth Braunstein's research on faith-based liberal advocacy, and her attention to stories is as astute as her analysis of other dimensions of religious practice. She recalls Rev. James Forbes speaking to a health-care-focused Interfaith Service of Witness and Prayer. He conjured this narrative scene for the crowd: "The Lord has asked me, 'How do you have the nerve to pray to me for yourself with respect to your health needs, and you show no concern for the other 46 million of your brothers and sisters who have no coverage'" (quoted in Braunstein 2012, 119). Rather than presenting a theological treatise justifying movement activism, leaders draw on grassroots stories, including their own, and frame them symbolically as stories of faith that carry within them the promise of change.

Studying religious practices that put forward a narrative of change can be done with a wide variety of methods. Seeing a narrative on the page or on the screen may fall short in capturing the emotional impact of the words or the response of the audience, but from internet archives to the old-fashioned kind stored in boxes, the practice of storytelling leaves traces that can be studied. Sociologist Michael Young was interested in the earliest national social movements in the United States, namely, the nineteenth-century temperance and antislavery movements. How did they manage to strike a chord and spread throughout the country? He utilized archival data on Protestant benevolent societies along with a wide range of historical newspapers and other publications to create a state-by-state picture of the link between the presence of religious institutions and social movement activity. The institutions were providing the network of resources necessary for leadership and mobilization. But more important for our purposes is Young's exploration of what leaders were saying and doing. All his digging through boxes paid off in both the storytelling he captured and the geographic patterns that reveal its spread. Note his astute ear for the difference between an argument based on health and one that utilizes an entirely different, religious, mode of narrating.

Confessing Sin and Organizing for Change in Nineteenth-Century New York

The American Temperance Society promoted a pledge as a ritual for joining the society. Initially the temperance pledge included a moderate statement that alcohol consumption was "injurious" and that intemperance promoted "evils." . . . It was not a confession. Reports from auxiliaries within New York reveal that by the early 1830s, the pledge had changed to a confession of sin and faith. Unlike the temperance publications of the 1820s, these reports are filled with claims of repentant merchants, reformed tipplers, and reclaimed sots taking the pledge. . . . In 1833, the magazine of the state society compared the temperance pledge to "the Sabbath, circumcision, baptism, the Lord's supper." They were "all pledges or covenants." . . . The society exhorted the individual "to deny himself, to abandon his prejudices and error, and become a firm, active, and a pledged friend of TEMPERANCE." (Young 2002, 676, citations to original sources omitted)

Young linked the geographies and resources of the movements to show how they spread, but the heart of his argument is about how particular religious practices, drawn from different parts of US religious culture, proved especially adaptable. He calls these practices "schemas" to denote the way they organized people's perceptions and actions:

[These] social movements emerged as particular variants of the schemas of sin and confession combined. The two schemas came from different and competing religious contexts. Extending from the populist
institutions of upstart sects [Baptists and Methodists] was a schema or
practice of public confession. Extending from the orthodox institutions
of benevolence was a schema of the special sins of the nation. As they
combined in the consciences of many evangelicals, they triggered confessional protests aimed at transforming individuals and national institutions. (Young 2002, 666)

Alcohol and then slavery were defined not simply as harmful but as sin,
not just individual sin but the sin of a nation. Confessing and repenting
were established practices in revival culture, but now they were tied to
new causes. Narratives can be both pliable and powerful in producing
new futures for individuals and societies.

A new narrative interpretation, linked to a religious practice, can
often have powerful effects on how people act in the moment and into
the future. As we have seen, such adaptations are likely to include themes
and plots drawn from a wide array of sources, taking existing practices
and envisioning a new ending. Because the underlying narratives may
not be right on the surface, it is often useful to engage in an iterative
process of listening, analyzing, and trying out what we think we have
heard. That is what sociologist Arlie Russell Hochschild (2016b) did as
she listened to the talk of Louisiana Tea Party activists, then constructed
a "deep story" and took it back to them to see if it resonated. It was a
story about being left behind in US political and economic life. Hochschild could have said it with stark statistics, but she painted a narrative
picture instead, a picture of other people unfairly skipping ahead in line;
and that resonated with her participants. But she also heard strands of
a religious story in their conversation, namely, the "left behind" narrative found in the massively popular series of books that fictionalized
biblical accounts of the end-time (Frykholm 2004). Interwoven with the
political and economic story about the indignities of contemporary life
were stories of the Rapture, featuring a messianic figure who radically
alters history, rewarding the deserving ones and punishing the evildoers. Those stories helped Hochschild explain these activists' reaction to
Donald Trump, then a candidate for US president. As they saw him de-

scending a golden escalator or sitting at the head of the table casting out failed apprentices, they saw a powerful savior punishing those who had gained unfair advantage. Interlocked stories explained the present and allowed them to imagine a new future.

The narrative dimension of religious practice includes telling stories that constitute, motivate, and interpret both everyday and extraordinary social action. Religious communities and traditions provide vocabularies and genres, but stories and images from throughout the culture can be adapted to give shape to what people see and experience. Like all elements of lived religious practice, narrative practice is both structured and creative. It can unite, and it can divide. For students of lived religious practice, it is useful to examine the ways in which collective narratives allow people to explain their behavior and their desires to themselves and to others.

Putting It All Together

Attention to narrative religious practices brings our multidimensional exploration to completion, so it is time to recap and put it all together. What might be the payoff in studying lived religion in the ways laid out in this book? What new questions arise? What do we see when we take contexts into better account? How can each of the dimensions of practice enrich the study of the others? To do that, let's return to the Chinese Qingming festival, the "tomb sweeping" rituals that take place in early April each year. While the Chinese government seeks to define this as "tradition" and "culture" rather than "religion," what might we see if we analyzed contemporary festival practices as lived religious practice? Taking our cue from an account written by a young Chinese Canadian, Christopher Cheung, let's take a close look at the social structures of the practice, the cultural and legal contexts in which it happens, and the multiple human dimensions that constitute Qingming practice.

Sweeping Tombs in Vancouver

Cheung's (2019) blog recounts scenes at the Vancouver cemetery where his grandfather is buried, full of Chinese families tidying the graves on the appointed day. He describes the activity itself as relatively easy, but "the physicality of the tasks forces you to be quite intimate with death. If crouching in a garden makes you feel close to the earth, crouching to clean a grave reminds you that you are earth." His contemporary interpretation is accompanied by learning the proper modern practice of bowing (rather than prostration). He notes, "My older uncle went first because the order, by seniority, is important. When it was my turn, the adults taught me how to do it, 'Three times. With good posture.'" He ends his blog this way: "There are times I can't help but cry when we talk about happy days they weren't around to see. But I also can't help but laugh at times like when my grandmother shouts to the dead about the A's we got on our report cards. Because the tour goes on, I feel like they're still with us." He notes, as well, his feeling of connection to the larger Chinese community: "It's hard not to think about other Chinese-Canadian families on Qingming when we see them at the cemetery. I love seeing how they pay their respects."

Like all practices, Qingming is co-created by the social participants, using the traditions they know and the habits that just seem natural. Cheung's (2019) blog post notes how the sight of Chinese families tidying the graves heightened his feeling of connection to the larger Chinese community: "It's hard not to think about other Chinese-Canadian families on Qingming when we see them at the cemetery. I love seeing how they pay their respects." Participating in this practice was collective and social. The presence of others provided models for action, but there is a mix of inherited structure and collective agency. Older people may have some memory of the tradition, but they are all reinventing it in a new time and place. When new situations challenge habits and traditions, people improvise. That is as true for religious practice as for any other social practice.

What is also true is that religious practices are as much shaped by forces of status, identity, and division as are any other practices. The capacity to improvise and resist is always there, but so are the tendencies to reproduce existing lines of class and race and privilege. For the grave sweepers, the most obvious distinctions are those based on age, but judgments about social class are embedded in the stories they tell and the objects they use. Understanding social position enlightens understanding of the practice, but observing the practice deepens understanding of how those positions work. Note also that this festival becomes a marker of Chinese ethnicity in the diaspora. It is *Chinese* Canadians who are at the cemetery on this day. Religious practices are, that is, implicated in social identity.

Studying lived religion means paying attention to the places where people recognize a layer of nonordinary reality, and that is certainly the case here. Even though neither the Chinese state nor these "modern" Canadians might call their practice religious, there is nevertheless a spiritual dimension in the way time is collapsed, bringing together past and present, but also in the way participants interact with ancestors and use material objects (willow branches) to drive evil spirits (ghosts) away. In modern Vancouver, our blogger noted that for his family, the older traditions (as he put it) that were focused on spiritual presence—bringing food and gifts for the dead, the willow branches to scare off evil spirits—were not part of their ritual. "But we did clean the grave, and we did bring flowers, and we did bow to my grandfather in respect" (Cheung 2019). Even if the participants are not involved in any organized religious group and do not identify with a single religious tradition, the practices themselves—by invoking awareness of a spiritual reality—can be analyzed as religious practices.

In an earlier time, all these practices might have been part of a highly entangled religious social world, but today they are perhaps best understood as happening within a fluid but highly regulated set of state-sanctioned activities.[13] While traditional popular ancestor practices are not part of the major recognized religions in China, they are generally tolerated. Where practices are being absorbed into one of the official religions (Buddhist or Daoist), both state and religious authorities might attempt to exercise oversight. Indeed, the establishment of Qingming as one of the four public holidays celebrating Chinese traditional culture demonstrates its quasi-establishment status on the mainland. As a relatively newly revived and rapidly evolving set of customs, however, there are also a variety of interstitial innovations. Wherever religious practices are being developed and redeveloped in interstitial social circumstances, we have a window on the social mechanisms through which innovation happens. The tug between tight state regulation and churning social innovation, in fact, mirrors the way much of the rest of Chinese society is changing.

It is important, that is, to place this and any other religious practice in its historical and legal context. That leads us to wonder how the experience of Canadian Chinese is different from that of Chinese people in China. In China, the holiday appears on the official national calendar, while in Canada, Chinese Canadians must create holiday time on their own. Back in China, one might imagine some older participants telling stories about the years when they were forbidden to sweep the graves, while younger Canadians have no such memory. In China, the material items necessary for the festival are readily available, while Canadians may have a harder time assembling the right flowers. As for immigrants everywhere, religious practices are social occasions of both memory and invention. Even the same religious practice is shaped by its cultural context.

Then, examining the practices themselves as multidimensional social interactions both deepens our understanding and opens questions for comparison. We can begin by observing that this practice involves human *bodies* and prescribed movements. Cheung describes the activity itself as relatively easy but notes that the physicality of it evokes encounters with mortality. That suggests thinking about where else we might observe embodied religious practice that brings practitioners into contact with death. Cheung also speaks of learning the "modern" practice of bowing, rather than prostrating himself in obeisance. Where else are postures and movements adapting to new expectations? Observing embodied practice might also suggest comparisons to expressions of reverence within Chinese experience toward the Buddha or Mao Zedong (Tatlow 2016). What might we learn about relations of authority by taking each of those embodied practices seriously?

The material character of Qingming practices is equally striking. Not only are people engaged in tending to a *material space*, but the locations of those spaces have both ritual and practical significance. We might wonder about how the places themselves evoke spiritual experience, as well as ancestral memory. New graves were traditionally situated according to rules of feng shui, but that is more possible in rural areas than in cities. So how do specific places continue to play a part in this and other practices? That question also suggests asking about other burial practices, in China and beyond. Other research tells us that cremation is required in Chinese cities, with most residents then practicing cremains burial or the more expensive option of a columbarium. What happens when there are no graves to tidy in the usual ways? How might the festival encompass these material changes? The arduous journey to the ancestral countryside is another challenge, but some younger generations in China's cities are now using apps for virtual commemoration (Kong 2011) instead. Those who do travel can combine the trip with new tourism opportunities, often advertised as a "spring outing." But travel also brings transportation nightmares (and, in a pandemic, travel restrictions) as millions leave the cities for the countryside. Noting the material dimension of this religious practice—and its intersection with other parts of society such as tourism and transportation—can prompt contrasts and comparisons to other places where religious practices have practical impacts beyond the religious field itself.

Because we do not yet have extensive data on the personal experiences of Qingming practitioners, questions about *emotion* are more speculative. Students of Chinese funeral practices have documented a range of emotional expression and performance (Kipnis 2017, X. Liu 2000, H.-M. Liu 2020), but performance of emotion at Qingming does not necessarily seem to follow the same rules. Our young Vancouver participant, however, was sufficiently moved to create his blog post and to end it by describing his feelings of both joy and sadness. His experience suggests that practices of commemoration may be especially fruitful sites for the study of the emotional dimensions of religious practice. How do cultural expectations channel individual feelings? And how do spiritual and emotional forces combine to shape action?

The *aesthetic* dimensions of Qingming practice are more easily observable, as we saw in chapter 7. There are kites with lanterns lighting the night sky, the pleasant smell of incense, and the less pleasant smells of burning paper money or firecrackers; and especially, there are the flowers that are chosen for their beauty. Again, it is worth remembering that aesthetic judgments are both cultural and status based. A closer study of Qingming would surely ask about how beauty was being judged and by whom.

Moral judgments in these practices are also relatively easy to see. The grandmother told the deceased grandfather all about how the family is doing, reinforcing a tacit statement of the moral compass by which they were living. Not only were they accomplishing important things; they were fulfilling social obligations (by getting married and having children, for example), and they were showing proper moral respect for those who have gone before. If asked to explain these things, they might well point to their grounding in Confucian ethics of filial piety (Pang 2012). But in the People's Republic of China, official state guidelines play a role, as well. Proper respect and commemoration is codified into suggestions for the virtues to be celebrated in tombstone carvings (Kipnis 2017). The moral dimension of Qingming practice is carried by family expectation, social striving, and state guidelines, which might lead us to wonder about how those social forces are at work in less obvious ways elsewhere. How are spiritually infused acts of commemoration shaping how we think about what is right and wrong?

The grandmother's recitation of family accomplishments was accompanied, of course, by a rich array of other storytelling. As with any festival gathering, there are *narrative practices*, stories of past celebrations and of what memorable things extended family members did—which uncle was drunk at the Hanukah party or the memorable time a long-estranged brother came home for Christmas. Cheung (2019) recalled, "On some of those Qingming visits, as my family reminisced, I'd hear new snippets of information about my departed relatives." That suggests that Qingming narratives might be analyzed alongside other family-focused religious practice and other accounts of the filial piety that characterizes the social heritage of Confucianism. One might also wonder how those stories conveyed expectations about proper practice or what one does or does not have to believe. Sometimes narrative practices include official theological writing about how commemoration should happen, but even more often, the narratives are recorded in something like Cheung's blog, recounting, "On Qingming My Family Tidies the Graves." Especially when practices are dislodged, challenged, and changing, there will be many stories—official and unofficial—explaining why and how a lived religious practice matters.

If you wanted to learn more about this practice, then, you might look for official guides, but you would also want to observe and interview ordinary people. That is especially true where religion is not being carried primarily by organized institutions, either those established by a state or those organized into a professionalized religious sector. In entangled contexts, religious practices are pervasive, and no single set of experts is in charge. In interstitial contexts, whatever religious practices exist have been improvised (often in spite of the experts).

Whether we look primarily to ordinary everyday action or to special-ized expert action depends in part on the type of context to be studied. In a Chinese society that still officially establishes atheism, Qingming is largely being reinvented at the grassroots, but within what the state makes possible.

Whether at Qingming or an ordinary funeral, whether in China or elsewhere in the world, finding ways to hear stories—understood as part of multidimensional religious practices—is the goal of studying lived religion. Thinking about how social practices work and placing them in cultural context is the foundation for your work, but looking for all the dimensions of human experience is the rest of the challenge. Lived religion is more than the improvisation of people who can choose every-thing about how they live. Wherever people are engaging in interaction that recognizes a spiritual presence in life, there are questions to ask. Having more answers about religious practice—wherever it happens—can be valuable for understanding both the larger social world and the individual actors we encounter. The embodied actions, along with the words themselves, tell stories about spiritual presence and contempo-rary life. They may be automatic and habitual, but they may also exhibit remarkable improvisation. Shared material surroundings both enable and constrain what people do. The emotional, aesthetic, and moral as-pects of the action tell us how and why people seek new experiences and maintain old boundaries. Like all the lived religious practices we have encountered in this book, each one reminds us how much there still is to learn.

Ideas for Further Study

1. This dramaturgical way of thinking about social interaction was famously devel-oped by Erving Goffman, especially in his *Presentation of Self in Everyday Life* (1959).
2. Margaret Somers (1994) calls this internal narrative "ontological." As I have pointed out elsewhere, I think that gives it more stability than is warranted. I am building in this chapter both on Somers's framework and on my earlier thinking about "narrative identity" (Ammerman 2003).
3. If you are interested in approaching communication from a "critical discourse analysis" perspective, the work of Norman Fairclough (2003) can be a helpful guide, and Alexa Hepburn and Jonathan Potter (2004) have written an accessible

introduction to the methodological options for pursuing a discourse analysis strategy. Robert Wuthnow's (2011) call to "take talk seriously" shows why discourse is important in the study of religion, and one good example is the study by Jean-Pierre Reed and Sarah Pitcher (2015), who show how particular forms of speaking helped to form a revolutionary identity in the Solentiname community in 1970s Nicaragua. In sociology, Paul Lichterman (2008, 2012) has been an especially astute analyst of how ways of talking shape and are shaped by the settings and groups in which they take place.

4. Many of the standard ways of defining religion emerged in mid-twentieth-century US social science. Anthropologist Clifford Geertz says that "a religion is: (1) a system of symbols which acts to (2) establish powerful, pervasive, and long-lasting moods and motivations in men by (3) formulating conceptions of a general order of existence and (4) clothing these conceptions with such an aura of factuality that (5) the moods and motivations seem uniquely realistic" (1973, 90). Despite Peter Berger's devoting an appendix in his classic 1967 book to the variety of sociological definitions of religion, he largely avoided offering one of his own. Treating religion as the creation of a "sacred cosmos," he says that "religion is the audacious attempt to conceive of the entire universe as being humanly significant" (Berger 1967, 28). Robert Bellah, writing at about the same time, took a similar tack, defining religion as "a set of symbolic forms and acts that relate man to the ultimate conditions of his existence" (1963, 21). Note that all of them emphasize the symbolic, explanatory nature of religion. In contrast, a 2013 issue of the *Journal of Contemporary Religions* focused on belief in practice terms, as a "cultural performance" (e.g., Day 2013).

5. Religious communities can also use digital tools to facilitate collective storytelling. Lynn Schofield Clark and Jill Dierberg (2013) studied a church youth group that developed a set of identifying themes about who they are and produced a video account expressing them. Similarly, "photovoice" is a technique for eliciting storytelling through photographs (Williams 2019).

6. As we have noted, the studies by J. Kwabena Asamoah-Gyadu (2007, 2010) are an excellent introduction to what this process looks like outside the West. From his base in Accra, Ghana, he has examined the role of multiple media in African and transnational Christian communities.

7. Studies of "media and religion" have expanded enormously in the past generation. For broad overviews, in addition to Lynn Schofield Clark's extensive work (for example, 2007a), Claire Badaracco (2005) has brought together a collection of articles by both journalists and academics that examine the way religion is reported in public media. Mia Lövheim's (2018) overview article outlines many of the key issues at the intersection of media studies and religion studies, and she has also brought needed attention to the role of gender in media production and use (Lövheim 2013; Lövheim and Lundmark 2019). Heidi Campbell's (2013) edited book offers a sampling of what people have learned about the relationship between religion and digital media. Stewart Hoover (2006) was an early pio-

neer, starting with studies of religion on television and continuing to be a major contributor to our understanding of what people are doing when they do religion through mediated platforms. Former religion reporter Diane Winston (2009), who now teaches at the Annenberg School at the University of Southern California, is especially attuned to how media become part of lived religion.

8. Philip Gorski's (2017) history of US civil religion traces the early racist and colonialist nature of our founding stories, even as he remains optimistic about the possibilities of a morally grounded national story. To explore the way the Black Church tradition has its own civil-religion role to play, Omar McRoberts's work is a good place to start. As he writes, the Black Church's kind of "bottom-up" civil religion articulates "the mythic significance of Black peoplehood" and the way it challenges US national power (McRoberts 2020, 53).

9. Memorials have been examined by scholars in a number of disciplines, from art history to semiotics, but there are also good places to look for research that examines the lived practices of constructing and interacting with such sites. Street-side spontaneous memorials are among the most fascinating, and Sylvia Grider's (2006) work is a helpful analysis on that score, as is Avril Maddrell's (2009) analysis of cairns along a pilgrimage route. Janet Jacobs's (2010) courageous exploration of Holocaust memorials asks how gender is portrayed. What sorts of women and men do we see in them? Jacobs's work is also an excellent example of using visual methods in analyzing religion. A larger collection of articles on the links between religion, violence, memory, and place is found in the book edited by Oren Stier and Shawn Landres (2006).

10. Many studies of conversion come from the religious upheavals of the 1960s and '70s, when youths were unexpectedly joining new religious movements and conservative groups were seemingly on the rise. Among the best of those are the books by Mary Jo Neitz (1987) on the Catholic Charismatic renewal and Lynn Davidman (1991) on the journey of Jewish women into Orthodox communities. In addition to David Smilde's (2007) work in Venezuela, Elizabeth Brusco (1995) has produced excellent analyses of evangelical conversions in Latin America, paying special attention to how family life and gender are transformed. Various Pentecostal groups and offshoots have also grown explosively across Africa and Asia, and that has meant attention to conversion in those settings. Two interesting places to start in the African cases are Nicolette Manglos's (2010) work in Malawi and Andre Droogers's (2001) reflection on the phenomenon in its global context. In China, as Fenggang Yang (2005) has documented, conversion is complicated by political and economic factors but is a widespread phenomenon there, as well. The social processes of identity change are also brought into relief when the "conversion" goes the other way. Both Dianne Vaughn ("uncoupling"; 1986) and Helen Rose Ebaugh (becoming an "ex"; 1988) have done classic studies of what it looks like to leave.

11. C. Wright Mills (1976) famously described the "sociological imagination" as the ability to link personal troubles to historical realities. Biblical studies scholar

Walter Brueggemann (1978) made the link to religious life in his book on the "prophetic imagination."

12. As we have seen, researchers interested in religious practices in social movements have many excellent sources to work with. Marshall Ganz's (2009) study of the California farmworkers is especially attentive to storytelling and includes an important look at the use of Catholic ritual practices. The religious practices of the US civil rights movement have gotten good attention, as well, including the books by sociologist Aldon Morris (1984) and by theologian Charles Marsh (1997).

13. For excellent overviews of recent religious changes in China, including folk religious practice, see the article by Richard Madsen (2011) and the volume edited by David Palmer, Glenn Shive, and Philip Wickeri (2011).

Concluding and Beginning

Methods for Studying Lived Religion

Having explored dozens of examples of what can be learned when we take the complexity and situatedness of religious practice seriously, perhaps you are thinking about doing your own research. If so, there are choices to make and resources to gather. This final chapter is intended as an initial set of suggestions to consider as you decide among the tools available to you. Throughout this book, we have emphasized that there are many ways to study lived religion. You have seen examples from multiple disciplines and multiple modes of analysis. How you proceed will depend on both the question you want to answer and the audience you wish to reach—from a particular scholarly discipline to a broad public.

If your curiosity has been piqued, start by thinking small and close. There are undoubtedly interesting people and places near you, and you may just want to explore what they are doing. What sorts of religious practices are out there, both in religious institutions and out in everyday life? You might pick a place to try out your observational skills, paying attention to all the dimensions of practice outlined in this book. You might also pay attention to the gendered differences you see and the particular cultural context of the practice. That sort of initial descriptive foray is an excellent place to start.

If you want a more serious research project, it's time to expand your methodological repertoire. As we have noted, many authors write detailed accounts of how they did their work. You have perhaps already begun to think about which of the studies you've read about provides a model for something you'd like to do; it's now worth checking that study more closely to see what you can learn.

Venturing out to learn about the religious practices of others is more of a craft in which one apprentices than a skill to be learned by the book.

It helps to read about what others have done, but it is even more helpful to have a mentor and guide to talk with along the way. One never anticipates all the issues from the start, and flexibility will be critical. Think about the skilled researchers you know, and find conversation partners who can help you through the inevitable difficulties.

Most of the methods used by people who study lived religion fall under the umbrella of "qualitative research," and the study of religion can be thought of as an aspect of studying culture; so those are methodological starting points. The book *Measuring Culture* has brought together some of the most innovative scholars in the sociology of culture to reflect on the methodological choices available when studying practices of any kind.

Mohr, John W., Christopher A. Bail, Margaret Frye, Jennifer C. Lena, Omar Lizardo, Terence E. McDonnell, Ann Mische, Iddo Tavory, and Frederick F. Wherry. 2020. *Measuring Culture*. New York: Columbia University Press.

Another good way to start is to familiarize yourself with one or more of the excellent comprehensive handbooks that can guide you from design to analysis to writing. Annette Lareau has provided an excellent new summary of the process, while several older handbooks are among the most trusted guides.

Denzin, Norman, and Yvonna S. Lincoln, eds. 2011. *Sage Handbook of Qualitative Research*. Thousand Oaks, CA: Sage.
Lareau, Annette. 2021. *Listening to People: A Practical Guide to Interviewing, Participant Observation, Data Analysis, and Writing It All Up*. Chicago: University of Chicago Press.
Ragin, Charles C., and Lisa M. Amoroso. 2011. *Constructing Social Research: The Unity and Diversity of Method*. Thousand Oaks, CA: Pine Forge.
Seale, Clive, Giampietro Gobo, Jaber F. Gubrium, and David Silverman. 2004. *Qualitative Research Practice*. London: Sage.

Each of these handbooks contains many articles by experienced researchers, and they cover most of the specific methods we will discuss throughout this chapter.

Who and Where?

One of the first questions you will confront is "sample selection." That is, whom will you study? That obviously starts with determining the questions you want to answer and the practices that will be your focus, but choosing where to locate yourself for a study that involves in-person observation and conversation is different from choosing a sample for a survey. The latter is likely to be governed by procedures of random selection that are not easy to replicate when it's just you and your eyes and ears (or even a small team working together). It can nevertheless be useful to think about the logic behind the procedures that produce a "representative" sample. How will you know that you are covering the range of differences you need to see?

Deciding whom and where to study is always a matter of both substantive and practical significance. You want to have opportunities to learn about specific things, but you will also have to determine how many interviews you have time for and how many sites you can visit for how long, how many websites you can follow and analyze or how many texts you can gather, and so on. You will also need to build in the difficulties of contacting and arranging appointments with interviewees, the sporadic nature of some kinds of events, and other contingencies. And don't forget that those interviews will have to be transcribed and coded. All that will have to happen long before you ever outline your first bit of writing.

The practical realities have to be balanced with the substantive focus of your study. Too many people settle for a "convenience sample" that is not well suited to the questions at hand. Not only do you need to situate yourself so that you can see the relevant practices "in action," but you also need to think about what kinds of social factors you want to be able to weigh as you do your analysis. Do you want to be able to talk about gendered differences? Then you need to be able to observe and talk with *both* men and women (and depending on your questions, trans and queer people, as well). Do you want to be able to talk about the effects of education? Then it will help to have educational variation in your sample. A quantitative model might posit that for every year of additional education, people are more or less likely to engage in a given practice. The practicalities of direct observation often mean that we can't account for that kind of fine-grained assertion (and it is frankly not especially helpful anyway). What we can do, however, is show in intimate detail how differences in something like education show up in how people practice religion—but only if our sample includes those differences.

Sampling is not just an issue for people who are interviewing and observing. Historians who work with documents and artifacts from the past have to think about their sources and about who is and is not present in the texts they study. Whose words and possessions were considered worthy of preserving? And what has been the role of institutions in archiving this material? Who is visible, and what counts as "evidence"? Both Bonnie Smith and Joan Scott have written critical reflections on those questions and, in the process, provided lots of help in thinking about what historians do.

Scott, Joan W. 1991. "The Evidence of Experience." *Critical Inquiry* 17 (4): 773–797.
Smith, Bonnie G. 1998. *The Gender of History: Men, Women, and Historical Practice.*
    Cambridge, MA: Harvard University Press.

People who study contemporary texts from the internet face a similar question—compounded by the sheer volume of material available to analyze. Who produces these texts, and what interests do they serve? Is the volume of data really reflective of the size and influence of a given group?

Being Aware of Your Own Position

No matter the form of the data, it will also be important to consider your own position relative to the people you will study. Researchers looking back in time also face a cultural gulf in understanding. Researchers of every sort need "reflexivity." We need to analyze our own presence and experiences right alongside our analysis of others. That is especially important when we belong to social groups that have had difficult histories with the groups we are studying, whether that is a history of colonization or a history of racism or a history of patriarchy or interreligious conflict. Even if we have managed to come to terms with our own privilege, that does not change the reality that we will be perceived—at least initially—as part of that dominant group. The research itself is likely to change us, and reflecting on how that unfolds is an important part of the research process. Still, as Charlotte Davies outlines in her book on "reflexive ethnography," it is also important to do this work without falling into the trap of a "radical reflexivity" that ends up eclipsing the voices of others in the shadow of our own ruminations.

Davies, Charlotte Aull. 2008. *Reflexive Ethnography: A Guide to Researching Selves and Others*. 2nd ed. New York: Routledge.

Studying lived religion, then, means having a disciplined awareness of how mutual perceptions and different positions in society shape what we see and hear, something that is explored well in a book edited by James Spickard, Shawn Landres, and Meredith McGuire. Several of those essays give attention to the role of feminism in shaping this kind of critical stance toward our own work, and James Spickard's later work extends that critical lens to include our place in the cultural world order.

Spickard, James V., J. Shawn Landres, and Meredith McGuire, eds. 2002. *Personal Knowledge and Beyond: Reshaping the Ethnography of Religion*. New York: New York University Press.
Spickard, James V. 2017. *Alternative Sociologies of Religion: Through Non-Western Eyes*. New York: New York University Press.

Into the Field: Participant Observation

Participant observation is the most common method chosen by students of lived religion. Being directly present as a practice is being enacted allows the researcher access to the sensory and kinetic experiences of the moment, as well as what is said and the material spaces and objects that are used. The researcher can often reflect on their own experience, as well as observing what others are doing.

That is never sufficient, however. We can never infer that others are feeling what we are feeling. Nor can we assume that everyone in a place is experiencing the same thing. Nor can we account for the people and things that are absent. Paying attention to absence can send us to other sites and occasions to fill in the gaps. Tapping the range of different experiences is likely to require interviewing. And checking the meanings we are inferring from our own perceptions is likely to require a set of cultural guides—people we come to trust as informants, who can explain the things we find mysterious and correct us when we make assumptions.

Methods of recording observations will vary depending on the constraints of the setting. In many situations, it is perfectly possible to jot notes as things happen. In other situations, the notes have to wait for a later moment. In still other situations, sound and video recording may add layers of data. No matter how you record the moment, always turn your memories and notes into a full-fledged set of field notes as soon as possible. A good rule of thumb is "never sleep on your notes." Even one night's sleep will begin to shift how you remember what happened.

People have been writing about the craft of participant observation for a long time, so there are some classic guides. Two of my favorites are these:

Jorgensen, Danny L. 1989. *Participant Observation: A Methodology for Human Studies.* Newbury Park, CA: Sage.

Lofland, John, and Lyn H. Lofland. 1984. *Analyzing Social Settings: A Guide to Qualitative Observation and Analysis.* Belmont, CA: Wadsworth.

In addition, of course, the methodological handbooks noted earlier include many articles that can be helpful. And if your "site" is actually on the internet, you will need to think through how that environment will shape your work. Christine Hine's book may be helpful for that.

Hine, Christine. 2015. *Ethnography for the Internet: Embedded, Embodied and Everyday.* London: Bloomsbury.

Talking to People

Interviewing is at least as common as direct observation in the study of lived religion. When we need accounts of things we can't have direct access to—or explanations of things we did observe—words have to suffice. While a direct face-to-face conversation may be the most common way to find out about what people do and experience in their religious practices, visual communications platforms like Skype and Zoom are now highly satisfactory alternatives when in-person meetings are not possible (and they may offer the advantage of built-in recording and transcribing).

Researchers also sometimes talk with people in small groups, taking advantage of the way people can prompt each other with recollections and details. There are challenges in taking this tack, however. The balance between paying attention and making a record of the conversation is always difficult, but it is doubly so when you are moderating a group conversation. Whatever recording device(s) you use will also have to be especially sensitive so that speakers can be identified. In addition, groups can often engender as much silence as conversation. Sensitive topics or underlying tensions may be better explored individually than in a setting where others are present. George Kamberelis and Greg Dimitriadis are good guides if you are thinking about using focus groups.

Kamberelis, George, and Greg Dimitriadis. 2013. *Focus Groups: From Structured Interviews to Collective Conversations*. London: Taylor and Francis.

Whatever means you use for communicating, you will need to have a clear but flexible strategy for asking your questions. Write them out in advance and practice, but be ready to rephrase and explain. It helps to have a condensed version of your interview guide handy so that you can easily remind yourself of what has and hasn't already been covered. There is no need to ask every question in exactly the same way and in the same order. In fact, people often answer some of your questions without you ever asking them. The more like a conversation it is, the more likely you are to hear stories in the participant's own frame. However, as every guide to interviewing will caution, what we get in an interview is very much an "account." It emerges from an interaction between two (or more) people, and their relationship and perceptions of each other matter. Words are never just words, nor are they self-explanatory.

One of the biggest temptations of interviewers is to ask questions that invite people to analyze their own behavior (rather than reporting it) in terms of some concept or category that is strange to them but native to the researcher. Sociologists ask about alienation or cohesion. Psychologists ask about anxiety or trauma. Theologians ask about redemption or ecclesiology. The challenge of interviewing is to know enough about your interlocutor's culture to ask your questions in their language. That usually means that some sort of preliminary exploration is advisable before encountering your first interview participant. And when you do have that first conversation, asking about actions and events is likely to tell you more than probing for interpretations.

All of this is covered in helpful detail in these guides:

Clandinin, D. Jean, and F. Michael Connelly. 2000. *Narrative Inquiry: Experience and Story in Qualitative Research*. San Francisco: Jossey-Bass.

Gerson, Kathleen, and Sarah Damaske. 2020. *The Science and Art of Interviewing*. New York: Oxford University Press.

Weiss, Robert S. 1995. *Learning from Strangers: The Art and Method of Qualitative Interview Studies*. New York: Free Press.

Getting Closer to the Everyday

Lived religion research asks what people are actually doing, and a variety of methods have emerged in recent years that allow students to get just a little closer to everyday practices. There are many things that we might not be able to observe and that might not make it into someone's answer when asked a general question in an interview. In our "spiritual narratives" project (Ammerman 2013a), we asked people to keep an oral diary. We gave them a recorder and a set of prompts and invited them to take us along as they went about their daily activities. We found that this kind of data-gathering effort worked best after we already had a relationship with a participant who could then imagine the person they were communicating with, even when we weren't there. There is more detail in this summary article:

Ammerman, Nancy T., and Roman R. Williams. 2012. "Speaking of Methods: Eliciting Religious Narratives through Interviews, Photos, and Oral Diaries." In *Annual Review of the Sociology of Religion: New Methods in Sociology of Religion*, edited by Luigi Berzano and Ole Riis, 117–134. Leiden: Brill.

A variation on those oral diaries is an email diary, a technique used by Paula Pryce (2018) in her study of contemplative practice. For people who are scattered and are comfortable with writing about their experiences, a set of routine questions about daily activities can provide rich insight into practices that might otherwise go under the radar. If you include prompts about the multiple dimensions of practice, you may find this especially fruitful. Material surroundings, emotions, and the like may be more easily recounted when the experience is fresh.

A more high-tech variation comes in the form of "time diaries" and using prompts that arrive via mobile phone. Researchers can ask participants to report on what they are doing in the moment to trace out when and where practices may be typically happening. If you are curious, you can look at these examples:

Bouma, Gary D., and Dan Lennon. 2003. "Estimating the Extent of Religious and Spiritual Activity in Australia Using Time-Budget Data." *Journal for the Scientific Study of Religion* 42 (1): 107–112.

Kucinskas, Jaime, Bradley R. E. Wright, D. Matthew Ray, and John Ortberg. 2017. "States of Spiritual Awareness by Time, Activity, and Social Interaction." *Journal for the Scientific Study of Religion* 56 (2): 418–437.

Visual Methods

Among the most exciting developments in lived religion research is the ability to incorporate a variety of visual methods. These vary from using visual means of data capture to supplement your note taking to inviting participants to create and curate their own visual archive. Photos are especially important in accessing the material dimension of practice. Participants can visually take us to see things and tell us stories about what happens there. This is called "photo elicitation" because talking together about a picture almost always elicits details about religious practice that might not emerge any other way.

A creative variation on this method was adopted by Gustavo Morello and his colleagues (2019) in their study of lived religion in three Latin American cities. They invited participants to bring a significant object with them to an interview, and if that object couldn't easily be brought, a photo substituted. Nor should we forget the visual presentations that many people make with their bodies, through tattoos, jewelry, and other adornment. Collecting images (with permission, of course) may be a rewarding part of your study; asking people to tell the stories behind the images is one of the most fruitful methods for learning about lived religious practice.

In other cases, such as Janet Jacobs's (2010) study of Holocaust memorials, the researcher may be the photographer, using both the images and the experience of encountering things and places to analyze the emotional and moral and aesthetic dimensions of the practices of remembering. Sources for exploring these visual methods include these:

Stanczak, Gregory C. 2007. *Visual Research Methods: Image, Society, and Representation.* Los Angeles: Sage.

Williams, Roman R., ed. 2015. *Seeing Religion: Toward a Visual Sociology of Religion.* London: Routledge.

One other kind of visualization is the spatial visualization that techniques such as Google Maps and geographic information systems (GIS) coding make possible. Location-tagged information is now a routine part of daily life for anyone who carries a smartphone, and that means that this "geoweb" can be both a source of data and an aspect of the materiality of practice. Sites of practices can be mapped and overlaid with representations of a variety of other aspects of the social environment. The study of lived religion has in fact blossomed in the field of geography, with Wilbur Zelinsky and Kim Knott as key contributors, but the more technical methods involved in GIS analysis are still relatively rare in the study of religion. David Bodenhamer was an early advocate, and his study with Etan Diamond of Indianapolis churches is an example that can pique your imagination about the possibilities.

Diamond, Etan, and David J. Bodenhamer. 2001. "Race and the Decline of Mainline Protestantism in American Cities: A GIS Analysis of Indianapolis in the 1950s." *History & Computing* 13 (1): 25–44.

Knott, Kim. 1998. "Issues in the Study of Religions and Locality." *Method and Theory in the Study of Religion* 10:279–290.

Zelinsky, Wilbur. 2001. "The Uniqueness of the American Religious Landscape." *Geographical Review* 91 (3): 565–585.

Analyzing Texts

As we have already noted, many students of lived religion begin with texts. Some of those are historical documents, such as sermons, diaries, newspapers and magazines, and various records of what people in another time and place were doing. Similarly, contemporary religious practices sometimes take the form of texts—journals, blogs, and devotional books, as well as the written records of religious groups. Any of these can be brought into our explorations of lived religious practices. The act of producing a religious text is itself a practice to be examined, as is the act of using it. But often, we want to know about the shared knowledge and patterns of action the texts themselves depict. Those explorations can be accomplished through various forms of content analysis.

Although many studies seem to casually invoke this method, it requires more rigor than a mere impressionistic reading. You should think about all the questions of representativeness and sampling that we have already noted but also about what concepts will guide your study and how you will look for evidence in the texts. Will it be found in specific words, in kinds of words (referring to spiritual things, for example), in themes found in larger units of text (paragraphs and longer)? You can find a good basic guide in the book by Klaus Krippendorff, and Kimberly Neuendorf's book goes a bit farther in treating electronic texts and computer-assisted analysis.

Krippendorff, Klaus. 2019. *Content Analysis: An Introduction to Its Methodology*. Thousand Oaks, CA: Sage.
Neuendorf, Kimberly A. 2017. *The Content Analysis Guidebook*. Thousand Oaks, CA: Sage.

It has become increasingly common to assemble very large bodies of texts with which it is possible to perform various forms of digital analyses. Huge digital archives have gathered texts of all sorts, making them available for researchers. Across the humanities, this sort of work is becoming more common, and it is worth considering what we might learn about everyday religious practice by these means. One could simply explore the frequency of a word or phrase over time, using Google's Ngram (https://books.google.com/ngrams). But digital archives such as Internet Archive (https://archive.org/index.php, including its "Wayback Machine" archive of websites) and Hathi Trust (www.hathitrust.org/) offer much richer possibilities. In addition, it is possible to "scrape" social media content to gain a body of user-generated data reflecting everyday thoughts and actions.

If you venture into these kinds of analyses, you may be tempted to let the technical possibilities take over, but if you keep your own questions at the fore, you may find that studying a large group of texts can help you see patterns that would not otherwise be apparent. These sources can help you get started and keep your perspective:

Berry, David M. 2012. *Understanding Digital Humanities*. London: Palgrave Macmillan.
Gold, Matthew K., and Lauren F. Klein, eds. 2016. *Debates in the Digital Humanities 2016*. Minneapolis: University of Minnesota Press.

Analyzing Your Own Texts

For ethnographers, the texts in question include field notes and journal entries and, of course, interview transcripts. For a generation now, we have had increasingly good data-analysis software to help us find and document the patterns we are seeing (or not seeing) in the field. Whether you use MaxQDA, nVivo, AtlasTi, or some other package, the process of analysis is similar. As you review your notes and what people have said to you, you will look for themes and mark the relevant text. That's the process we call "coding." You may start with a set of categories you are looking for—gender assumptions, descriptions of the deity, emotional gestures, physical movement, and the like. As you read and code, those categories will expand and become more nuanced, and in the end, you will be able to sort and countersort on those categories. You can extract, for example, the sections of text that are about women and contain accounts of ecstatic spiritual experiences and then compare them to the sections that are about men. Often you may even want to quantify—how many older people compared to how many younger people report a particular aesthetic judgment? By keeping track of the social "attributes" of the people whom your notes and texts describe, you have opportunities to carefully check your own hunches about how patterns of practice may differ across the social groups you are studying. There are excellent guides for doing this work. Among the most trusted are these:

Charmaz, Kathy. 2014. *Constructing Grounded Theory*. Thousand Oaks, CA: Sage.
Miles, Matthew B., and A. Michael Huberman. 1994. *Qualitative Data Analysis*. Thousand Oaks, CA: Sage.

Surveying Larger Populations

Surveys need not be abandoned in the study of lived religious practice, especially if we encourage cooperation between qualitative and quantitative researchers. If a survey asks good questions, it can provide valuable insight into the prevalence and systematic variation in lived religious practice. Lisa Pearce (2002) reflected on her own experience moving between her ethnographic observations and the creation of questions that could give her a bigger picture of religion and childbearing in Nepal. Two exemplary US examples of qualitative research informing a large-scale survey are the study of spirituality undertaken by Brian Steensland and his colleagues and the study of congregations developed by Mark Chaves (full details at the interactive website https://sites.duke.edu/ncsweb/.)

Steensland, Brian, Xiaoyun Wang, and Lauren Chism Schmidt. 2018. "Spirituality: What Does It Mean and to Whom?" *Journal for the Scientific Study of Religion* 57 (3): 450–472.

Exploring Mind and Body

Among the newest entrants into the study of lived religion are the researchers who situate themselves in cognitive science and related efforts to measure biological aspects of religious experience. While an MRI or oxytocin levels may not be able to provide a full account of what is happening in a religious practice, these studies can be an interesting adjunct, especially when we are asking about the emotional or cognitive dimensions of what we are seeing. As we noted in chapter 3, Kate Stockly (2020) has provided a good overview of the relationship between biological research and other studies of the emotional dimensions of religious experience.

One of the pioneering centers for this work is the Center for Mind and Culture in Boston (http://mindandculture.org). Among its projects is one that seeks to quantify religious experience by using an "Enhanced Phenomenology of Consciousness Inventory."

Putting Research to Work

Finally, what about the implications of our work for policy and social change? Many people who study lived religion do so as "action research." They often start with concerns that arise from a community, formulate their questions and strategies in conversation with community participants, and hope that their findings will help communities make positive changes. Strategic changes in religious practice are often the goal of practical theologians, for example. This work should be no less guided by rigorous considerations of sample selection and attention to how we gather and analyze data, but the questions and the reasons for asking are distinct. People who study religion and health often want to see more effective health-care practices. People who study religion and human rights want to see new policies that advance liberty and security. Religious leaders and theologians want to see individuals and religious communities thrive. Among the practical theologians who have thought carefully about this subject are Elaine Graham and Mary Moschella, along with the authors in the book edited by Dale Andrews and Robert London.

Andrews, Dale P., and Robert London Smith, Jr., eds. 2015. *Black Practical Theology.* Waco, TX: Baylor University Press.

Graham, Elaine. 2013. "Is Practical Theology a Form of 'Action Research'?" *International Journal of Practical Theology* 17: 148–178.

Moschella, Mary Clark. 2008. *Ethnography as a Pastoral Practice.* New York: Pilgrim.

Even if your study is not explicitly aimed at practical changes, every student of lived religion has an obligation to treat individuals and communities with respect and to communicate what we find in ways that advance human understanding. If religious practice is an integral part of many human lives, all of us can benefit when we see and learn from the practices of the myriad religious communities around the world.

ACKNOWLEDGMENTS

This book has emerged out of dozens of years of conversation and reading and observing, and the people who have been part of that form a much wider circle than I will be able to acknowledge here. I want to start where many acknowledgments end, with my family. My husband, Jack Ammerman, has heard about this stuff over more dinner tables than he'd probably like to remember, but what I remember is that he so faithfully and spectacularly fills those dinner tables with great food and deep love. Abbey Ammerman long since moved out into her own life, but I'm incredibly fortunate that she is the best friend a mom could want and a regular booster who seems to think what I do is interesting.

As these ideas have percolated, I've had wonderful opportunities to present them to students and colleagues. Harvard's Culture Workshop, Boston University's "Pizza and Politics" group, the IUPUI "Social Dimensions of Spirituality" conference, and the Religion and Society group at Uppsala University were among the places where smart questions pushed my thinking. I've also tried out ideas in talks at the Nordic Sociology of Religion conference and the Society for the Scientific Study of Religion; in colloquies at Boston College, the University of Massachusetts, Notre Dame, and Purdue; at the UK Conference on Congregational Music; and as my Morris Lecture to my own Sociology Department at Boston University. Each group helped me find the things that were the most important to say.

During these years, my own students have challenged and encouraged me, and their work has found its way into what I have written here. My participation in the Nordic "Religion-Values-Society" Program has especially stretched my intellectual and geographic horizons in highly productive ways. Director Geir Afdal's own writing on practice theory came at just the right moment to help me sharpen my own ideas. Working with students whose research stretched from Siberia to India to South Africa and Nigeria and Kazakhstan, to all of the Nordic countries helped me to become even more convinced of the utility of a practice approach to studying religion and of the importance of context.

A key problem I faced in conceiving this book was how to lay out the theoretical framework in sufficient detail without turning it into a theory book. It was a conversation with Mary Jo Neitz that helped me see that I might need a different venue for all that theoretical complexity. Why not a journal article? Then this book could draw on the thinking that went into the article but focus mostly on what we have learned and could better learn about studying lived religion. The resulting article was published in the *American Journal of Sociology* (Ammerman 2020). As I said there, I owe a debt to the people who made that theoretical work possible: Orit Avishai, Kira Ganga Kieffer, Jaime Kucinskas, Nicolette Manglos-Weber, Gerardo Marti, Mary Jo Neitz, Jim Spickard, Brian Steensland, Anna Sun, Steve Warner, and the anonymous AJS reviewers. Yes, even the reviewers pushed and sharpened the argument in extraordinarily helpful ways.

Once I began to draft chapters, I needed the critical eyes of people who know the fields I'm trying to write about. I am incredibly grateful for the generosity of Robert Brenneman, Janet Jacobs, Lance Laird, Mia Lövheim, Nicolette Manglos-Weber, Joyce Mercer, Mary Jo Neitz, Anthony Petro, Paula Pryce, John Schmaltzbauer, and Daniel Winchester. Each read one or more chapters or just answered my questions. They caught lots of mistakes, suggested shifts in focus, and provided suggestions of research to include. I haven't done everything they told me to, but this book is undoubtedly better for their attention to it.

I also got helpful advice from the reviewers to which NYU Press sent the almost final manuscript, as well as from editor Jennifer Hammer. In fact, Jennifer deserves an award for the vision she has had for this book and for her patience over many years as my teaching and administrative duties kept me from making any progress on actually producing it.

The vast majority of my research and writing on this project has taken place from home. Initially that was just because I finally retired and didn't have to go to campus every day. But in the final months, "WFH" became a necessity for all of us. Because of the coronavirus pandemic, I could no longer make occasional forays to the BU Library, so I became largely dependent on what was available online. I am incredibly grateful for JSTOR and Wiley and all the organizations that make remote access possible. Most especially, I'm grateful for ProQuest's e-books. It is no exaggeration to say that this book would not exist without all of them.

In my previous books, there have been organizations and participants to thank for their generous welcome as I asked them questions and observed their activities. In this book, that acknowledgment is indirect. Hundreds and thousands of people have welcomed dozens and dozens of observers into their lives, and it is those insights that populate these pages. My gratitude, then, is both to those communities and to the students of lived religion from whom I've been learning over these years. This book is both a tribute to what you have taught us and an invitation to the others who are about to follow in our footsteps. And judging from the young scholars I've seen emerging on Twitter, your numbers are legion. It is more than gratifying to see the study of religion gaining such good attention and to see the horizons of our inquiries continue to expand. I'm only sorry I couldn't squeeze in all the great new work that is coming along. I look forward to continuing to learn from you all.

REFERENCES

Abbington, James. 2001. *Let Mt. Zion Rejoice! Music in the African American Church.* Valley Forge, PA: Judson.

Abu-Ghazaleh, Faida N. 2011. *Ethnic Identity of Palestinian Immigrants in the United States: The Role of Cultural Material Artifacts.* El Paso, TX: LFB.

Abu-Lughod, Lila. 2002. "Do Muslim Women Really Need Saving? Anthropological Reflections on Cultural Relativism and its Others." *American Anthropologist* 104 (3): 783–790.

Ahmed, Sara. 2014. *The Cultural Politics of Emotion.* 2nd ed. Edinburgh: Edinburgh University Press.

Albanese, Catherine L. 1990. *Nature Religion in America: From the Algonkian Indians to the New Age.* Chicago: University of Chicago Press.

Alexander, Jeffrey C., Dominik Bartmanski, and Bernhard Giesen, eds. 2012. *Iconic Power: Materiality and Meaning in Social Life.* New York: Palgrave Macmillan.

Alimen, Nazli. 2018. *Faith and Fashion in Turkey.* London: I. B. Tauris.

Allahyari, Rebecca Anne. 2001. *Visions of Charity: Volunteer Workers and Moral Community.* Berkeley: University of California Press.

Ammerman, Nancy T. 1997a. *Congregation and Community.* New Brunswick, NJ: Rutgers University Press.

———. 1997b. "Golden Rule Christianity: Lived Religion in the American Mainstream." In *Lived Religion in America: Toward a History of Practice*, edited by David Hall, 196–216. Princeton, NJ: Princeton University Press.

———. 1998. "Culture and Identity in the Congregation." In *Studying Congregations: A New Handbook*, edited by Nancy T. Ammerman, Jackson Carroll, Carl Dudley, and William McKinney, 78–104. Nashville: Abingdon.

———. 2003. "Religious Identities and Religious Institutions." In *Handbook of the Sociology of Religion*, edited by Michele Dillon, 207–224. Cambridge: Cambridge University Press.

———. 2005. *Pillars of Faith: American Congregations and Their Partners.* Berkeley.: University of California Press.

———. 2013a. *Sacred Stories, Spiritual Tribes: Finding Religion in Everyday Life.* New York: Oxford University Press.

———. 2013b. "Spiritual but Not Religious? Beyond Binary Choices in the Study of Religion." *Journal for the Scientific Study of Religion* 52 (2): 258–278.

———. 2016. "Lived Religion as an Emerging Field: An Assessment of Its Contours and Frontiers." *Nordic Journal of Religion and Society* 29 (2): 83–99.

——. 2020. "Rethinking Religion: Toward a Practice Approach." *American Journal of Sociology* 126 (1): 6–51.

Andersson, Ruben. 2016. "Here Be Dragons: Mapping an Ethnography of Global Danger." *Current Anthropology* 57 (6): 707–731.

Annear, Steve. 2019. "'We Have Found the "Wow" Child!': Handel and Haydn Society Tracks Down Enthusiastic Concertgoer." *Boston Globe*, May 10, 2019. www.bostonglobe.com.

Appleby, R. Scott. 2000. *The Ambivalence of the Sacred: Religion, Violence, and Reconciliation*. New York: Littlefield.

Asad, Talal. 1993. *Genealogies of Religion: Discipline and Reasons of Power in Christianity and Islam*. Baltimore: Johns Hopkins University Press.

Asamoah-Gyadu, Kwabena. 2007. "'Blowing the Cover': Imaging Religious Functionaries in Ghanaian/Nigerian Films." In *Religion, Media, and the Marketplace*, edited by Lynn Schofield Clark, 224–243. New Brunswick, NJ: Rutgers University Press.

——. 2010. "Mediating Spiritual Power: African Christianity, Transnationalism and the Media." In *Religion Crossing Boundaries: Transnational Religious and Social Dynamics in Africa and the new African Diaspora*, edited by Afe Adogame and James V. Spickard, 87–106. Leiden: Brill.

Aune, Kristin. 2015. "Feminist Spirituality as Lived Religion: How UK Feminists Forge Religio-spiritual Lives." *Gender & Society* 29 (1): 122–145. doi:10.1177/0891243214545681.

Avishai, Orit. 2008. "Halakhic Niddah Consultants and the Orthodox Women's Movement in Israel: Evaluating the Story of Enlightened Progress." *Journal of Modern Jewish Studies* 7 (2): 195–216. doi:10.1080/14725880802124214.

Avishai, Orit, Afshan Jafar, and Rachel Rinaldo. 2015. "A Gender Lens on Religion." *Gender & Society* 29 (1): 5–25. doi:10.1177/0891243214548920.

Badaracco, Claire Hoertz, ed. 2005. *Quoting God: How Media Shape Ideas about Religion and Culture*. Waco, TX: Baylor University Press.

Baird, Ian G. 2009. "Identities and Space: The Geographies of Religious Change amongst the Brao in Northeastern Cambodia." *Anthropos* 104 (2): 457–468.

Barbalet, Jack. 2002. "Introduction: Why Emotions Are Crucial." *Sociological Review* 50 (S2): 1–9. doi:10.1111/j.1467-954X.2002.tb03588.x.

Barker, Eileen. 1984. *The Making of a Moonie: Choice or Brainwashing?* Oxford, UK: Blackwell.

Barnes, Linda, and Susan Sered, eds. 2004. *Religion and Healing in America*. New York: Oxford University Press.

Barnes, Sandra L. 2005. "Black Church Culture and Community Action." *Social Forces* 84 (2): 967–994.

Barr, Beth Allison. 2021. *The Making of Biblical Womanhood: How the Subjugation of Women Became Gospel Truth*. Waco, TX: Brazos.

Bartkowski, John. 2000. "Breaking Walls, Raising Fences: Masculinity, Intimacy, and Accountability among the Promise Keepers." *Sociology of Religion* 61 (1): 33–53.

Barton, Bernadette. 2012. *Pray the Gay Away: The Extraordinary Lives of Bible Belt Gays*. New York: New York University Press.

Bass, Dorothy C., ed. 1997. *Practicing Our Faith: A Way of Life for Searching People*. San Francisco: Jossey-Bass.

Bass, Dorothy C., and Craig Dykstra, eds. 2008. *For Life Abundant: Practical Theology, Theological Education, and Christian Ministry*. Grand Rapids, MI: Eerdmans.

Beamon, Benae. 2020. "Black Trans Women and Ploughing: Ethical Resistance and Postures for Life." PhD diss., Religious Studies, Boston University.

Beckford, James. 1985. *Cult Controversies: The Societal Response to New Religious Movements*. London: Tavistock.

———. 2003. *Social Theory and Religion*. New York: Cambridge University Press.

Bell, Catherine. 1997. *Ritual: Perspectives and Dimensions*. New York: Oxford University Press.

Bellah, Robert N. 1963. "Religious Evolution." In *Beyond Belief*, 20–50. Boston: Beacon.

———. 2011. *Religion in Human Evolution: From the Paleolithic to the Axial Age*. Cambridge, MA: Harvard University Press.

Bellah, Robert N., Richard Madsen, William M. Sullivan, Ann Swidler, and Steven M. Tipton. 1985. *Habits of the Heart*. Berkeley: University of California Press.

Bender, Courtney. 2010. *The New Metaphysicals: Spirituality and the American Religious Imagination*. Chicago: University of Chicago Press.

Bender, Courtney, Wendy Cadge, Peggy Levitt, and David A. Smilde, eds. 2012. *Religion on the Edge: De-centering and Re-centering the Sociology of Religion*. New York: Oxford University Press.

Berger, Peter L. 1967. *The Sacred Canopy*. Garden City, NY: Anchor Doubleday.

———. 1970. *A Rumor of Angels: Modern Society and the Rediscovery of the Supernatural*. Garden City, NY: Anchor.

———. 1997. *Redeeming Laughter: The Comic Dimension of Human Experience*. New York: De Gruyter.

———. 2014. *The Many Altars of Modernity: Toward a Paradigm for Religion in a Pluralist Age*. Boston: De Gruyter.

Berghuijs, Joantine, Jos Pieper, and Cok Bakker. 2013. "Conceptions of Spirituality among the Dutch Population." *Archive for the Psychology of Religion* 35 (3): 369–397. doi:10.1163/15736121-12341272.

Berns, Steph. 2016. "In Defense of the Dead: Materializing a Garden of Remembrance in South London." *Material Religion* 12 (2): 165–188. doi:10.1080/17432200.2016.1172759.

Berrelleza, Erick. 2020. "Exclusion in Upscaling Institutions: The Reproduction of Neighborhood Segregation in an Urban Church." *City and Community* 19. doi:10.1111/cico.12474.

Bivens, Jason C. 2008. *Religion of Fear: The Politics of Horror in Conservative Evangelicalism*. New York: Oxford University Press.

Bourdieu, Pierre. 1990. *The Logic of Practice*. Stanford, CA: Stanford University Press.

———. 1991. *Language and Symbolic Power*. Cambridge, MA: Harvard University Press.

———. 1993. *The Field of Cultural Production: Essays on Art and Literature*. New York: Columbia University Press.

Brasher, Brenda E. 1998. *Godly Women: Fundamentalism and Female Power*. New Brunswick, NJ: Rutgers University Press.

Bratton, Susan Power. 2012. *The Spirit of the Appalachian Trail: Community, Environment, and Belief*. Knoxville: University of Tennessee Press.

Braunstein, Ruth. 2012. "Storytelling in Liberal Religious Advocacy." *Journal for the Scientific Study of Religion* 51 (1): 110–127. doi:10.1111/j.1468–5906.2012.01634.x.

———. 2019. "Muslims as Outsiders, Enemies, and Others: The 2016 Presidential Election and the Politics of Religious Exclusion." In *Politics of Meaning/Meaning of Politics*, edited by Jason L. Mast and Jeffrey Alexander, 185–206. New York: Palgrave Macmillan.

Braunstein, Ruth, Todd Nicholas Fuist, and Rhys Williams, eds. 2017. *Religion and Progressive Activism: New Stories about Faith and Politics*. New York: New York University Press.

Braunstein, Ruth, Brad R. Fulton, and Richard L. Wood. 2014. "The Role of Bridging Cultural Practices in Racially and Socioeconomically Diverse Civic Organizations." *American Sociological Review* 79 (4): 705–725. doi:10.1177/0003122414538966.

Bremborg, Anna Davidsson. 2013. "Creating Sacred Space by Walking in Silence: Pilgrimage in a Late Modern Lutheran Context." *Social Compass* 60 (4): 544–560. doi:10.1177/0037768613503092.

Brenneman, Robert, and Brian J. Miller. 2020. *Building Faith: A Sociology of Religious Structures*. New York: Oxford University Press.

Brewer, John D., and Gareth I. Higgins. 1999. "Understanding Anti-Catholicism in Northern Ireland." *Sociology* 33 (2): 235–255. doi:10.1177/S0038038599000152.

Brown, Carolynne H. 2009. "Singing through Struggle: Music as a Mode of Cultural Exchange in African American Border City Churches after Emancipation, 1862–1890." ThD diss., Boston University School of Theology.

Brown, Michael F. 2002. "Moving toward the Light: Self, Other, and the Politics of Experience in New Age Narratives." In *Stories of Change: Narrative and Social Movements*, edited by Joseph E. Davis, 101–122. Albany: State University of New York Press.

Browning, Donald S. 1991. *A Fundamental Practical Theology*. Minneapolis: Fortress.

Bruce, Steve. 2011. *Secularization: In Defence of an Unfashionable Theory*. New York: Oxford University Press.

Brueggemann, Walter. 1978. *The Prophetic Imagination*. Philadelphia: Fortress.

Brusco, Elizabeth E. 1995. *The Reformation of Machismo: Evangelical Conversion and Gender in Colombia*. Austin: University of Texas Press.

Buggeln, Gretchen T. 2001. "Architecture as Community Service." In *The Visual Culture of American Religions*, edited by David Morgan and Sally M. Promey, 87–101. Berkeley: University of California Press.

Burke, Kelsy. 2016. *Christians under Covers: Evangelicals and Sexual Pleasure on the Internet*. Berkeley: University of California Press.

Burke, Kelsy, and Amy Moff Hudec. 2015. "Sexual Encounters and Manhood Acts: Evangelicals, Latter-Day Saints, and Religious Masculinities." *Journal for the Scientific Study of Religion* 54 (2): 330–344. doi:10.1111/jssr.12182.

Burkitt, Ian. 2012. "Emotional Reflexivity: Feeling, Emotion and Imagination in Reflexive Dialogues." *Sociology* 46 (3): 458–472. doi:10.1177/0038038511422587.

Butler, Anthea. 2011. *Women in the Church of God in Christ: Making a Sanctified World.* Chapel Hill: University of North Carolina Press.

Cadge, Wendy. 2013. *Paging God: Religion in the Halls of Medicine.* Chicago: University of Chicago Press.

Callahan, Richard J., Jr. 2009. *Work and Faith in the Kentucky Coal Fields: Subject to Dust.* Bloomington: Indiana University Press.

Campbell, Heidi A., ed. 2013. *Digital Religion: Understanding Religion in a New Media World.* New York: Routledge.

Campbell, Heidi A., and Michael W. DeLashmutt. 2014. "Studying Technology and Ecclesiology in Online Multi-site Worship." *Journal of Contemporary Religion* 29 (2): 267–285. doi:10.1080/13537903.2014.903662.

Carrette, Jeremy R. 1999. "Prologue to a Confession of the Flesh." In *Religion and Culture: Michel Foucault,* edited by Jeremy R. Carrett, 1–47. New York: Routledge.

Carrette, Jeremy R., and Richard King. 2005. *Selling Spirituality: The Silent Takeover of Religion.* London: Routledge.

Casanova, Jose. 1994. *Public Religions in the Modern World.* Chicago: University of Chicago Press.

Cassaniti, Julia L., and Tanya M. Luhrmann. 2014. "The Cultural Kindling of Spiritual Experiences." *Current Anthropology* 55 (S10): S333–S343. doi:10.1086/677881.

Center for Global Christianity and Mission. 2020. "Chinese Christian Posters." Boston University School of Theology. Accessed October 1, 2020. https://ccposters.com/.

Chambers, Paul. 2007. "Contentious Headscarves: Spirituality and the State in the Twenty-First Century." In *A Sociology of Spirituality,* edited by Kieran Flanagan and Peter C. Jupp, 127–144. Aldershot, UK: Ashgate.

Chaudhry, Ayesha S. 2019. "Body." In "A Universe of Terms," *The Immanent Frame,* Social Science Research Council. Accessed March 9, 2020. http://tif.ssrc.org.

Chen, Zhuo, Ralph W. Hood Jr., Lijun Yang, and P. J. Watson. 2011. "Mystical Experience among Tibetan Buddhists: The Common Core Thesis Revisited." *Journal for the Scientific Study of Religion* 50 (2): 328–338. doi:10.1111/j.1468-5906.2011.01570.x.

Cheung, Christopher. 2019. "On Qingming, My Family Tidies the Graves." *The Tyee,* April 5, 2019. https://thetyee.ca.

Chidester, David. 1988. *Salvation and Suicide: An Interpretation of Jim Jones, the Peoples Temple and Jonestown.* Bloomington: Indiana University Press.

———. 1996. *Savage Systems: Colonialism and Comparative Religion in Southern Africa.* Chicago: University of Chicago Press.

Chidester, David, and Edward T. Linenthal. 1995. Introduction to *American Sacred Space,* edited by David Chidester and Edward T. Linenthal, 1–42. Bloomington: Indiana University Press.

Cho, Sumi, Kimberlé Williams Crenshaw, and Leslie McCall. 2013. "Toward a Field of Intersectionality Studies: Theory, Applications, and Praxis." *Signs: Journal of Women in Culture and Society* 38 (4): 785–810. doi:10.1086/669608.

Christerson, Brad, Korie E. Edwards, and Michael O. Emerson. 2005. *Against All Odds: The Struggle for Racial Integration in Religious Organizations*. New York: New York University Press.

Clark, Lynn Schofield. 2003. *From Angels to Aliens: Teenagers, the Media, and the Supernatural*. New York: Oxford University Press.

———, ed. 2007a. *Religion, Media, and the Marketplace*. New Brunswick, NJ: Rutgers University Press.

———. 2007b. "Religion, Twice Removed: Exploring the Role of Media in Religious Understandings among 'Secular' Young People." In *Everyday Religion: Observing Modern Religious Lives*, edited by Nancy T. Ammerman, 69–82. New York: Oxford University Press.

Clark, Lynn Schofield, and Jill Dierberg. 2013. "Digital Storytelling and Collective Religious Identity in a Moderate to Progressive Youth Group." In *Digital Religion*, edited by Heidi Campbell, 147–154. New York: Routledge.

Collins, Randall. 2004. *Interaction Ritual Chains*. Princeton, NJ: Princeton University Press.

Comaroff, Jean. 1991. *Of Revelation and Revolution: Christianity, Colonialism, and Consciousness in South Africa*. Vol. 1. Chicago: University of Chicago Press.

Costen, Melva Wilson. 1999. "African-American Liturgical Music in a Global Context." *Journal of the Interdenominational Theological Center* 27:63–110.

Cowan, Douglas E. 2005. "Online U-Topia: Cyberspace and the Mythology of Placelessness." *Journal for the Scientific Study of Religion* 44 (3): 257–264.

Crenshaw, Kimberlé Williams. 1989. "Demarginalizing the Intersection of Race and Sex: A Black Feminist Critique of Antidiscrimination Doctrine, Feminist Theory and Antiracist Politics." *University of Chicago Legal Forum* 1989:139–167.

Crocker, Elizabeth Thomas. 2017. "Moral Geographies of Diasporic Belonging: Race, Ethnicity, and Identity among Haitian Vodou Practitioners in Boston." PhD diss., Anthropology, Boston University.

Csordas, Thomas J. 1990. "Embodiment as a Paradigm for Anthropology." *Ethos* 18:5–47.

Davalos, Karen Mary. 2002. "'The Real Way of Praying': The Via Crucis, Mexicano Sacred Space, and the Architecture of Domination." In *Horizons of the Sacred: Mexican Traditions in U.S. Catholicism*, edited by Timothy Matovina and Gary Riebe-Estrella, 41–68. Ithaca, NY: Cornell University Press.

Davidman, Lynn. 1991. *Tradition in a Rootless World*. Berkeley: University of California Press.

———. 2015. *Becoming Un-Orthodox: Stories of Ex-Hasidic Jews*. New York: Oxford University Press.

Davie, Grace. 2000. *Religion in Modern Europe: A Memory Mutates*. Oxford: Oxford University Press.

———. 2007. "Vicarious Religion: A Methodological Challenge." In *Everyday Religion: Observing Modern Religious Lives*, edited by Nancy T. Ammerman, 21–36. New York: Oxford University Press.

———. 2015. *Religion in Britain: A Persistent Paradox*. 2nd ed. Malden, MA: Wiley Blackwell.

Davis, Kathy. 1997. "Em-bodying Theory: Beyond Modernist and Postmodernist Readings of the Body." In *Embodied Practices: Feminist Perspectives on the Body*, edited by Kathy Davis, 1–23. Thousand Oaks, CA: Sage.

Day, Abby. 2013. "Varieties of Belief over Time: Reflections from a Longitudinal Study of Youth and Belief." *Journal of Contemporary Religion* 28 (2): 277–293. doi:10.1080/13537903.2013.783339.

———. 2017. *The Religious Lives of Older Laywomen: The Last Active Anglican Generation*. Oxford: Oxford University Press.

Dean, Melanie. 2013. "From 'Evil Eye' Anxiety to the Desirability of Envy: Status, Consumption and the Politics of Visibility in Urban South India." *Contributions to Indian Sociology* 47 (2): 185–216. doi:10.1177/0069966713482999.

de Certeau, Michel 1984. *The Practice of Everyday Life*. Translated by S. Rendall. Berkeley: University of California Press.

Decoteau, Claire Laurier. 2016. "The Reflexive Habitus: Critical Realist and Bourdieusian Social Action." *European Journal of Social Theory* 19 (3): 303–321. doi:10.1177/1368431015590700.

Delehanty, Jack, Penny Edgell, and Evan Stewart. 2018. "Christian America? Secularized Evangelical Discourse and the Boundaries of National Belonging." *Social Forces* 97 (3): 1283–1306. doi:10.1093/sf/soy080.

Diamond, Etan. 2000. *And I Will Dwell in Their Midst: Orthodox Jews in Suburbia*. Chapel Hill: University of North Carolina Press.

DiMaggio, Paul. 1997. "Culture and Cognition." *Annual Review of Sociology* 23:263–287.

DiMaggio, Paul, and John Mohr. 1985. "Cultural Capital, Educational Attainment, and Marital Selection." *American Journal of Sociology* 90 (6): 1231–1257.

Dodson, Jualynne E., and Cheryl Townsend Gilkes. 1995. "There's Nothing Like Church Food." *Journal of the American Academy of Religion* 63:519–538.

Dougherty, Beth L. 2018. "Somatic Coordination: An Ethnography of Religious Entrainment in Christian and Neo-Pagan Rituals." *Sociology of Religion* 79 (1): 108–128. doi:10.1093/socrel/srx054.

Dougherty, Kevin D., and Jerome R. Koch. 2019. "Religious Tattoos at One Christian University." *Visual Studies* 34:311–318. doi:10.1080/1472586X.2019.1687331.

Douglas, Mary. 1966. *Purity and Danger*. London: Routledge and Kegan Paul.

Droogers, Andre. 2001. "Globalisation and Pentecostal Success." In *Between Babel and Pentecost: Transnational Pentecostalism in Africa and Latin America*, edited by Andre Corten and Ruth Marshall-Fratani, 41–61. Bloomington: Indiana University Press.

———. 2014. *Religion at Play*. Eugene, OR: Cascade Books.

DuMez, Kristin Kobes. 2020. *Jesus and John Wayne: How White Evangelicals Corrupted a Faith and Fractured a Nation*. New York: Liveright.

Durkheim, Emile. (1898) 1975. "Individualism and the Intellectuals." In *Durkheim on Religion*, edited by W. S. F. Pickering, 59–73. London: Routledge and Kegan Paul.

———. (1912) 1964. *The Elementary Forms of the Religious Life*. Translated by Joseph Ward Swain. New York: Free Press.

Eade, John, and Michael J. Sallnow. 2000. *Contesting the Sacred: The Anthropology of Pilgrimage*. Urbana: University of Illinois Press.

Ebaugh, Helen Rose. 1988. *Becoming an Ex: The Process of Role Exit*. Chicago: University of Chicago Press.

Ebaugh, Helen Rose, and Janet Saltzman Chafetz, eds. 2000. *Religion and the New Immigrants: Continuities and Adaptations in Immigrant Congregations*. Walnut Creek, CA: AltaMira.

Edgell, Penny. 2012. "A Cultural Sociology of Religion: New Directions." *Annual Review of Sociology* 38:247–265.

Edgell, Penny, Joseph Gerteis, and Douglas Hartmann. 2006. "Atheists as 'Other': Moral Boundaries and Cultural Membership in American Society." *American Sociological Review* 71 (2): 211–234.

Edwards, Korie L. 2008. *The Elusive Dream: The Power of Race in Interracial Churches*. New York: Oxford University Press.

———. 2009. "Race, Religion, and Worship: Are Contemporary African-American Worship Practices Distinct?" *Journal for the Scientific Study of Religion* 48 (1): 30–52.

Edwards, Korie L., and Rebecca Kim. 2019. "Estranged Pioneers: The Case of African American and Asian American Multiracial Church Pastors." *Sociology of Religion* 80 (4): 456–477. doi:10.1093/socrel/sry059.

Eiesland, Nancy. 1994. *The Disabled God: Toward a Liberatory Theology of Disability*. Nashville: Abingdon.

Ellemers, Naomi, Jojanneke van der Toorn, Yavor Paunov, and Thed van Leeuwen. 2019. "The Psychology of Morality: A Review and Analysis of Empirical Studies Published from 1940 through 2017." *Personality and Social Psychology Review* 23 (4): 332–366. doi:10.1177/1088868318811759.

Ellis, Stephen, and Gerrie ter Haar. 2007. "Religion and Politics: Taking African Epistemologies Seriously." *Journal of Modern African Studies* 45 (3): 385–401.

Elver, Hilal. 2012. *The Headscarf Controversy: Secularism and Freedom of Religion*. New York: Oxford University Press.

Emerson, Michael O., and Christian Smith. 2000. *Divided by Faith: Evangelical Religion and the Problem of Race in America*. New York: Oxford University Press.

Emirbayer, Mustafa, and Ann Mische. 1998. "What Is Agency?" *American Journal of Sociology* 103 (4): 962–1023.

Fadiman, Anne. 1997. *The Spirit Catches You and You Fall Down: A Hmong Child, Her American Doctors, and the Collision of Two Cultures*. New York: Farrar, Straus and Giroux.

Fairclough, Norman. 2003. *Analysing Discourse: Textual Analysis for Social Research*. London: Routledge.

Fanon, Frantz. (1963) 1968. *The Wretched of the Earth [Damnes de la terre]*. Translated by Richard Philcox. New York: Grove.

Fetzer Institute. 2020. "Study of Spirituality in the United States." Accessed October 15, 2020. https://spiritualitystudy.fetzer.org/.

Fields, Karen E. 1982. "Charismatic Religion as Popular Protest: The Ordinary and the Extraordinary in Social Movements." *Theory and Society* 11:321–361.

———. 1985. *Revival and Rebellion in Colonial Central Africa*. Princeton, NJ: Princeton University Press.

Finlayson, Caitlin Cihak. 2012. "Spaces of Faith: Incorporating Emotion and Spirituality in Geographic Studies." *Environment and Planning A* 44 (7): 1763–1778.

Fisk, Anna. 2018. "'So That You've Got Something for Yourself': Knitting as Implicit Spirituality." In *Foundations and Futures in the Sociology of Religion*, edited by Luke Doggett and Alp Arat, 133–148. New York: Routledge.

Fogelin, Lars. 2003. "Ritual and Presentation in Early Buddhist Religious Architecture." *Asian Perspectives* 42 (1): 129–154.

Foucault, Michel. (1980) 1999. "About the Beginning of the Hermeneutics of the Self." In *Religion and Culture: Michel Foucault*, edited by Jeremy R. Carrett, 158–181. New York: Routledge.

Fox, Jonathan. 2004. "Religion and State Failure: An Examination of the Extent and Magnitude of Religious Conflict from 1950–1996." *International Political Science Review* 25 (1): 55–76.

Frederick, Marla F. 2003. *Between Sundays: Black Women and Everyday Struggles of Faith*. Berkeley: University of California Press.

Friedman, Asia M. 2015. "Perceptual Construction: Rereading the Social Construction of Reality through the Sociology of the Senses." *Cultural Sociology* 10 (1): 77–92. doi:10.1177/1749975515615149.

Frykholm, Amy Johnson. 2004. *Rapture Culture: Left Behind in Evangelical America*. New York: Oxford University Press.

Fulkerson, Mary McClintock. 2007. *Places of Redemption: Theology for a Worldly Church*. New York: Oxford University Press.

Fuller, Martin G., and Martina Löw. 2017. "Introduction: An Invitation to Spatial Sociology." *Current Sociology* 65 (4): 469–491. doi:10.1177/0011392117697461.

Gallego, Francisco A., and Robert Woodberry. 2010. "Christian Missionaries and Education in Former African Colonies: How Competition Mattered." *Journal of African Economies* 19 (3): 294–329. doi:10.1093/jae/ejq001.

Gamm, Gerald. 1999. *Urban Exodus: Why the Jews Left Boston and the Catholics Stayed*. Cambridge, MA: Harvard University Press.

Ganga Kieffer, Kira. 2020. "Why Some Vaccine Skeptics Are Fighting Covid-19 Restrictions." *Religion & Politics*, June 16, 2020. https://religionandpolitics.org.

Ganz, Marshall. 2009. *Why David Sometimes Wins: Strategy, Leadership, and the California Agricultural Movement*. New York: Oxford University Press.

Ganzevoort, R. Ruard, and Johan Roeland. 2014. "Lived Religion: The Praxis of Practical Theology." *International Journal of Practical Theology* 18 (1): 91–101. doi:10.1515/ijpt-2014-0007.

Garfinkel, Harold. 1967. *Studies in Ethnomethodology*. Englewood Cliffs, NJ: Prentice-Hall.

Geertz, Clifford. 1973. "Religion as a Cultural System." In *The Interpretation of Cultures*, 87–125. New York: Basic Books.

Gerber, Lynne. 2009. "My Body Is a Testimony: Appearance, Health, and Sin in an Evangelical Weight-Loss Program." *Social Compass* 56 (3): 405–418.

———. 2011. *Seeking the Straight and Narrow: Weight Loss and Sexual Reorientation in Evangelical America*. Chicago: University of Chicago Press.

Gifford, Paul. 2004. "Persistence and Change in Contemporary African Religion." *Social Compass* 51 (2): 169–176. doi:10.1177/0037768604043004.

Gilkes, Cheryl Townsend. 2001. *If It Wasn't for the Women . . . : Black Women's Experience and Womanist Culture in Church and Community*. Maryknoll, NY: Orbis Books.

Glassman, Lindsay W. 2018. "'In the Lord's Hands': Divine Healing and Embodiment in a Fundamentalist Christian Church." *Sociology of Religion* 79 (1): 35–57. doi:10.1093/socrel/srx046.

Goffman, Erving. 1959. *Presentation of Self in Everyday Life*. New York: Doubleday.

———. 1963. *Stigma; Notes on the Management of Spoiled Identity*. Englewood Cliffs, NJ: Spectrum.

———. 1967. *Interaction Ritual: Essays on Face-to-Face Behavior*. New York: Doubleday.

Goodhew, David, and Anthony-Paul Cooper, eds. 2019. *The Desecularisation of the City: London's Churches, 1980 to the Present*. London: Routledge.

Gorski, Philip. 2017. *American Covenant: A History of Civil Religion from the Puritans to the Present*. Princeton, NJ: Princeton University Press.

Gould, Rebecca Kneale. 2005. *At Home in Nature: Modern Homesteading and Spiritual Practice in America*. Berkeley: University of California Press.

Graham, Jesse, Brian A. Nosek, Jonathan Haidt, Ravi Iyer, Spassena Koleva, and Peter H. Ditto. 2011. "Mapping the Moral Domain." *Journal of Personality and Social Psychology* 101 (2): 366–385. doi:10.1037/a0021847.

Grainger, Brett Malcolm. 2019. *Church in the Wild: Evangelicals in Antebellum America*. Cambridge, MA: Harvard University Press.

Graw, Knut. 2012. "Divination and Islam: Existential Perspectives in the Study of Ritual and Religious Praxis in Senegal and Gambia." In *Ordinary Lives and Grand Schemes: An Anthropology of Everyday Religion*, edited by Samuli Schielke and Liza Debevec, 17–32. New York: Berghahn Books.

Gray, Edward R., and Scott L. Thumma. 1997. "The Gospel Hour: Liminality, Identity, and Religion in a Gay Bar." In *Contemporary American Religion*, edited by Penny Edgell Becker and Nancy L Eiesland, 79–98. Walnut Creek, CA: AltaMira.

Graybill, Beth, and Linda Boynton Arthur. 1999. "The Social Control of Women's Bodies in Two Mennonite Communities." In *Religion, Dress and the Body*, edited by Linda Boynton Arthur, 9–29. Oxford, UK: Berg.

Graziano, Frank. 2007. *Cultures of Devotion: Folk Saints of Spanish America*. New York: Oxford University Press.

Grider, Sylvia. 2006. "Spontaneous Shrines and Public Memorialization." In *Death and Religion in a Changing World*, edited by Kathleen Garces-Foley, 246–264. Armonk, NY: M. E. Sharpe.

Griffith, R. Marie. 1997. *God's Daughters: Evangelical Women and the Power of Submission*. Berkeley: University of California Press.

———. 2004. *Born Again Bodies: Flesh and Spirit in American Christianity*. Berkeley: University of California Press.

Gross, Neil. 2009. "A Pragmatist Theory of Social Mechanisms." *American Sociological Review* 74 (3): 358–379.

Guhin, Jeffrey. 2016. "Why Worry about Evolution? Boundaries, Practices, and Moral Salience in Sunni and Evangelical High Schools." *Sociological Theory* 34 (2): 151–174. doi:10.1177/0735275116649220.

Ha, Hyun Jeong. 2017. "Emotions of the Weak: Violence and Ethnic Boundaries among Coptic Christians in Egypt." *Ethnic and Racial Studies* 40 (1): 133–151. doi:10.1080/01419870.2016.1201586.

Hackett, Rosalind I. J., ed. 2008. *Proselytization Revisited: Rights Talk, Free Markets and Culture Wars*. New York: Routledge.

Haddad, Yvonne Yazbeck. 2007. "The Post-9/11 Hijab as Icon." *Sociology of Religion* 68 (3): 253–267.

Hagan, Jacqueline Maria. 2008. *Migration Miracle: Faith, Hope, and Meaning on the Undocumented Journey*. Cambridge, MA: Harvard University Press.

Haidt, Jonathan. 2012. *The Righteous Mind: Why Good People Are Divided by Politics and Religion*. New York: Vintage.

Hall, David, ed. 1997. *Lived Religion in America*. Princeton, NJ: Princeton University Press.

Hall, John R. 1987. *Gone from the Promised Land: Jonestown in American Cultural History*. New Brunswick, NJ: Transaction.

Hammarberg, Melvin. 2013. *The Mormon Quest for Glory: The Religious World of the Latter-Day Saints*. New York: Oxford University Press.

Harrison, Douglas. 2012. *Then Sings My Soul: The Culture of Southern Gospel Music*. Urbana: University of Illinois Press.

Heelas, Paul, and Linda Woodhead. 2004. *The Spiritual Revolution: Why Religion Is Giving Way to Spirituality*. Malden, MA: Blackwell.

Heider, Anne, and R. Stephen Warner. 2010. "Bodies in Sync: Interaction Ritual Theory Applied to Sacred Harp Singing." *Sociology of Religion* 71 (1): 76–97.

Hepburn, Alexa, and Jonathan Potter. 2004. "Discourse Analytic Practice." In *Qualitative Research Practice*, edited by Clive Seale, Giampietro Gobo, Jaber F. Gubrium, and David Silverman, 168–184. London: Sage.

Higginbotham, Evelyn Brooks. 1993. *Righteous Discontent: The Women's Movement in the Black Baptist Church, 1890–1920*. Cambridge, MA: Harvard University Press.

Highmore, Ben. 2010. "Social Aesthetics." In *Handbook of Cultural Sociology*, edited by John R. Hall, Laura Grindstaff, and Ming-Cheng M. Lo, 155–163. London: Routledge.

Hinson, Glenn. 2000. *Fire in My Bones: Transcendence and the Holy Spirit in African American Gospel*. Philadelphia: University of Pennsylvania Press.

Hitlin, Steven, and Stephen Vaisey. 2010. *Handbook of the Sociology of Morality*. New York: Springer Science and Business Media.

———. 2013. "The New Sociology of Morality." *Annual Review of Sociology* 39 (1): 51–68. doi:10.1146/annurev-soc-071312-145628.

Hochschild, Arlie Russell. 1979. "Emotion Work, Feeling Rules, and Social Structure." *American Journal of Sociology* 85 (3): 551–575.

———. 1983. *The Managed Heart: Commercialization of Human Feeling*. Berkeley: University of California Press.

———. 2016a. "The Ecstatic Edge of Politics: Sociology and Donald Trump." *Contemporary Sociology* 45 (6): 683–689.

———. 2016b. *Strangers in Their Own Land*. New York: New Press.

Hoover, Brett C. 2014. *Shared Parish: Latinos, Anglos, and the Future of U.S. Catholicism*. New York: New York University Press.

Hoover, Stewart. 2006. *Religion in the Media Age*. New York: Routledge.

Hout, Michael, and Claude S. Fischer. 2014. "Explaining Why More Americans Have No Religious Preference: Political Backlash and Generational Succession, 1987–2012." *Sociological Science* 1:423–447. doi:10.15195/v1.a24.

Howes, David. 2003. *Sensual Relations: Engaging the Senses in Culture and Social Theory*. Ann Arbor: University of Michigan Press.

Hudec, Amy Moff. 2015. "Courting Eternity: LDS Dating, Courtship, and Celestial Marriage in and out of Utah." PhD diss., Sociology, Boston University.

Hughes, Jennifer Scheper. 2010. *Biography of a Mexican Crucifix: Lived Religion and Local Faith from the Conquest to the Present*. New York: Oxford University Press.

Hume, Lynne. 2000. "The Dreaming in Contemporary Aboriginal Australia." In *Indigenous Religions: A Companion*, edited by Graham Harvey, 125–138. London: Bloomsbury.

Hurd, Elizabeth Shakman. 2015. *Beyond Religious Freedom: The Global Politics of Religion*. Princeton, NJ: Princeton University Press.

Idler, Ellen L., Marc Musick, Christopher Ellison, G., Linda K. George, Neal Krause, Marcia G. Ory, Kenneth I. Pargament, Lynn G. Underwood, and David R. Williams. 2003. "Measuring Multiple Dimensions of Religion and Spirituality for Health Research: Conceptual Background and Findings from the 1998 General Social Survey." *Research on Aging* 25 (4): 327–365.

Ignatow, Gabriel. 2007. "Theories of Embodied Knowledge: New Directions for Cultural and Cognitive Sociology?" *Journal for the Theory of Social Behaviour* 37 (2): 115–135. doi:10.1111/j.1468-5914.2007.00328.x.

———. 2010. "Morality and Mind-Body Connections." In *Handbook of the Sociology of Morality*, edited by Steven Hitlin and Stephen Vaisey, 411–424. New York: Springer Science and Business Media.

Ivakhiv, Adrian. 2001. *Reclaiming Sacred Ground: Pilgrims and Politics at Glastonbury and Sedona*. Bloomington: Indiana University Press.

Izard, Susan S. 2003. "A History of the Shawl-Knitting Ministry." In *Knitting into the Mystery: A Guide to the Shawl-Knitting Ministry*, edited by Susan S. Izard and Susan S. Jorgensen, 11–16. Harrisburg, PA: Morehouse.

Jacobs, Janet. 2010. *Memorializing the Holocaust: Gender, Genocide and Collective Memory*. New York: I. B. Tauris.

James, William. (1936) 1994. *Varieties of Religious Experience: A Study in Human Nature*. New York: Modern Library. Original published 1902.

Jennings, Mark. 2008. "'Won't You Break Free?': An Ethnography of Music and the Divine-Human Encounter at an Australian Pentecostal Church." *Culture and Religion* 9:161–174. doi:10.1080/14755610802211544.

Joshi, Khyati Y. 2006. *New Roots in America's Sacred Ground: Religion, Race, and Ethnicity in Indian America*. New Brunswick, NJ: Rutgers University Press.

Juergensmeyer, Mark, Margo Kitts, and Michael Jerryson, eds. 2013. *The Oxford Handbook of Religion and Violence*. New York: Oxford University Press.

Kanter, Rosabeth Moss. 1972. *Commitment and Community*. Cambridge, MA: Harvard University Press.

Kaufmann, Debra. 1991. *Rachel's Daughters*. New Brunswick, NJ: Rutgers University Press.

Kearns, Laurel, and Rosemary Skinner Keller, eds. 2007. *Ecospirit: Religions and Philosophies for the Earth*. New York: Fordham University Press.

Kelner, Shaul. 2010. *Tours That Bind: Diaspora, Pilgrimage, and Israeli Birthright Tourism*. New York: New York University Press.

Keltner, Dacher, and Jonathan Haidt. 2003. "Approaching Awe: A Moral, Spiritual, and Aesthetic Emotion." *Cognition & Emotion* 17 (2): 297–314. doi:10.1080/02699930302297.

Kenna, Margaret E. 1985. "Icons in Theory and Practice: An Orthodox Christian Example." *History of Religions* 24 (4): 345–368.

———. 2005. "Why Does Incense Smell Religious? Greek Orthodoxy and the Anthropology of Smell." *Journal of Mediterranean Studies* 15 (1): 50–69.

Kipnis, Andrew B. 2017. "Governing the Souls of Chinese Modernity." *HAU: Journal of Ethnographic Theory* 7 (2): 217–238.

Klassen, Pamela. 2009. "Ritual." In *Oxford Handbook of Religion and Emotion*, edited by John Corrigan, 143–162. New York: Oxford University Press.

Knott, Kim. 2005. *The Location of Religion: A Spatial Analysis*. London: Equinox.

———. 2016. "Living Religious Practices." In *Intersections of Religion and Migration: Issues at the Global Crossroads*, edited by Jennifer B. Saunders, Elena Fiddian-Qasmiyeh, and Susanna Snyder, 71–90. New York: Palgrave Macmillan.

Kollman, Paul. 2012. "Generations of Catholics in Eastern Africa: A Practice-Centered Analysis of Religious Change." *Journal for the Scientific Study of Religion* 51 (3): 412–428. doi:10.1111/j.1468-5906.2012.01667.x.

Kong, Lily. 2001. "Mapping 'New' Geographies of Religion: Politics and Poetics in Modernity." *Progress in Human Geography* 25 (2): 211–233.

———. 2011. "No Place, New Places: Death and Its Rituals in Urban Asia." *Urban Studies* 49 (2): 415–433.

Konieczny, Mary Ellen. 2009. "Sacred Places, Domestic Spaces: Material Culture, Church, and Home at Our Lady of the Assumption and St. Brigitta." *Journal for the Scientific Study of Religion* 48 (3): 419–442.

Kucinskas, Jaime. 2019. *The Mindful Elite: Mobilizing from the Inside Out*. New York: Oxford University Press.

Kuiper, Esgo, and Anders Bryn. 2012. "Forest Regrowth and Cultural Heritage Sites in Norway and along the Norwegian St. Olav Pilgrim Routes." *International Journal of Biodiversity Science, Ecosystem Services & Management* 9 (1): 54–64. doi:10.1080/215 13732.2012.711774.

Lakoff, George. 1996. *Moral Politics: How Liberals and Conservatives Think*. Chicago: University of Chicago Press.

Laliberté, André. 2016. "The Five Worlds of Religious Establishment in Taiwan." In *Varieties of Religious Establishment*, edited by Winnifred Fallers Sullivan and Lori G. Beaman, 147–162. Abingdon, UK: Taylor and Francis.

Lamont, Michèle. 1992. *Money, Morals, and Manners*. Chicago: University of Chicago Press.

Lamont, Michèle, and Marcel Fournier. 1992. *Cultivating Differences: Symbolic Boundaries and the Making of Inequality*. Chicago: University of Chicago Press.

Lamont, Michèle, and Laurent Thévenot. 2000. *Rethinking Comparative Cultural Sociology: Repertoires of Evaluation in France and the United States*. Cambridge: Cambridge University Press.

Lareau, Annette. 2021. *Listening to People: A Practical Guide to Interviewing, Participant Observation, Data Analysis, and Writing It All Up*. Chicago: University of Chicago Press.

Lee, Tong Soon. 1999. "Technology and the Production of Islamic Space: The Call to Prayer in Singapore." *Ethnomusicology* 43 (1): 86–99.

Lefebvre, Henri. 1991. *Production de l'espace*. Oxford, UK: Blackwell.

Levitt, Peggy. 2007. *God Needs No Passport*. New York: New Press.

Lewis, Reina. 2015. *Muslim Fashion: Contemporary Style Cultures*. Durham, NC: Duke University Press.

Lichterman, Paul. 2005. *Elusive Togetherness: Church Groups Trying to Bridge America's Divisions*. Princeton, NJ: Princeton University Press.

———. 2008. "Religion and the Construction of Civic Identity." *American Sociological Review* 73 (1): 83–104.

———. 2012. "Religion in Public Action: From Actors to Settings." *Sociological Theory* 30 (1): 15–36. doi:10.1177/0735275112437164.

Lincoln, C. Eric, and Lawrence H. Mamiya. 1990. *The Black Church in the African American Experience*. Durham, NC: Duke University Press.

Liu, Huwy-Min Lucia. 2020. "Ritual and Pluralism: Incommensurable Values and Techniques of Commensurability in Contemporary Urban Chinese Funerals." *Critique of Anthropology* 40 (1): 102–124. doi:10.1177/0308275X19899447.

Liu, Xin. 2000. *In One's Own Shadow: An Ethnographic Account of the Condition of Post-Reform Rural China*. Berkeley: University of California Press.

Lizardo, Omar, and Michael Strand. 2010. "Skills, Toolkits, Contexts and Institutions: Clarifying the Relationship between Different Approaches to Cognition in Cultural Sociology." *Poetics* 38 (2): 205–228. doi:10.1016/j.poetic.2009.11.003.

Longman, Timothy. 2009. *Christianity and Genocide in Rwanda*. New York: Cambridge University Press.

Longman, Timothy, and Théoneste Rutagengwa. 2006. "Religion, Memory, and Violence in Rwanda." In *Religion, Violence, Memory, and Place*, edited by Oren Baruch Stier and J. Shawn Landres, 132–149. Bloomington: Indiana University Press.

Lövheim, Mia. 2013. *Media, Religion and Gender: Key Issues and New Challenges*. London: Taylor and Francis.

———. 2018. "Media and Religion: Bridging 'Incompatible Agendas.'" In *Foundations and Futures in the Sociology of Religion*, edited by Luke Doggett and Alp Arat, 39–52. New York: Routledge.

Lövheim, Mia, and Evelina Lundmark. 2019. "Gender, Religion and Authority in Digital Media." *Journal for Communication Studies* 12 (2): 23–38.

Löw, Martina. 2008. "The Constitution of Space: The Structuration of Spaces through the Simultaneity of Effect and Perception." *European Journal of Social Theory* 11 (1): 25–49. doi:10.1177/1368431007085286.

Luhrmann, Tanya M. 2012. *When God Talks Back: Understanding the American Evangelical Relationship with God*. New York: Knopf.

———. 2020a. *How God Becomes Real: Kindling the Presence of Invisible Others*. Princeton, NJ: Princeton University Press.

———. 2020b. "Mind and Spirit: A Comparative Theory." Special issue. *Journal of the Royal Anthropological Institute* 26 (S1): 1–166.

Mackie, Diane M., Lisa A. Silver, and Eliot R. Smith. 2004. "Intergroup Emotions: Emotion as an Intergroup Phenomenon." In *The Social Life of Emotions*, edited by Larissa A. Tiedens and Colin Wayne Leach, 227–245. Cambridge: Cambridge University Press.

Maddrell, Avril. 2009. "A Place for Grief and Belief: The Witness Cairn, Isle of Whithorn, Galloway, Scotland." *Social & Cultural Geography* 10 (6): 675–693. doi:10.1080/14649360903068126.

Madsen, Richard. 2011. "Religious Renaissance in China Today." *Journal of Current Chinese Affairs* 40 (2): 17–42. doi:10.1177/186810261104000202.

Maffly-Kipp, Laurie F., Leigh E. Schmidt, and Mark Valeri, eds. 2006. *Practicing Protestants: Histories of Christian Life in America, 1630–1965*. Baltimore: Johns Hopkins University Press.

Mahmood, Saba. 2005. *Politics of Piety: The Islamic Revival and the Feminist Subject*. Princeton, NJ: Princeton University Press.

Maldonado-Estrada, Alyssa. 2019. "Tattoos as Sacramentals." *American Religion*, Center for Religion and the Human, Indiana University. https://american-religion.org.

Manglos, Nicolette D. 2010. "Born Again in Balaka: Pentecostal versus Catholic Narratives of Religious Transformation in Rural Malawi." *Sociology of Religion* 71 (4): 409–431.

Markowitz, Harvey. 2001. "From Presentation to Representation in Sioux Sun Dance Painting." In *The Visual Culture of American Religions*, edited by David Morgan and Sally M. Promey, 160–175. Berkeley: University of California Press.

Marsh, Charles. 1997. *God's Long Summer: Stories of Faith and Civil Rights*. Princeton, NJ: Princeton University Press.

———. 2017. "Introduction: Lived Theology: Method, Style, and Pedagogy." In *Lived Theology: New Perspectives on Method, Style, and Pedagogy*, edited by Charles Marsh, Peter Slade and Sarah Azaransky, 1–20. New York: Oxford University Press.

Marshall, Katherine, and Sally Smith. 2015. "Religion and Ebola: Learning from Experience." *Lancet* 386 (10005): e24–e25. doi:10.1016/S0140-6736(15)61082-0.

Marti, Gerardo. 2012. *Worship across the Racial Divide*. New York: Oxford University Press.

———. 2020. *American Blindspot: Race, Class, Religion, and the Trump Presidency*. Lanham, MD: Rowman and Littlefield.

Martin, Bernice. 2006. "The Aesthetics of Latin American Pentecostalism: The Sociology of Religion and the Problem of Taste." In *Materializing Religion: Expression, Performance and Ritual*, edited by Elisabeth Arweck and William Keenan, 139–160. Farnham, UK: Ashgate.

Martin, John Levi. 2003. "What Is Field Theory?" *American Journal of Sociology* 109 (1): 1–49. doi:10.1086/375201.

———. 2010. "Life's a Beach but You're an Ant, and Other Unwelcome News for the Sociology of Culture." *Poetics* 38 (2): 229–244. doi:10.1016/j.poetic.2009.11.004.

———. 2011. *The Explanation of Social Action*. New York: Oxford University Press.

Marx, Karl. (1844) 1963. "Contribution to a Critique of Hegel's Philosophy of Right." In *Karl Marx: Early Writings*, edited by T. B Bottomore, 43–59. New York: McGraw-Hill.

Mayrl, Damon. 2015. "How Does the State Structure Secularization?" *Archives Européennes de Sociologie / European Journal of Sociology* 56 (2): 207–239. doi:10.1017/S0003975615000119.

McDannell, Colleen. 1995. *Material Christianity*. New Haven, CT: Yale University Press.

———. 2011. *The Spirit of Vatican II: A History of Catholic Reform in America*. New York: Basic Books.

McGuire, Meredith B. 2008. *Lived Religion: Faith and Practice in Everyday Life*. New York: Oxford University Press.

McQueeney, Krista. 2014. "'We Are God's Children, Y'All': Race, Gender, and Sexuality in Lesbian- and Gay-Affirming Congregations." *Social Problems* 56 (1): 151–173. doi:10.1525/sp.2009.56.1.151.

McRoberts, Omar Maurice. 2003. *Streets of Glory: Church and Community in a Black Urban Neighborhood*. Chicago: University of Chicago Press.

———. 2004. "Beyond Mysterium Tremendum: Thoughts toward an Aesthetic Study of Religious Experience." *Annals of the American Academy of Political and Social Science* 595 (1): 190–203. doi:10.1177/0002716204267111.

———. 2020. "Civil Religion and Black Church Political Mobilization." In *Religion Is Raced: Understanding American Religion in the Twenty-First Century*, edited by Grace Yukich and Penny Edgell, 40–57. New York: New York University Press.

Mercer, Joyce Ann. 2005. *Welcoming Children: A Practical Theology of Childhood*. St. Louis: Chalice.

Messenger, Troy. 1999. *Holy Leisure: Recreation and Religion in God's Square Mile*. Minneapolis: University of Minnesota.

Meyer, Birgit. 2004. "Christianity in Africa: From African Independent to Pentecostal-Charismatic Churches." *Annual Review of Anthropology* 33:447–474. doi:10.2307/25064861.

———. 2008. "Religious Sensations: Why Media, Aesthetics, and Power Matter in the Study of Contemporary Religion." In *Religion: Beyond a Concept*, edited by Hent de Vries, 704–723. New York: Fordham University Press.

———. 2012. "Religious and Secular, 'Spiritual' and 'Physical' in Ghana." In *What Matters? Ethnographies of Value in a Not So Secular Age*, edited by Courtney Bender and Ann Taves, 86–117. New York: Columbia University Press.

Michaels, Axel. 2016. *Homo Ritualis*. New York: Oxford University Press.

Miller, Rowland W. 2004. "Emotion as Adaptive Interpersonal Communication." In *The Social Life of Emotions*, edited by Larissa A. Tiedens and Colin Wayne Leach, 87–104. Cambridge: Cambridge University Press.

Mills, C. Wright. 1976. *The Sociological Imagination*. New York: Oxford University Press.

Mitchell, Kerry. 2016. *Spirituality and the State: Managing Nature and Experience in America's National Parks*. New York: New York University Press.

Moon, Dawne. 2004. *God, Sex, and Politics: Homosexuality and Everyday Theologies*. Chicago: University of Chicago Press.

Mooney, Margarita. 2009. *Faith Makes Us Live: Surviving and Thriving in the Haitian Diaspora*. Berkeley: University of California Press.

Morello, Gustavo, SJ, Hugo Rabbia, Néstor Da Costa, and Catalina Romero. 2019. *La religión como experiencia cotidiana: Creencias, prácticas y narratives espirituales en Sudamérica*. Cordoba, Argentina: Editorial de la Universidad Católica de Córdoba; Editorial Pontificia Universidad Católica del Perú; Universidad Católica del Uruguay.

Morgan, David. 1996. Introduction to *Icons of American Protestantism: The Art of Warner Sallman*, edited by David Morgan, 1–23. New Haven, CT: Yale University.

————. 1998. *Visual Piety: A History and Theory of Popular Religious Images*. Berkeley: University of California Press.

Morris, Aldon D. 1984. *The Origins of the Civil Rights Movement: Black Communities Organizing for Change*. New York: Free Press.

Moschella, Mary Clark. 2008. *Ethnography as a Pastoral Practice*. New York: Pilgrim.

Moser, Sarah. 2013. "New Cities in the Muslim World: The Cultural Politics of Planning an 'Islamic' City." In *Religion and Place: Landscape, Politics and Piety*, edited by Peter Hopkins, Lily Kong, and Elizabeth Olson, 39–55. Dordrecht: Springer Netherlands.

Munson, Ziad. 2007. "When a Funeral Isn't Just a Funeral: The Layered Meaning of Everyday Action." In *Everyday Religion: Observing Modern Religious Lives*, edited by Nancy T. Ammerman, 121–136. New York: Oxford University Press.

————. 2008. *The Making of Pro-Life Activists: How Social Movement Mobilization Works*. Chicago: University of Chicago Press.

Nabhan-Warren, Kristy. 2011. "Embodied Research and Writing: A Case for Phenomenologically Oriented Religious Studies Ethnographies." *Journal of the American Academy of Religion* 79 (2): 378–407.

Nason-Clark, Nancy. 2004. "When Terror Strikes at Home: The Interface between Religion and Domestic Violence." *Journal for the Scientific Study of Religion* 43 (3): 303–310.

Nasr, Seyyed Hossein. 1987. *Islamic Art and Spirituality*. Albany: State University of New York Press.

Neal, Lynn S. 2019. *Religion in Vogue: Christianity and Fashion in America*. New York: New York University Press.

Neitz, Mary Jo. 1987. *Charisma and Community*. New Brunswick, NJ: Transaction.

————. 2000. "Queering the Dragonfest: Changing Sexualities in a Post-patriarchal Religion." *Sociology of Religion* 61 (4): 369–392.

————. 2003. "Dis/Location: Engaging Feminist Inquiry in the Sociology of Religion." In *Handbook of the Sociology of Religion*, edited by Michele Dillon, 276–293. Cambridge: Cambridge University Press.

————. 2005. "Reflections on Religion and Place: Rural Churches and American Religion." *Journal for the Scientific Study of Religion* 44 (3): 243–248.

————. 2011. "Lived Religion: Signposts of Where We Have Been and Where We Can Go from Here." In *Religion, Spirituality and Everyday Practice*, edited by Giuseppe Giordan and William H. Swatos Jr., 45–55. New York: Springer.

Nelson, Timothy J. 2005. *Every Time I Feel the Spirit: Religious Experience and Ritual in an African American Church*. New York: New York University Press.

Niebuhr, H. Richard. 1929. *The Social Sources of Denominationalism*. New York: World.

Nieman, James R. 2008. *Knowing the Context*. Minneapolis: Fortress.

Norris, Pippa, and Ronald Inglehart. 2004. *Sacred and Secular: Religion and Politics Worldwide*. New York: Cambridge University Press.

O'Brien, John. 2017. *Keeping It Halal: The Everyday Lives of Muslim American Teenage Boys*. Princeton, NJ: Princeton University Press.

Ojo, Olatunji. 2019. "Performing Trauma: The Ghosts of Slavery in Yoruba Music and Ritual Dance." *Journal of West African History* 5 (1): 1–27.

Olivier, Jill. 2015. "Religion at the Intersection of Development and Public Health in Development Contexts: From Advocacy about Faith-Based Organizations to Systems Thinking." In *The Routledge Handbook of Religions and Global Development*, edited by Emma Tomalin, 346–358. London: Routledge.

Olupona, Jacob K. 2011. *City of 201 Gods: Ilé-Ifè In Time, Space, and the Imagination.* Berkeley: University of California Press.

O'Neal, Gwendolyn S. 1999. "The African American Church, Its Sacred Cosmos and Dress." In *Religion, Dress and the Body*, edited by Linda Boynton Arthur, 117–134. Oxford, UK: Berg.

Orsi, Robert A. 1985. *The Madonna of 115th Street: Faith and Community in Italian Harlem, 1880–1950.* New Haven, CT: Yale University Press.

———. 2005. *Between Heaven and Earth: The Religious Worlds People Make and the Scholars Who Study Them.* Princeton, NJ: Princeton University Press.

———. 2016. *History and Presence.* Cambridge, MA: Harvard University Press.

Pagis, Michal. 2019. *Inward: Vipassana Meditation and the Embodiment of the Self.* Chicago: University of Chicago Press.

Palmer, David A., Glenn Shive, and Philip L. Wickeri, eds. 2011. *Chinese Religious Life.* New York: Oxford University Press.

Palmisano, Stefania. 2010. "Spirituality and Catholicism in Italy." *Journal of Contemporary Religion* 25 (2): 221–241.

Pang, Qin. 2012. "A Socio-Political Approach to Cultural Resurgence in Contemporary China: Case Study of the Approval of Traditional Festivals as Public Holidays." *International Journal of China Studies* 3 (1): 79–92.

Parks, Richard C. 2012. *Hygiene, Regeneration, and Citizenship: Jews in the Tunisian Protectorate.* Minneapolis: University of Minnesota Press.

Parvez, Z. Fareen. 2017. *Politicizing Islam: The Islamic Revival in France and India, Religion and Global Politics.* New York: Oxford University Press.

Pattillo-McCoy, Mary. 1998. "Church Culture as a Strategy of Action in the Black Community." *American Sociological Review* 63:767–784.

Pearce, Lisa D. 2002. "Integrating Survey and Ethnographic Methods for Systematic Anomalous Case Analysis." *Sociological Methodology* 32 (1): 103–132. doi:10.1111/1467-9531.00113.

Pearce, Tola Olu. 2002. "Cultural Production and Reproductive Issues: The Significance of the Charismatic Movement in Nigeria." In *Religion and Sexuality in Cross-Cultural Perspective*, edited by Stephen Ellingson and M. Christian Green, 21–50. New York: Routledge.

Petro, Anthony M. 2015. *After the Wrath of God: AIDS, Sexuality, and American Religion.* New York: Oxford University Press.

Pew Research Center. 2015. "America's Changing Religious Landscape." May 12, 2015. www.pewforum.org.

————. 2016. "The Gender Gap in Religion Around the World." Pew Forum on Religion and Public Life, March 22, 2016. www.pewforum.org.

————. 2019. "In U.S., Decline of Christianity Continues at Rapid Pace." October 17, 2019. www.pewforum.org.

Pink, Sarah. 2012. *Situating Everyday Life: Practices and Places*. Los Angeles: Sage.

Plate, S. Brent, ed. 2002. *Religion, Art, and Visual Culture: A Cross-Cultural Reader*. New York: Palgrave.

Poindexter, Cynthia Cannon, Nathan L. Linsk, and R. Stephen Warner. 1999. "'He Listens . . . and Never Gossips': Spiritual Coping without Church Support among Older, Predominantly African-American Caregivers of Persons with HIV." *Review of Religious Research* 40 (3): 230–243.

Post, Paul. 2011. "Profiles of Pilgrimage: On Identities of Religion and Ritual in the European Public Domain." *Studia Liturgica* 41 (2): 129–155.

Pryce, Paula. 2018. *The Monk's Cell: Ritual and Knowledge in American Contemplative Christianity*. New York: Oxford University Press.

Qian, Ding. 2019. "Four Popular Mourning Flowers during Qingming Festival." Beijing: Chinese Global Television Network, April 5, 2019. https://news.cgtn.com.

Read, Jen'nan Ghazal. 2007. "Muslim Integration in the United States and France." Special issue. *Sociology of Religion* 68 (3).

Read, Jen'nan Ghazal, and John Bartkowski. 2000. "To Veil or Not to Veil? A Case Study of Identity Negotiation among Muslim Women in Austin, Texas." *Gender and Society* 14 (3): 395–417.

Reckwitz, Andreas. 2002. "Toward a Theory of Social Practices: A Development in Culturalist Theorizing." *European Journal of Social Theory* 5 (2): 243–263. doi:10.1177/13684310222225432.

Reed, Jean-Pierre, and Sarah Pitcher. 2015. "Religion and Revolutionary We-ness: Religious Discourse, Speech Acts, and Collective Identity in Prerevolutionary Nicaragua." *Journal for the Scientific Study of Religion* 54 (3): 477–500.

Reimer-Kirkham, Sheryl. 2009. "Lived Religion: Implications for Nursing Ethics." *Nursing Ethics* 16 (4): 406–417. doi:10.1177/0969733009104605.

Repstad, Pål, ed. 2019. *Political Religion, Everyday Religion: Sociological Trends*: Leiden: Brill.

Richardson, James T., ed. 2004. *Regulating Religion: Case Studies from Around the Globe*. New York: Kluwer/Plenum.

Riis, Ole, and Linda Woodhead. 2010. *A Sociology of Religious Emotion*. Oxford: Oxford University Press.

Rinaldo, Rachel. 2013. *Mobilizing Piety: Islam and Feminism in Indonesia*. New York: Oxford University Press.

Rogers, Douglas. 2008. "Old Belief between 'Society' and 'Culture': Remaking Moral Communities and Inequalities on a Former State Farm." In *Religion, Morality, and Community in Post-Soviet Societies*, edited by Mark D. Steinberg and Catherine Wanner, 115–147. Washington, DC: Woodrow Wilson Center Press.

Roof, Wade Clark. 1999. *Spiritual Marketplace: Baby Boomers and the Remaking of American Religion*. Princeton, NJ: Princeton University Press.

Roy, Olivier. 2020. *Is Europe Christian?* Translated by Cynthia Schoch. New York: Oxford University Press.

Saliers, Don E. 2005. "Sound Spirituality: On the Formative Expressive Power of Music for Christian Spirituality." In *Minding the Spirit: The Study of Christian Spirituality*, edited by Elizabeth A. Dreyer and Mark S. Burrows, 334–340. Baltimore: Johns Hopkins University Press.

Sample, Tex. 1996. *White Soul: Country Music, the Church and Working Americans*. Nashville: Abingdon.

Scharen, Christian, and Aana Marie Vigen, eds. 2011. *Ethnography as Christian Theology and Ethics*. New York: Continuum.

Schatzki, Theodore R. 2001. Introduction to *The Practice Turn in Contemporary Theory*, edited by Karin Knorr Cetina, Theodore R. Schatzki, and Eike von Savigny, 10–24. New York: Routledge.

Scheer, Monique. 2012. "Are Emotions a Kind of Practice (and Is That What Makes Them Have a History)? A Bourdieuian Approach to Understanding Emotion." *History and Theory* 51 (2): 193–220. doi:10.1111/j.1468-2303.2012.00621.x.

Schmidt, Leigh Eric. 1995. *Consumer Rites: The Buying and Selling of American Holidays*. Princeton, NJ: Princeton University.

———. 2003. "The Making of Modern 'Mysticism.'" *Journal of the American Academy of Religion* 71 (2): 273–302.

Schutz, Alfred. 1945. "On Multiple Realities." *Philosophy and Phenomenological Research* 5 (4): 533–576. doi:10.2307/2102818.

Schwadel, Philip. 2006. "Current Expressions of American Jewish Identity: An Analysis of 114 Teenagers." In *Passing on the Faith: Transforming Traditions for the Next Generation of Jews, Christians, and Muslims*, edited by James L. Heft, 135–144. New York: Fordham University Press.

———. 2008. "Poor Teenagers' Religion." *Sociology of Religion* 69 (2): 125–149.

Seligman, Adam, Robert P. Weller, Michael J. Puett, and Bennett Simon. 2008. *Ritual and Its Consequences: An Essay on the Limits of Sincerity*. New York: Oxford University Press.

Sells, Michael. 2003. "Crosses of Blood: Sacred Space, Religion, and Violence in Bosnia-Hercegovina." *Sociology of Religion* 64 (3): 309–331.

Sered, Susan Starr. 1988. "Food and Holiness: Cooking as a Sacred Act among Middle-Eastern Jewish Women." *Anthropological Quarterly* 61 (3): 129–139.

Sewell, William H., Jr. 1992. "A Theory of Structure: Duality, Agency, and Transformation." *American Journal of Sociology* 98:1–29.

Shelton, Jason E., and Michael O. Emerson. 2012. *Blacks and Whites in Christian America: How Racial Discrimination Shapes Religious Convictions*. New York: New York University Press.

Shusterman, Richard. 2000. *Pragmatist Aesthetics: Living Beauty, Rethinking Art*. Lanham, MD: Rowman and Littlefield.

Sigalow, Emily. 2019. *American JewBu: Jews, Buddhists, and Religious Change*. Princeton, NJ: Princeton University Press.

Sinha, Vineeta. 2008. "Merchandizing Hinduism: Commodities, Markets and Possibilities for Enchantment." In *Religious Commodifications in Asia*, edited by Pattana Kitiarsa, 169–185. New York: Routledge.

Smelser, Neil J. 2009. *The Odyssey Experience: Physical, Social, Psychological, and Spiritual Journeys*. Berkeley: University of California Press.

Smilde, David A. 2003. "Skirting the Instrumental Paradox: Intentional Belief through Narrative in Latin American Pentecostalism." *Qualitative Sociology* 26 (3): 313–329.

———. 2007. *Reason to Believe: Cultural Agency in Latin American Evangelicalism*. Berkeley: University of California Press.

Smith, Christian. 2003a. *Moral, Believing Animals*. New York: Oxford University Press.

———, ed. 2003b. *The Secular Revolution: Power, Interests, and Conflict in the Secularization of American Public Life*. Berkeley: University of California Press.

———. 2010. *What Is a Person? Rethinking Humanity, Social Life, and the Moral Good from the Person Up*. Chicago: University of Chicago Press.

Smith, Christian, and Melinda Lundquist Denton. 2005. *Soul Searching: The Religious and Spiritual Lives of American Teenagers*. New York: Oxford University Press.

Smith, Christian, with Patricia Snell Herzog. 2009. *Souls in Transition: The Religious and Spiritual Lives of Emerging Adults*. New York: Oxford University Press.

Snyder, Samuel. 2007. "New Streams of Religion: Fly Fishing as a Lived Religion of Nature." *Journal of the American Academy of Religion* 75 (4): 896–922. doi:10.1093/jaarel/lfm063.

Snyder, Timothy K. 2013. "Twitter and Tragedy: A Revamped American Religious Experience." *Washington Post*, September 15, 2013. www.washingtonpost.com.

Sointu, Eeva, and Linda Woodhead. 2008. "Spirituality, Gender, and Expressive Selfhood." *Journal for the Scientific Study of Religion* 47 (2): 259–276.

Somers, Margaret R. 1994. "The Narrative Constitution of Identity: A Relational and Network Approach." *Theory and Society* 23:605–649.

Soper, J. Christopher, and Joel S. Fetzer. 2018. *Religion and Nationalism in Global Perspective*. Cambridge: Cambridge University Press.

Spurrier, Rebecca F. 2020. *The Disabled Church: Human Difference and the Art of Communal Worship*. New York: Fordham University Press.

Srinivas, Tulasi. 2018. *The Cow in the Elevator: An Anthropology of Wonder*. Durham, NC: Duke University Press.

Steensland, Brian. 2006. "Cultural Categories and the American Welfare State: The Case of Guaranteed Income Policy." *American Journal of Sociology* 111 (5): 1273–1326.

Steensland, Brian, Xiaoyun Wang, and Lauren Chism Schmidt. 2018. "Spirituality: What Does It Mean and to Whom?" *Journal for the Scientific Study of Religion* 57 (3): 450–472.

Steets, Silke. 2014. "Multiple Realities and Religion: A Sociological Approach." *Society* 51 (2): 140–144. doi:10.1007/s12115-014-9753-6.

Stets, Jan E. 2010. "The Social Psychology of the Moral Identity." In *Handbook of the Sociology of Morality*, edited by Steven Hitlin and Stephen Vaisey, 385–409. New York: Springer Science and Business Media.

Stets, Jan E., and Jonathan H. Turner, eds. 2014. *Handbook of the Sociology of Emotions*. New York: Springer Science.

Stier, Oren Baruch, and J. Shawn Landres, eds. 2006. *Religion, Violence, Memory, and Place*. Bloomington: Indiana University Press.

Stockly, Kate. 2020. "Appendix B: How Is God 'Like a Drug'? Exploring the Evolution of Social Affects and Oxytocin." In *High on God: How Megachurches Won the Heart of America*, by James Wellman, Katie Corcoran, and Kate Stockly, 251–292. New York: Oxford University Press.

Stringer, Martin. 1999. *On the Perception of Worship*. Birmingham, UK: University of Birmingham.

Sullivan, Susan Crawford. 2011. *Living Faith: Everyday Religion and Mothers in Poverty*. Chicago: University of Chicago Press.

Sullivan, Winnifred Fallers, and Lori G. Beaman, eds. 2016. *Varieties of Religious Establishment*. Abingdon, UK: Taylor and Francis.

Sun, Anna. 2013. *Confucianism as a World Religion: Contested Histories and Contemporary Realities*. Princeton, NJ: Princeton University Press.

Swartz, David. 1998. *Culture and Power: The Sociology of Pierre Bourdieu*. Chicago: University of Chicago Press.

Swidler, Ann. 1986. "Culture in Action: Symbols and Strategies." *American Sociological Review* 51:273–286.

———. 2010a. "Access to Pleasure: Aesthetics, Social Inequality, and the Structure of Culture Production." In *Handbook of Cultural Sociology*, edited by John R. Hall, Laura Grindstaff, and Ming-Cheng M. Lo, 285–294. London: Routledge.

———. 2010b. "The Return of the Sacred: What African Chiefs Teach Us about Secularization." *Sociology of Religion* 71 (2): 157–171.

Tatlow, Didi Kirsten. 2016. "Venerating Mao, Even Where Famine Remains a Memory." *New York Times*, January 13, 2016. www.nytimes.com.

Tavory, Iddo, and Ann Swidler. 2009. "Condom Semiotics: Meaning and Condom Use in Rural Malawi." *American Sociological Review* 74 (2): 171–189. doi:10.1177/000312240907400201.

Taylor, Charles. 2007. *A Secular Age*. Cambridge, MA: Harvard University Press.

ter Kuile, Casper. 2020. *The Power of Ritual: Turning Everyday Activities into Soulful Practices*. New York: Harper One.

ter Kuile, Casper, and Angie Thurston. 2014. *How We Gather*. Sacred Design Lab. https://sacred.design/insights.

Thumma, Scott. 1991. "Negotiating a Religious Identity." *Sociological Analysis* 52 (4): 333–347.

Thumma, Scott, and Edward R. Gray, eds. 2004. *Gay Religion*. Walnut Creek, CA: AltaMira.

Thurfjell, David, Cecilie Rubow, Atko Remmel, and Henrik Ohlsson. 2019. "The Relocation of Transcendence: Using Schutz to Conceptualize the Nature Experiences of Secular People." *Nature and Culture* 14 (2): 190–214.

Toft, Monica Duffy, Daniel Philpott, and Timothy S. Shah. 2011. *God's Century: Resurgent Religion and Global Politics*. New York: Norton.

Trinitapoli, Jenny, and Alexander Weinreb. 2012. *Religion and AIDS in Africa*. New York: Oxford University Press.

Turner, Bryan S. 2008. *The Body and Society: Explorations in Social Theory*. 3rd ed. London: Sage.

Turner, John G., and Lincoln Mullen. 2020. "Pandemic Religion: A Digital Archive." George Mason University. Accessed October 15, 2020. https://pandemicreligion.org.

Turner, Victor. 1977. *The Ritual Process*. Ithaca, NY: Cornell University Press.

Turowetz, Jason J., and Douglas W. Maynard. 2010. "Morality in the Social Interactional and Discursive World of Everyday Life." In *Handbook of the Sociology of Morality*, edited by Steven Hitlin and Stephen Vaisey, 503–526. New York: Springer Science and Business Media.

Vanderslice, Kendall. 2019. *We Will Feast: Rethinking Dinner, Worship, and the Community of God*. Grand Rapids, MI: Eerdmans.

van Gennep, Arnold. 1960. *The Rites of Passage*. Chicago: University of Chicago Press.

Vannini, Phillip, Dennis Waskul, and Simon Gottschalk. 2011. *The Senses in Self, Society, and Culture: A Sociology of the Senses*. London: Routledge.

Van Zandt, David E. 1991. *Living in the Children of God*. Princeton, NJ: Princeton University Press.

Vasquez, Manuel A., and Marie Friedmann Marquardt. 2003. *Globalizing the Sacred; Religion across the Americas*. New Brunswick, NJ: Rutgers University Press.

Vaughan, Diane. 1986. *Uncoupling: Turning Points in Intimate Relationships*. New York: Oxford University Press.

Vincett, Giselle. 2013. "'There's Just No Space for Me There': Christian Feminists in the UK and the Performance of Space and Religion." In *Religion and Place: Landscape, Politics and Piety*, edited by Peter Hopkins, Lily Kong, and Elizabeth Olson, 167–184. Dordrecht: Springer Netherlands.

Warner, R. Stephen. 1993. "Work in Progress toward a New Paradigm for the Sociological Study of Religion in the United States." *American Journal of Sociology* 98 (5): 1044–1093.

Warner, R. Stephen, and Judith G. Wittner, eds. 1998. *Gatherings in Diaspora: Religious Communities and the New Immigration*. Philadelphia: Temple University Press.

Weber, Max. (1922) 1946. "The Sociology of Charismatic Authority." In *From Max Weber*, edited by Hans Gerth and C. Wright Mills, 245–252. New York: Oxford University Press.

———. 1947. *The Theory of Social and Economic Organization*. Translated by A. M Henderson and Talcott Parsons. New York: Free Press.

———. 1958. *From Max Weber: Essays in Sociology*. Edited by H. H. Gerth and C. Wright Mills. New York: Oxford University Press.

Wedow, Robbee, Landon Schnabel, Lindsey K. D. Wedow, and Mary Ellen Konieczny. 2017. "'I'm Gay and I'm Catholic': Negotiating Two Complex Identities at a Catholic University." *Sociology of Religion* 78 (3): 289–317. doi:10.1093/socrel/srx028.

Wellman, James K., Katie E. Corcoran, and Kate Stockly-Meyerdirk. 2014. "'God Is Like a Drug . . .': Explaining Interaction Ritual Chains in American Megachurches." *Sociological Forum* 29 (3): 650–672. doi:10.1111/socf.12108.

Wertheimer, Jack. 2018. *The New American Judaism: How Jews Practice Their Religion Today*. Princeton, NJ: Princeton University Press.

West, Traci C. 2019. *Solidarity and Defiant Spirituality: Africana Lessons on Religion, Racism, and Ending Gender Violence*. New York: New York University Press.

White, Heather Rachelle. 2015. *Reforming Sodom: Protestants and the Rise of Gay Rights*. Chapel Hill: University of North Carolina Press.

Whitehead, Andrew L., and Samuel L. Perry. 2020. *Taking America Back for God: Christian Nationalism in the United States*. New York: Oxford University Press.

Whitehouse, Harvey. 2009. "Terror." In *Oxford Handbook of Religion and Emotion*, edited by John Corrigan, 260–276. New York: Oxford University Press.

Wigner, Dann. 2018. "Icons: A Case Study in Spiritual Borrowing between Eastern Orthodoxy and the Emergent Church." *Spiritus: A Journal of Christian Spirituality* 18 (Spring): 78–100.

Wilcox, Melissa M. 2003. *Coming Out in Christianity: Religion, Identity, and Community*. Bloomington: Indiana University Press.

———. 2009. *Queer Women and Religious Individualism*. Bloomington: Indiana University Press.

———. 2012. "'Spiritual Sluts': Uncovering Gender, Ethnicity, and Sexuality in the Postsecular." *Women's Studies* 41 (6): 639–659.

Williams, Roman R. 2010. "Space for God: Lived Religion at Work, Home, and Play." *Sociology of Religion* 71 (3): 257–279.

———. 2019. "Facilitating Understanding through Photographs." Interfaith Photovoice, October 2, 2019. https://interfaithphotovoice.org/.

Williams-Jones, Pearl. 1975. "Afro-American Gospel Music: A Crystallization of the Black Aesthetic." *Ethnomusicology* 19 (3): 373–385. doi:10.2307/850791.

Winchester, Daniel. 2008. "Embodying the Faith: Religious Practice and the Making of a Muslim Moral Habitus." *Social Forces* 86:1753–1780. doi:10.1353/sof.0.0038.

———. 2016. "A Hunger for God: Embodied Metaphor as Cultural Cognition in Action." *Social Forces* 95 (2): 585–606.

———. 2017. "'A Part of Who I Am': Material Objects as 'Plot Devices' in the Formation of Religious Selves." *Journal for the Scientific Study of Religion* 56 (1): 83–103. doi:10.1111/jssr.12318.

Winchester, Daniel, and Kyle D. Green. 2019. "Talking Your Self into It: How and When Accounts Shape Motivation for Action." *Sociological Theory* 37 (3): 257–281. doi:10.1177/0735275119869959.

Winston, Diane H. 2009. *Small Screen, Big Picture: Television and Lived Religion*. Waco, TX: Baylor University Press.

Wolff, Janet. 1983. *Aesthetics and the Sociology of Art*. London: George Allen and Unwin.

Wood, Richard L. 2002. *Faith in Action: Religion, Race, and Democratic Organizing in America*. Chicago: University of Chicago Press.

Woods, Orlando. 2018. "Spaces of the Religious Economy: Negotiating the Regulation of Religious Space in Singapore." *Journal for the Scientific Study of Religion* 57 (3): 531–546.

Wright, Stuart A. 1995. *Armageddon in Waco: Critical Perspectives on the Branch Davidian Conflict*. Chicago: University of Chicago Press.

Wuthnow, Robert. 1998. *After Heaven: Spirituality in America since the 1950s*. Berkeley: University of California Press.

———. 2001. *Creative Spirituality: The Way of the Artist*. Berkeley: University of California Press.

———. 2011. "Taking Talk Seriously: Religious Discourse as Social Practice." *Journal for the Scientific Study of Religion* 50 (1): 1–21. doi:10.1111/j.1468-5906.2010.01549.x.

———. 2020. *What Happens When We Practice Religion? Textures of Devotion in Everyday Life*. Princeton, NJ: Princeton University Press.

Yang, Fenggang. 2005. "Lost in the Market, Saved at McDonald's: Conversion to Christianity in Urban China." *Journal for the Scientific Study of Religion* 44 (4): 423–441.

———. 2006. "The Red, Black, and Gray Markets of Religion in China." *Sociological Quarterly* 47 (1): 93–122.

———. 2012. *Religion in China: Survival and Revival under Communist Rule*. New York: Oxford University Press.

Young, Michael P. 2002. "Confessional Protest: The Religious Birth of U.S. National Social Movements." *American Sociological Review* 67 (5): 660–688.

Yukich, Grace, and Ruth Braunstein. 2014. "Encounters at the Religious Edge: Variation in Religious Expression across Interfaith Advocacy and Social Movement Settings." *Journal for the Scientific Study of Religion* 53 (4): 791–807. doi:10.1111/jssr.12142.

Yukich, Grace, and Penny Edgell, eds. 2020. *Religion Is Raced: Understanding American Religion in the Twenty-First Century*. New York: New York University Press.

Zhou, Winting. 2017. "Large Crowds Expected for Qingming Festival." *China Daily (USA)*, March 31, 2017. www.pressreader.com.

Zigon, Jarrett. 2010. "Moral and Ethical Assemblages." *Anthropological Theory* 10 (1–2): 3–15. doi:10.1177/1463499610370520.

Zubair, Shirin, and Maria Zubair. 2017. "Situating Islamic Feminism(s): Lived Religion, Negotiation of Identity and Assertion of Third Space by Muslim Women in Pakistan." *Women's Studies International Forum* 63:17–26.

Zubrzycki, Genevieve. 2016. *Beheading the Saint: Nationalism, Religion, and Secularism in Quebec*. Chicago: University of Chicago Press.

INDEX

ABOUT THE AUTHOR

Nancy Tatom Ammerman is Professor of Sociology of Religion, Emerita, at Boston University and the author of *Sacred Stories, Spiritual Tribes: Finding Religion in Everyday Life* and *Pillars of Faith: American Congregations and Their Partners.*